Attitudes toward Rape

Gender and Psychology
Feminist and Critical Perspectives
Series editor: Sue Wilkinson

This international series provides a forum for research focused on gender issues in – and beyond – psychology, with a particular emphasis on feminist and critical analyses. It encourages contributions which explore psychological topics where gender is central; which critically interrogate psychology as a discipline and as a professional base; and which develop feminist interventions in theory and practice. The series objective is to present innovative research on gender in the context of the broader implications for developing both critical psychology and feminism.

Sue Wilkinson teaches social psychology and women's studies at Loughborough University. She is also Editor of *Feminism and Psychology: An International Journal*.

Also in this series

Subjectivity and Method in Psychology
Wendy Hollway

Feminists and Psychological Practice
edited by Erica Burman

Feminist Groupwork
Sandra Butler and Claire Wintram

Motherhood: Meanings, Practices and Ideologies
edited by Ann Phoenix, Anne Woollett and Eva Lloyd

Emotion and Gender: Constructing Meaning from Memory
June Crawford, Susan Kippax, Jenny Onyx, Una Gault and Pam Benton

Women and AIDS: Psychological Perspectives
edited by Corinne Squire

Talking Difference: On Gender and Language
Mary Crawford

Feminism and Discourse: Psychological Perspectives
edited by Sue Wilkinson and Celia Kitzinger

Attitudes toward Rape

Feminist and Social Psychological Perspectives

Colleen A. Ward

SAGE Publications

London • Thousand Oaks • New Delhi

SAGE Publications Ltd
6 Bonhill Street
London EC2A 4PU

SAGE Publications Inc
2455 Teller Road
Thousand Oaks, California 91320

SAGE Publications India Pvt Ltd
32, M-Block Market
Greater Kailash - I
New Delhi 110 048

British Library Cataloguing in Publication data

A catalogue record for this book
is available from the British Library

ISBN 0 8039 8593 2
ISBN 0 8039 8594 0 (pbk)

Typeset by Photoprint, Torquay, S. Devon
Printed in Great Britain by Biddles Ltd, Guildford, Surrey

For Marge and Brenda,
mother and sister,
in hopes we can all share
our little bits of wisdom

Contents

List of Tables and Figures viii

Introduction 1

Part I   A Circle in the Making 9
1   Feminist Visions 18
2   Attitudes toward Rape and Rape Victims: Survey Research 38
3   Rape Perceptions and Attributions: Experimental Research 66
4   Social and Institutional Responses to Rape: Field Research 90
5   Returning to the Victim: Theory and Research on
    Psychological Reactions to Sexual Violence 116

Part II   A Circle in the Breaking 136
6   Changing Attitudes 139
7   Changing Systems: Feminist Action-Oriented Research 154

Conclusion 180

Appendices 193

References 205

Name Index 224
Subject Index 226

List of Tables and Figures

Tables

2.1 Attitudes toward rape (Barnett and Feild, 1977)   44
2.2 Attitudes toward rape (Giacopassi and Dull, 1986)   44
2.3 Attitudes toward rape victims (Ward, 1988a)   44
2.4 Attitudes toward rape (Holcomb et al., 1991)   45
2.5 ARVS scores in 15 countries   55
2.6 Knowledge about sexual offences   59
2.7 Attitudes toward rape victims   60

Figures

5.1 Stress and coping framework (Ward, 1988b)   119

Introduction

> They demanded to have sex with me. I refused but I couldn't do
> anything. They had weapons. . . . There were two of them and
> they wanted to take turns. I was very frightened.

May and her boyfriend David had gone out for an evening together.[1]
After a stroll through a public garden they sat on a park bench to
talk. About 11 p.m. they were confronted by two masked men
carrying knives. After searching May and David for money and
valuables, one man restrained David while the other dragged May
to a deserted public toilet and raped her at knifepoint. After the
rape May was returned to the park bench, but the second robber
brought her back to the toilet and also forced her to have intercourse. David managed to escape at this point, leaving May alone
with the two men; however, she was able to attract the attention of a
passing police patrol car shortly afterwards.

The offenders were apprehended and were taken with May to the
police station. There May's initial relief turned to despair. After
being held at the station most of the night she explained:

> I was very angry with them. At that moment I was very sad and angry.
> Angry because the police treated me like nothing. Sad because I was
> raped. Their attitude was very bad. I used to respect policemen a lot.
> You know, when a girl is raped, it is very traumatic for her. But they had
> a 'laugh it off' kind of attitude. Now I don't have a shred of respect for
> them.

May received medical attention the next day at a government
hospital. The medical examination confirmed the occurrence of
intercourse, but as May submitted under threat of violence, the
physician could not find evidence to corroborate the use of force.
May worked with the police and public prosecutors over the next six
months while she awaited the preliminary hearing which would
determine if the offenders would be tried for rape in the High
Court. She indicated that the police 'made me feel like I was the
criminal'. She also found interaction with the prosecutors very
difficult. To prepare her for the trial they would argue that she
actually consented to intercourse. She found the notion that she
would voluntarily have sex with strangers in a filthy public toilet
completely ridiculous. At times she remarked, 'I could not decide
whose side they were on'. She also feared that the additional stress

of a court appearance would exacerbate her epileptic condition and bring on a seizure.

The six months between the sexual assault and the hearing were particularly stressful for May. Although her family members were very supportive, her boyfriend had deserted her. She was extremely angry about this and considered that he may have actually conspired with the offenders. May was very fearful, had problems sleeping and often experienced vivid nightmares. She felt 'spoiled' and contaminated after the sexual assault, was very much ashamed of what had happened and experienced extreme anxiety over her upcoming court appearance.

On the day of the preliminary hearing May was restless and understandably agitated. She was accompanied to the court by her family and a social worker. They waited for over three hours to be called into the session. Eventually, the social worker was able to locate an officer from the appropriate courtroom and was told that the men had pleaded guilty, that there was no need for May to have her statement read in court, and that she could go home. May was extremely relieved by the news and went home with her family in hopes of putting the incident behind her. The next morning the following appeared in the newspaper:

Woman offered sex to two robbers

A woman, a victim in an armed robbery, offered sex to two robbers, a court heard yesterday. The 22-year-old woman followed the robbers after telling her boyfriend to return home. Because of this evidence, a district court judge said he might drop the rape charges. (*Straits Times*, September 26, 1985, p. 11)

May's story is typical in many ways. She was victimized by a brutal rape, deserted by her boyfriend, exploited further in an insensitive criminal justice system and cruelly exposed in the public media. Her interactions with both individuals and social systems were coloured by a common and pervading ideology about rape and rape victims: women secretly desire to be raped; they consent to sex and change their minds afterwards; and allegations of rape are easy to make and difficult to disprove. Or women are to blame; they get what they deserve; raped women are worthless; rape is only sex so what's the big deal? Although these attitudes are founded on misconceptions about sexual assault, they have a long-standing history and are resistant to change. They function at both the interpersonal and the societal levels as prescribed beliefs shared by individuals and reflected in social institutions. They are interwoven with social norms about male and female relations and directly and indirectly influence the prevalence, prevention and treatment of sexual violence. Rape ideology is ubiquitous, powerful, both subtle and overt – and it has devastating effects on victims of sexual assault.

Visions of Rape in the Words of . . .

The Victims[2]

I felt guilty. I felt it was my fault because I had been drinking. I felt angry at myself for not having fought or screamed louder. (English rape victim, cited in Hanmer and Saunders, 1983, p. 37)

I have been prejudiced against since I was 10 years old. I've been at a disadvantage. I've been trying to live for 25 years feeling like I was the bottom of a scum bucket. (New Zealand incest survivor, cited in Ward, 1992)

At the police station once it was established that I had been hitch-hiking, they really lost interest in whether or not I had been raped. They felt that I had somehow been asking for it by being alone on the road. (18-year-old Canadian victim raped in Europe, cited in Levine and Koenig, 1983)

The Offenders

Don't go with a group of guys because that is the stupidest thing a girl could do. She's just inviting herself to get raped. What would a group of guys want with a girl anyway, other than sex? (Canadian rapist, in therapy, cited in Levine and Koenig, 1983)

The Family

Maybe it was my fault. See, that's where I get when I think about it. My father always said whatever a man did to a woman, she provoked it. (American rape victim, cited in Burgess and Holmstrom, 1974a, p. 983)

My daughter has never been the same since the attack. What makes it even worse is that some of our own family members even shunned her because of the incident. Instead of understanding, they treated her as if she was a criminal, whose very presence could only taint them. (Singaporean mother of a 10-year-old rape victim, cited in *Straits Times*, March 12, 1986, p. 20)

He (my husband) doesn't want me around his family. He told his mother on Sunday and said he was ashamed of me. (American rape victim, cited in Holmstrom and Burgess, 1979, p. 323)

The Public

I am concerned about the increase of the number of ladies wearing see-through blouses, low cut necklines and low backs, mini skirts and very short shorts. These sexily-dressed ladies 'invite' and tempt men to turn into molesters and rapists for as we know, man is by nature easily aroused sexually by sight. (Singaporean man, newspaper editorial, cited in *Straits Times*, July 26, 1983, p. 21)

The Authorities

The offence of rape is extremely unlikely to have been committed against a woman who does not immediately show signs of extreme violence. (British Detective Sergeant on investigation, cited in Firth, 1975, p. 1507)

Women who say no do not always mean no. It is not just a question of saying no, it is a question of how she says it, how she shows and makes it clear. If she doesn't want it she only has to keep her legs shut and she would not get it without force and there would be marks of force being used. (Judge Wild at Cambridge Crown Court, cited in Temkin, 1986, pp. 19–20)

Women are responsible for causing about 40 per cent of reported rape cases. (Deputy Home Affairs Minister of Malaysia, Radzi Tan Sri Sheik Ahmad, cited in Consumers' Association of Penang, 1988, pp. 8 and 16.)

The Experts

In a way, the victim is always the cause of the crime. (Menachim Amir [1971, p. 258], sociologist and expert on rape)

Women ask for or invite rape by their behaviours or dress style; women are ambivalent about sex and capricious; men are oversexed and not responsible for their own behaviour; raped women are shameful, disgraceful and blameworthy; women can easily prevent rape; 'nice' people should not associate with sexually assaulted women – these myths are espoused by the police, the courts, rape experts, the general public, victims' families and even victims themselves.[3]

Concern about these rape myths and their consequences is not new. It has been almost 20 years since Susan Brownmiller (1975) highlighted the significance of rape ideologies and their role in mediating the sexual exploitation of women. Feminist analysis has argued that the patriarchal system of gender inequalities which empowers men and oppresses women underpins sexual violence and that stratification and social control are fundamental elements in the sexual domination of women. Associated values and attitudes prop up the patriarchal system. They are so pervasive and deeply ingrained that they are rarely subjected to critical scrutiny in everyday life. Rather, they are taken for granted, as givens which direct the manner in which men and women relate to each other. While much of the feminist literature has concentrated on the explanation and prediction of rape in a patriarchal society, rape-supportive beliefs, held by individuals and reinforced by institutions, have also merited analysis. In fact feminist scholarship has made two major contributions to the rape literature: (1) it has introduced rape to the scientific and professional community as a topic for serious investigation, and (2) it has increased awareness of the prevalent myths and stereotypes about sexual violence (Bourque, 1990).

This, in turn, has attracted substantial attention from the discipline of psychology. Prompted by feminist critiques and underpinned by a traditional interest in attitude theory and measurement, extensive empirical research on social cognition and rape victimology has recently emerged. Psychologists have further examined feminist claims of sexist ideology in society and have attempted to refine theory which elaborates the associations amongst rape-related attitudes and predicts rape-related behaviour (Donat and D'Emilio, 1992).

Applied psychological research and field studies have also emerged, and the relationship between attitudes and behaviour has been further explored. Psychologists have taken particular note of feminist scholarship which has implicated rape ideologies in rape proclivity (Mahoney et al., 1986), prevalence of reporting (Bourque, 1990), the formulation of rape laws (LeGrand, 1973), the likelihood of criminal conviction (Burt and Albin, 1981), the institutional processing of rape cases (Galton, 1975–6), the community response to victims of sexual violence (Koss and Harvey, 1991), policy decisions (Burgess and Holmstrom, 1974a; Schwendinger and Schwendinger, 1983), the quality of victim care (LeBourdais, 1976; McGuire and Stern, 1976), victims' self-perceptions and well-being (Libow and Doty, 1979), and recommended prevention strategies (Brodsky, 1976). Psychological research has begun to pursue these applied topics as well as the important issue of attitude change.

What Do We Know about Rape and How Do We Know It? Feminism and Psychology

> Accounting for the ordinary is often the most difficult of tasks, particularly when the ordinary is not at all obvious. Sexual coercion is woven into the fabric of our cultural, social and personal psychologies and is not easily defined or disentangled from this context. Thus, although so common as to be ordinary, it is not at all obvious how sexual coercion should be understood.
>
> (Burkhart and Fromuth, 1991, p. 88)

Feminist scholarship has argued that rape ideology encourages and justifies sexual coercion, trivializes sexual violence and demeans and devalues women who have experienced sexual assault. The foundation of this argument is based on women's experiences in patriarchal societies. Because feminist knowledge is rooted in experience, it is often criticized as being subjective, value-laden and a vehicle for feminist propaganda. Because feminist research is designed for social change, its association with politics often proves uncomfortable for those in the scientific arena.

Feminist theory and research differs from that found in mainstream psychology on several counts. Although there are many voices within feminism and a variety of perspectives in psychology, the general characteristics of a feminist approach can be identified and contrasted with those of contemporary social psychology. Feminist research is broad and expansive, rather than reductionist and narrow. It is often interdisciplinary, rather than strictly defined by the pressures to imitate, yet distinguish itself from, the natural sciences. It commences with the recognition that science is situated within society and, as such, reflects pervading social values. Acknowledging that it is impossible to shed our cultural baggage at the threshold of the research enterprise, feminist scholarship adopts a view of conscious partiality – being explicit in the statement of underlying values and straightforward in admitting to the limitations of this perspective. Psychological science, in contrast, has its roots in logical positivism and has traditionally laid claims to value-neutrality and the objective pursuit of knowledge.

Contrasts between feminist and psychological perspectives often translate into differences in specific methodological preferences. Feminists, for example, often follow an experiential route to knowledge and believe that women should be studied non-intrusively in their natural contexts. Psychologists, on the other hand, frequently opt for more controlled research settings and experimental manipulations. There are also traditional differences in power-sharing in the implementation of research with feminists favouring a more egalitarian relationship between the researcher and the researched and psychologists typically preferring more hierarchical arrangements.

Despite these methodological distinctions, feminism and psychology have mutually influenced each other. Certainly many of the topics chosen for investigation in contemporary social psychology mirror the concerns of the feminist movement. Similarly, developments in psychology have added fuel to the feminist fire by identifying and assessing these insidious rape myths and ideologies. In light of this interdependent relationship, this book attempts to blend feminist scholarship and social psychology to consider both *what* we know about rape and *how* we know it. On the one hand, empirical studies on rape and rape victims in current social psychology are evaluated from a feminist perspective. On the other hand, feminist claims about women's experiences of rape in patriarchal societies are assessed in light of empirical research findings from social psychology.

Outline of the Book

No one book can be all things to all people. This work emerges after a journey of undertaking a research and intervention project on sexual violence in Singapore, teaching feminist theory and methods in psychology in New Zealand, organizing a symposium on violence against women in Australia, coordinating cross-cultural research on attitudes toward rape victims in 15 countries, returning to Singapore to run training seminars on working with victims of sexual violence, and preparing to participate in an international symposium on sexual violence in Spain. Coloured very much by my own experiences in the field, the major objectives of this book are:

1 to introduce feminist theory and research on rape myths in society;
2 to review and synthesize what we know about all-pervasive rape ideologies through empirical studies in contemporary social psychology, incorporating research on attitudes, stereotypes, prejudice, attributions and values, including a range of methods such as case studies, surveys, experiments and field studies;
3 to consider practical applications of this research such as the psychological effects, both direct and indirect, of rape myths on victims of sexual assault and the strategies for changing attitudes toward sexual violence;
4 to incorporate, where possible, a cross-cultural perspective in the study of rape myths and attitudes; and
5 to evaluate psychological research from a feminist perspective and feminist theory via psychological research, including an analysis of what psychology and feminism may have to offer each other.

In achieving these objectives the work interweaves international and cross-cultural threads from both psychology and feminism. Given the diversity of resources, the production of a coherent tapestry depicting the sources, description, explanation and consequences of rape attitudes becomes a major challenge. The following is an honest attempt at the loom.

The book is divided into two major parts. Part I examines empirical evidence on attitudes toward rape. It commences with an introduction of early feminist theory and research on rape and goes on to describe social psychological investigations of attitudes toward and perceptions of victims of sexual violence. A range of methodological approaches to the study of rape myths are described: feminist ethnographic studies, survey research, experimental investigations, case studies and field research. A variety of subjects and research contexts are also included: legal, medical and social service professionals' attitudes toward sexual violence, views of the general public, rapists' perceptions of sexual coercion, trial outcome research and cross-cultural differences in attitudes toward rape victims are described and evaluated. In addition, a range of feminist and contemporary social psychological theories such as socio-cultural theories of rape, the 'just world' hypothesis, the attitude–behaviour link, attribution theory and the principles of cognitive dissonance are presented. The section concludes with a chapter which synthesizes the theoretical and empirical bases of feminist and psychological scholarship and assesses the impact of rape myths on victims' self-perceptions and recovery from sexual assault.

Part II is composed of two chapters which are focused on applied aspects of psychological and feminist research. The first chapter presents social psychological theories of attitude formation and change and evaluates the outcomes of educational interventions on changing individuals' attitudes toward sexual assault. The second chapter describes feminist action-oriented research which attempts to alter attitudes through political activity and changing social systems. These micro- and macro-levels of intervention and analysis represent complementary approaches to improving attitudes toward victims of sexual violence.

Finally, the Conclusion contains a critical analysis of theory and research on attitudes toward rape. Theoretical, methodological and epistemological issues are viewed from both social psychological and feminist perspectives. In the end, with the merger of feminism and psychology, it is hoped that some light can be shed on the causes and consequences of rape ideologies.

Notes

1 The names of the victim and her boyfriend have been changed to protect their identities. The interview and case study were taken from our research on sexual violence in Singapore.

2 In recent times victims have come to be called rape survivors. This acknowledges the seriousness of sexual assualt and credits the woman with the strength and courage needed to go on with her life. The term victim is retained here, however, because rape myths and attitudes further victimize survivors of sexual assault.

3 A brief description of the actual characteristics of sexual offences, in contrast with popular rape myths, is presented in Appendix A – Rape: Fact and Fiction.

PART I
A CIRCLE IN THE MAKING

Feminism, Psychology and Research on Rape

In 1975 Susan Brownmiller published *Against Our Will: Men, Women and Rape*. In the last 20 years the book has come to merit the status of a classic, and its social, psychological and political significance has been widely recognized. *Against Our Will* pioneered the documentation of a previously ignored topic and provided a major impetus for raising social and political consciousness about sexual violence. It represented a critical force in the development of feminist literature by focusing on the uniqueness of the female experience and interpreting women's realities from a female perspective. The work also sparked psychological interest in sexual violence and went on to provide the theoretical underpinnings of psychological research on rape.

Although in recent years feminism and psychology have converged in theory and research on rape, the generative work of Brownmiller and others demonstrated that the two shared very little common ground in the 1970s. Feminist scholars criticized psychological science first for its neglect of half the population and second for its androcentric perspective and misrepresentation of women in its meagre research endeavours (Kaplan and Sedney, 1980). Although these criticisms were applied to theory and research pertaining to most areas of women's lives – development, family roles, work, relationships, health and sexuality – sexual violence received particular attention. The first onslaught of feminist writings noted the invisibility of rape-related topics in the professional literature. Susan Griffin (1979), for example, was quick to point out that rape was not widely discussed by male intellectuals who described almost every other form of male activity! The second wave went on to criticize the theoretical content of what limited literature was available.

The academic and clinical literature of the time placed emphasis on the psychopathological nature of sexual offenders – suggesting that they were inherently different from other men – and the clinical characteristics of victims – implying that their traits or dispositions contributed to sexual victimization. Freud was especially notorious, postulating that masochism and penis envy are essential components

of healthy female development and that women possess an unconscious desire to be overwhelmed and subjected to painful sexual
encounters. Experts often dismissed the high incidence of sexual
violence yet frequently made reference to 'victim-precipitated'
rape. While feminists considered ignorance 'the benchmark' of
scientific theories of rape (Schwendinger and Schwendinger, 1983),
scientific sentiments were in line with social attitudes of the day
which suggested that offenders were generally sex-starved deviants
and that the rape of virtuous women was practically impossible.

Not only did feminist scholars point to the neglect and misrepresentation of sexual violence in the psychological literature, they
were also vocal in challenging the traditional and cherished representation of science as an objective and value-free enterprise.
They argued that science, including psychology, does not exist in a
cultural vacuum; rather, the questions we choose to ask, the solutions
we choose to reach and the methods we choose to employ are
influenced by social values. As psychology, like society, has been
traditionally dominated by men, inevitably the positions assumed,
the theories advanced and the research undertaken have been those
that inherently reflect a pervading androcentric bias. Historically,
science and philosophy, moulded from a masculine perspective,
conspired to reflect patriarchal values and to maintain the social and
political status quo.

Feminist critiques of science and theorizing on sexual violence
have contributed to a more comprehensive understanding of rape
by incorporating an interdisciplinary perspective and a wide range
of research methods in the investigation of sexual assault. Feminist
authors have also proposed alternative conceptual explanations for
sexual violence. On the theoretical level feminists have argued that
rape is the consequence of deep-rooted social traditions of male
dominance and female exploitation. In essence, rape is the result of
differentiated and unequal gender roles and social stratification
(Rose, 1977). While feminist theory has not concerned itself with
attitudes in the same way as social psychology, certain rape myths
have been identified, and arguments have been advanced that
attitudes, norms, values and traditions of inequality constitute a
world view which promotes 'rape-supportive' cultures (Russell,
1982). Feminists have also maintained that attitudes toward men,
women and their sexual interactions underpin the social conceptualization of rape and are reflected in the institutional treatment of
sexual violence.

In documenting these attitudes feminists have relied largely on
observation. This has occurred on the macro-level in terms of the
analysis of legal aspects of sexual crimes, the institutional policies

and practices regarding the treatment of sexual abuse victims by legal, medical and social services, the portrayal of rape in the media, and the academic and expert writings on sexual violence. Because feminist scholars maintain that knowledge is rooted in experience, they have also relied upon the experiences of individual survivors of sexual assault to elaborate the phenomenology of rape and to identify the attitudes which affect that experience. In the course of their research on sexual violence feminists have identified a number of rape myths which are harmful to women, men and society. These myths and the ethnographic approaches undertaken to understand and explain sexual violence are discussed in Chapter 1.

Feminism has been credited by a number of scholars with defining rape as a significant social problem, and feminist writing on sexual violence has had a major influence on the reconceptualization of rape (for example, Berger, 1977; Deming and Eppy, 1981). Undoubtedly feminism has affected theory and research in a range of disciplines and in a number of ways; however, the identification of rape myths has, in particular, attracted the attention of contemporary psychologists who have begun to examine feminist arguments via empirical studies. Their research endeavours have been diverse and are discussed in the following chapters. These include survey research on attitudes toward rape victims (Chapter 2), experimental attribution research (Chapter 3), multi-method field research (Chapter 4) and clinical case studies (Chapter 5).

In more recent years psychology and feminism have shared a somewhat more comfortable relationship. Inspired by feminist writings, psychologists have generated empirical data to test feminist theory. These data, in turn, have been cited by feminists as substantiating their claims and have been integrated into their knowledge base for the advancement of theory. The synthesis of feminist theory and psychological empiricism has contributed to a broader understanding of sexual violence; however, the feminist critiques of scientific method remain a controverisal topic. These critiques and the intersection of psychology and feminism will be considered in the concluding chapter.

A Note on Methodology

In reviewing and synthesizing what we know about attitudes toward rape victims, a fundamental distinction has been drawn between feminist and psychological research. This arrangement may neatly fit on the pages of the book, but the distinction between what is feminist and what is psychological research is often difficult to make. The content of the studies is essentially the same, that is, attitudes toward rape victims. The methods are more likely to differ, but even this criterion for distinction has limitations. Discrepancies in methodological preferences by feminists and psychologists are commonly observed, but the set of research techniques employed by the two are by no means exclusive.

Feminists tend to favour descriptive methods set in real life contexts and to emphasize the value of qualitative data. Psychologists, on the whole, are more comfortable with experimental methods, controlled research settings, statistical tools and quantitative techniques. Feminist scholarship emphasizes the importance of studying women in their natural contexts. While naturalistic techniques are likewise available to psychologists, they have conventionally favoured making use of laboratory research to achieve the rigorous control required for experimental studies. Feminists prefer to work with women in the real world, in familiar situations which reflect everyday life, sacrificing the 'control' necessary for a well-designed experiment, but achieving a study which has meaning and value for the participants.

The issue of control often extends to the relationship between the researcher and the researched. In the majority of psychological studies the investigator is involved in a hierarchical relationship with 'subjects', choosing and implementing the research strategy, directing subject participation and activities, and interpreting data according to pre-existing theoretical frameworks. Feminist scholars, in contrast, aim to perpetuate an egalitarian relationship between the researched and the researcher. Participants often assume substantial responsibility for the direction of projects, the research methods and in some instances the release of the findings. In addition, feminist research is designed to empower women, to improve their social realities and to change the status quo. This is often troublesome to psychologists, who generally believe that politics and science should not be mixed.

Not only may feminist and psychological studies of attitudes toward rape victims be contrasted in terms of a general approach or epistemological perspective, but differences may be further elaborated in relationship to the selection and implementation of specific research methods. Along these lines three methodological domains which are particularly relevant to the early interdisciplinary feminist research on rape may be identified: ethnography, content analysis and action research (Reinharz, 1992). Ethnography is a naturalistic descriptive technique akin to field studies in psychology; however, in contrast to psychologists, feminist researchers prefer non-interventionist strategies, qualitative data, researcher integration into the field context, and interpretation of women's lives from an explicitly feminist viewpoint. Feminists have used ethnographic techniques, including interviews, to monitor the interaction of rape victims with social institutions and to draw inferences about rape myths and attitudes. These techniques, along with content analysis and action-oriented research, are described in Chapter 1.

Content analysis is also a descriptive research technique; however, in this instance, public records or archives are the primary data sources. Certainly, archival methods have been used in psychological research. Even when sharing a common archival source, however, feminists and psychologists appear to have different priorities. Again feminists opt for reliance on qualitative data and latent analysis; psychologists prefer quantitative, manifest analysis. In the context of rape research feminists have examined the depiction of rape in the popular press, including news reports and magazines, as well as the professional literature from law, medicine and psychology.

Finally, feminist action-oriented research, defined primarily by its goals rather than its methods, has been implemented in the study of attitudes toward rape victims. Incorporating a variety of research techniques, action-oriented research is designed to empower women and to change social systems. Much of the early scholarship on rape emerged from direct work with rape victims and consciousness-raising activities such as public speak-outs and feminist campaigns to establish services for victims of sexual assault. While obviously significant in the formation of early feminist theories of rape, action-oriented research is discussed in greater detail in Part II in relation to feminist research and changing social systems.

All of these methods are available to social scientists; however, psychologists have generally preferred to rely on experiments, surveys, quasi-experiments and case studies (White and Farmer, 1992). Survey research, discussed in Chapter 2, is based upon non-interventionist techniques and generally involves the examination of pre-existing attitudes or behaviours. Surveys rely upon self-reports and typically include large numbers of subjects; many surveys employ standardized questionnaires and tap general rape-related attitudes either in the community at large or in a more limited and specific sample such as university students. Surveys have also been used to determine the prevalence and incidence of sexual assault.

In contrast, experiments, whether field- or lab-based, go beyond mere description and are used to draw inferences about causal relationships. In the context of research on rape perceptions and attitudes, experimental studies typically involve the presentation of hypothetical sexual assault cases in which characteristics of the victim and/or the offender are systematically varied to assess their impact on responses such as the attribution of blame, fault or responsibility for rape. In some studies attempts are made to simulate real cases of sexual assault by presenting mock newspaper descriptions of sexual violence or court transcripts and asking subjects to indicate an innocent or guilty verdict or to recommend length of sentencing for a convicted offender. This type of experimental research on rape perceptions is detailed in Chapter 3.

Field studies encompass a wide variety of research techniques, although in the context of psychological and sociological research on attitudes toward sexual assault their format is often similar to that of experiments. Indeed, these investigations are frequently referred to as natural or quasi-experiments. In a portion of field studies outcomes such as the likelihood of rape cases reaching trial or successful prosecution of sexual assault may be examined in conjunction with victim or offender attributes. This information may indirectly tell us about underlying perceptions of or attitudes toward rape. In these instances, however, the researcher has no control over the victim and offender traits, but merely monitors their presence or absence in relationship to outcome variables. Field studies, however, rely on multiple methods; they are not confined to quasi-experiments and may also include naturalistic observations and interviews in addition to archival research; in this domain they share methods favoured by feminist researchers.

Interpretative studies, presented in Chapter 5, rely largely on case study methods, interviews or other techniques which are designed to elaborate the victim's phenomenological experience of sexual violence. In these instances victims describe their experiences of sexual violence, their psychological responses to rape-related events, their treatment by social and legal institutions, the responses of friends and family, and the consequences for self-concept and psychological well-being. Both psychologists and feminists have used these methods, but psychological investigations have been conducted somewhat more systematically than early feminist studies on rape.

Obviously, there are a wide diversity of methods available for the study of attitudes toward rape victims. Each method has its strengths and weaknesses, and its overall effectiveness can be best gauged in relation to a specific research question and objective. In some instances the primary research objective is description. This is particularly the case when scholars approach a new area of investigation and must concentrate on examining a phenomenon, describing it and differentiating it from other phenomena. Early feminist studies, for example, characterized by well-developed observational descriptions of rape and rape myths, have given the impetus for later predictive and explanatory research on sexual violence.

In contrast to descriptive studies, predictive research examines the relationship between two phenomena and works toward predicting one by knowing the other. In short, the relationships among various phenomena are examined. This is conventionally achieved through correlational studies and typically involves the use of statistical analysis. Finally, explanatory research is concerned with cause and effect relationships. It is experimental in nature and is also reliant upon the use of statistical techniques. Although there are different objectives in individual studies of attitudes toward rape, the overall objectives become intermingled in the evolution of the research domain. For example, the research process often commences with observation, working through description, prediction and explanation as the field of investigation broadens and develops.

A Note on Social Psychological Theory

With the exception of the following chapter on feminist theory and research, the empirical investigations which are subsequently described fall, for the most part, within the domain of social psychology, the psychological study of individual, interpersonal and group processes. While social psychology encompasses a variety of topics, the study of attitudes, person perception and attributions is considered central to the field. Despite the proximity of attitudinal and perceptual research, there are some differences in their theoretical and methodological underpinnings. As such, it is useful to position the theoretical and empirical approaches to these topics within their respective social psychological traditions.

The survey studies of rape-related attitudes reported in Chapter 2 rely on theory and research techniques which are derived from classic (and older) social psychological studies of attitudes. In this tradition attitudes are conceptualized as relatively stable dispositions to respond in a certain way to persons or objects. Classic theory acknowledges that attitudes have three components – cognitive, conative and affective – and emphasizes the procedures for the development of reliable instruments for the measurement of attitudinal dispositions. Although this area of theory and research sits squarely within the purview of social psychology, it is, in essence, akin to work in personality which similarly emphasizes stable dispositional traits and their measurement.

In contrast, the experimental research presented in Chapter 3 is more strongly affected by the evolving influence of cognitive psychology within the discipline and consequently falls within the more contemporary purview of social cognition. This tradition in social psychology emphasizes the active processing of cognitive information, including the influence of transient situational factors on social perceptions and explanations. The investigation of situational influences on perceptions is particularly amenable to an experimental approach and is often undertaken within the conceptual framework provided by attribution theory, which examines the way in which people generate causal explanations. In considering the differences between research on rape attitudes and perceptions, then, two major distinctions can be drawn between the research domains. The first is the theoretical emphasis on dispositional versus situational factors in cognitive and behavioural responses to rape; the second is the general methodological preference for descriptive versus experimental techniques.

Chapter 4 introduces a new distinction, that is, the differences between basic and applied research. Although the division between the two is not always clear, basic research is more substantially grounded in theory. Applied research, while informed by theory, is more concerned with practical questions and issues. In some instances it is specifically designed to solve a particular problem, as in the case of action-oriented research. In the context of attitudes toward rape victims, the 'real world' provides a suitable context for asking practical questions. Are police less likely to clear sexual assault cases when the victim shows no sign of physical resistance? Are sexual offenders likely to receive shorter sentences in acquaintance rape? These and similar questions are addressed in Chapter 4 on field research.

Chapter 5 presents a combination of basic and applied research in the examination of victims' psychological responses to sexual violence. In doing so it reflects the influence of cognitive psychology in the merger of social and clinical theory and research. The majority of the studies described in this section concern victims' cognitive appraisal of rape and its consequences; this includes effects on both self-concept and mental health. Underpinning these effects are general attitudes toward sexual violence – attitudes held by society at large, embodied in social institutions and internalized by the victim herself. This line of research draws specifically on the clinical literature on stress and coping as well as social psychological theory on self-concept and attributional thinking; in this way it exemplifies an emerging area in contemporary psychology which straddles the boundary of clinical and social spheres.

A final word is offered in reference to the presentation of empirical studies of attitudes toward sexual violence. Rape attitudes are believed by many to be part of a wider implicit ideology about the relations between women and men and the structure of society as a whole. On one level laypersons, feminists and other social scientists have argued that these attitudes exert influence on and are reflected in social institutions and political legislation. On another level attitudes have also been assumed both to underpin behavioural responses to individual victims of sexual assault and to be influenced by these interactions. When seen from these perspectives it becomes apparent that theory and research on attitudes may be framed in relation to the antecedents or predictors of attitudes, the correlates of attitudes and the consequences of attitudes.

Attitudes and perceptions, however, are hypothetical constructs. They cannot be observed directly but are inferred from other sources such as self-report, behavioural observations or archival records. Given the nature of attitudes and the nature of attitudinal research, it is difficult to design studies which are able to distinguish antecedent and consequential factors. For example, is one more likely to have supportive attitudes toward victims because of discussions on sexual violence with survivors of sexual assault or is one more likely to discuss these experiences because of pre-existing supportive attitudes? While these questions are problematic to answer empirically, this does not prevent psychologists (or feminists) from hypothesizing about the direction of the relationship amongst variables or from conceptualizing the issues surrounding rape-related attitudes in terms of antecedents and consequences. Along these lines the organization of the following chapters is based on specific conceptual assumptions. Chapter 2 on survey research and Chapter 3 on experimental studies implicitly highlight the antecedents and correlates of attitudes toward and perceptions of rape victims. In contrast, Chapter 4 on field research and Chapter 5 on psychological responses of survivors are implicitly laid out in terms of the correlates and consequences of attitudes toward rape victims. Nevertheless, the chapters are finely intertwined and, taken as a whole, illustrate the circular relationship between the causes and consequences of rape myths.

1

Feminist Visions

In the beginning . . .

> Do women want to be raped? Do we crave humiliation, degradation and
> violation to our bodily integrity? Do we psychologically need to be
> seized, taken, ravished and ravaged? Must a feminist deal with this
> preposterous question?
>
> The sad answer is yes, it must be dealt with, because the popular
> culture that we inhabit, absorb and even contribute to, has so decreed.
> Actually, as we examine it, the cultural messages often conflict. Some-
> times the idea is floated that all women want to be raped and sometimes
> we hear that there is no such thing as rape at all, that the cry of rape is
> merely the cry of female vengeance in postcoital spite. Either way the
> woman is at fault. (Brownmiller, 1975, pp. 347–8)

Brownmiller's quote gives some insight into the essence of early
feminist writings on sexual violence. Images of rape in popular culture
were explored, and incidences of sexual assault were recounted.
The influence of male ideology on the definition, perception and
encouragement of sexual violence was highlighted. Situating rape
and other forms of sexual abuse in the context of an oppressive
patriarchy, feminists attempted to reconceptualize sexual violence
and to represent it in terms of women's realities.

This chapter features selected early feminist writings on rape. The
literature forms an appropriate starting point for the consideration
of rape myths and attitudes in that it has not only been credited with
raising social and political consciousness about sexual violence but
has also been cited as providing impetus for later psychological
investigations of rape attitudes and attributions. While the historical
significance of this feminist scholarship is widely accepted, it is
difficult to define precisely the boundaries of the early feminist
literature. In the main these writings fall into three areas. The first
and most important includes the 'classic' works by feminist theorists
Susan Brownmiller and Susan Griffin; these are the most powerful
and frequently cited writings on rape in the 1970s. Beyond these
writings there is a second strand of feminist literature which arose
from direct practice with victims of sexual violence. Psychiatrists,
counsellors, women's rights advocates and lawyers contributed to
this literature, combining their personal experiences of working
with sexual assault with professional training to produce commentaries on rape, rape myths and the institutional treatment of rape

victims. Finally, there is a small body of interdisciplinary writings in the 1970s which focused on the critical review of the limited academic and professional literature on rape and rape victims.

To cite the interdisciplinary 1970s feminist literature on rape as a 'starting point' for understanding attitudes toward sexual violence is to present only part of the total picture. Indeed, feminist scholarship does underpin much of the social psychological research on rape attitudes and attributions. But this depiction of the relationship between feminism and psychology does not tell the whole tale. Illustrating the impact of social movements on the production of science, feminism has certainly exerted significant influence on psychology; however, psychological theory and research have also affected feminist thought. The relationship between feminism and psychology may be more appropriately represented as a circle in the making.

Feminist Understanding and Feminist Consciousness

> Feminist consciousness is the consciousness of victimization.
>
> (Bartky, 1990, p. 15)

In her writings on the phenomenology of oppression Sandra Lee Bartky strongly argues that feminist consciousness, while complex and contradictory, is primarily dependent upon seeing things about self and society that were previously hidden: discovering and rediscovering, encountering the painfully familiar in new and different ways. The first waves of feminist writings shared this vision, acknowledging injustices, inequalities and victimization that were always present but viewing and representing these experiences from different vantage points. The topics of discussion were wide and varied – women's work, family, relationships, sexuality, health and social status. The emerging perspective, however, was decisively a female perspective, rooted in female experience. It relied on the interpretation of social reality from women's point of view and contributed to the awakening of a new feminist consciousness.

Although feminist scholarship on sexual violence provided only one avenue for the raising of feminist consciousness, these writings are particularly appropriate for identifying and elaborating the victimization of women. In this context Susan Brownmiller's *Against Our Will* (1975) has been recognized as the cornerstone of feminist scholarship on rape. The book considers the history and politics of rape, psychological aspects of sexual violence, the presentation of rape in the popular media and professional literature, rape and the law, victims' perspectives on sexual violence and feminist responses to it. The work was also one of the first to identify classic rape myths in society. *Against Our Will* provides a powerful feminist perspective on sexual violence and an extensive documentation of sexual assault; however, with respect to attitudes toward rape one of the most significant contributions is contained in the personal statement which prefaces the book. Brownmiller's open declaration describes the dynamics of feminist consciousness-raising. In short, she wrote *Against Our Will* because her visions of rape had changed.

Before commencing the work Brownmiller held many of the traditional rape myths; she 'knew' that rape was a sex crime and that it was the product of deranged minds. However, in working with victimized women she became aware that rape is a feminist issue and that something had been missing in her social education – 'a way of looking at male–female relations' (1975, p. xii). In reformulating her own understanding of rape and setting out her new perspectives, Brownmiller provided insight into the emergence of feminist consciousness. She demonstrated that the personal is political and that knowledge is rooted in experience. Then, in sharing a personal transition, she precipitated a political transformation.

Brownmiller's contribution to the study of sexual violence is notable not only in providing a resource book on rape but also in serving to define and illustrate a feminist approach to the topic. First, the book emerged from grassroots work with women, from shared experiences of victimization. She particularly credited the New York Radical Feminist Speak-out on Rape (January 24, 1971), the New York Radical Feminist Conference on Rape (April 17, 1971) and the joint New York Radical Feminist–National Black Feminist Organization Speak-out on Rape and Sexual Abuse (August 25, 1974) as shaping her writings. Secondly, the work was motivated by practical, real-life concerns, and directed toward describing and highlighting a social problem with an ultimate, long-range goal of changing the status quo and ameliorating the oppression of women. Thirdly, *Against Our Will* illustrates feminist scholarship as a new way of 'seeing', a reinterpretation of familiar phenomena from a woman's perspective. It offers feminist theory which evolved from attempts to describe sexual violence in society, to highlight its significance as a social problem and then to reinterpret it in terms of women's realities. Finally, the work is reliant upon feminist method. Theory and data were largely based on observations of sexual violence and cultural responses to it. The observations derived from a variety of sources including direct contact with sexually abused women, analytical observations of social trends and traditions, and the use of archival records for data on sexual violence.

Multi-method Techniques in Feminist Research

As feminists believe that are many routes to knowledge and have emphasized the importance of experience in understanding women's realities, it is not surprising that Brownmiller and other feminist scholars have relied heavily on ethnographic methods in their studies of sexual violence. Ethnographic methods are primarily based on naturalistic observations. In feminist ethnography the researcher often participates in a social system, rather than remaining aloof and detached from it, and typically relies on interviews to supplement observations and to gain more comprehensive pictures of women's lives. Ethnographic methods share a number of the features of psychological field research; however, feminists emphasize the importance of qualitative data while psychologists prefer quantitative approaches. Another defining feature of feminist ethnography is the significance of understanding the world from women's perspective. Feminist ethnographers draw on feminist theory and often adopt flexible and creative formats for the presentation of their data. As in the case of Susan Brownmiller, they are also more likely to examine the reflexive impact of their research activities on themselves. Exemplifying a naturalistic, qualitative approach to the study of women's worlds the major objectives of feminist ethnographic research are: (1) the documentation of women's activities; (2) the representation of women's experiences in their own terms; and (3) the situation of women's behaviours in social context (Reinharz, 1992).

Early feminist scholars also relied extensively on the study of cultural artefacts, particularly public records or archives, often as part of a broader ethnographic approach. Archival research is similarly descriptive and naturalistic; in this case, however, the study of public documents does not require direct interaction with research participants. A variety of archival sources have been used in feminist studies of sexual violence, but most significant are the popular press, including newspapers and magazines, and academic and professional writings from law, medicine, psychology and social science.

After identifying these documents as potentially rich sources for tapping the cultural expression, production and perpetuation of the patriarchy, feminist scholars subject archives to content analysis, an interpretative process also referred to as text analysis or, in some instances, as literary criticism. In feminist analyses the emphasis is generally on latent, rather than manifest, content and on qualitative rather than quantitative interpretations. In the research process cultural documents such as scientific texts or institutional records are reread from a feminist perspective, deconstructed and reconstructed in terms of what the documents do and do not say about women, and then contextualized in feminist theory (Reinharz, 1992).

While feminist methods in early rape research predominantly relied on field observations and archival methods, it should also be acknowledged that a portion of the scholarship emerged from feminist action-oriented research. This multi-faceted research tradition is politically motivated and directed toward changing the status quo, empowering women on both the individual and societal levels. As such, action-oriented research is more accurately defined by its objectives – social change – than by its methods per se. In her excellent discussion of feminist approaches to social research Shulamit Reinharz (1992) identifies some unconventional methods in action-oriented research. For example, she describes consciousness-raising techniques such as speak-outs or public seminars as not only a form of activism but also a method of data collection. In addition, Reinharz emphasizes the significance of *demystification* in feminist research, acknowledging that the very act of obtaining knowledge creates a potential for change because the paucity of research perpetuates powerlessness. Certainly this is the case in research on sexual violence, an almost totally neglected topic before the pioneering feminist literature in the 1970s.

Early Feminist Theory

Feminist theories of sexual violence have concerned themselves with the definition, nature, causes, functions and consequences of rape. However, theoretical perspectives on rape derived from broader feminist theory which emphasizes gender differentials in power that affect all social interactions between men and women. Feminists have maintained that violence against women is an integral part of a patriarchal society; rape is a social tradition of male domination and female exploitation (Brownmiller, 1975).

A major theme in feminist literature on rape centres on power (Griffin, 1971). Consistent with sociological theories of conflict, it has been argued that rape is a direct function of the degree to which women are socially, politically and economically powerless in comparison to men. Not only does rape derive from power differentials, but sexual violence also serves to maintain the status quo. A number of authors have noted that women have some level of consciousness about the fear of sexual assault and that this serves to restrict and constrain their behaviours (Griffin, 1971).

Feminist scholars have borrowed from psychology as well as

politics and sociology in their theorizing and have incorporated aspects of social learning theory in the analysis of sexual violence. Along these lines it has been emphasized that rape is the result not only of social stratification but also of differentiated gender roles and socialization (Rose, 1977; Russell, 1975). Setting the acquisition of gender-related behaviours in the overarching social context of the patriarchy, feminists have argued that men learn to be aggressors and women learn to be victims. In highlighting the social control aspect of sexual violence feminists have also made the point that rape is a crime of violence and hostility rather than a sexual crime per se.

The power and control issues associated with sexual violence have been further considered in relationship to sexual access and male ownership of females. From this viewpoint women are seen as property, and female sexuality is recognized as a commodity to be used and enjoyed by men (Millett, 1969). This perspective is enshrined in both historical and traditional rape legislation. For example, under Anglo-Saxon law the penalty for rape was a fine to be paid to a husband or father for loss of value to property (Clark and Lewis, 1977). In parts of the Arab world legal proceedings against rape are dropped if the assailant agrees to marry the victim (Nawal El Saadawi, 1980). The current debate over marital rape suggests that rape is generally perceived not as violent, unwanted sex but as illegal sex – assault by a man who has no legal 'property' rights over a woman (Herman, 1989).

Although feminist theories have concentrated on the construction, causes and consequences of rape, a notable body of literature has commented on attitudes and myths about rape. A number of the early authors argued that sexist attitudes and the acceptance of violence, shaped by patriarchal values, directly contribute to sexual assault (Brownmiller, 1975; Griffin, 1971; Mehrhof and Kearon, 1973). Others have emphasized the significance of cultural values in shaping the responses of social institutions to sexual violence (Burt and Estep, 1977). Maintaining that power and privilege mould the cultural pattern of beliefs about and definition of victimization, feminists noted the negative effects of rape myths on interpersonal and institutional levels. They also highlighted the effects of rape myths on victims' perceptions of sexual violence and on psychological consequences of sexual assault (Medea and Thompson, 1974).

Feminist Visions: Identifying Rape Myths

Susan Brownmiller (1975) was one of the first to identify 'deadly male myths of rape' which distort and govern female sexuality.

Working directly with survivors of sexual assault and surveying the representation of sexual violence in historical writings, psychology, the popular press and in legal circles, she recounted four fundamental misconceptions:

1   All women want to be raped.
2   No woman can be raped against her will.
3   She was asking for it.
4   If you are going to be raped you might as well enjoy it. (1975, p. 246)

As well as reflecting popular views of sexual violence, these myths were cited as forming the cornerstone of pseudoscientific inquiries into female sexuality. Their consequences were discussed in political terms with emphasis on the control and subordination of women. Brownmiller was also one of the first to recognize that this unconscious rape ideology was strongly ingrained, widespread and accepted without question. Not only do rape myths disadvantage and oppress women, but they also subtly encourage sexual violence without awareness of moral wrongdoing.

In her reconceptualization of rape Brownmiller argued that rape is not a crime of irrational, impulsive and uncontrollable lust but a deliberate, hostile, violent act of degradation which inspires fear and intimidation. She recommended that we critically examine the elements in our culture which promote and reinforce popular rape myths so that we can go on to consider ways of changing society. Through her forceful writings on rape victimization she has been credited with making rape a speakable crime, demystifying sexual violence and paving the road toward social change.

Although Brownmiller's work is by far the best known of the early feminist writings on rape, a literature on rape myths was also emerging from feminists in other fields. In some instances this literature evolved from grassroots consciousness-raising activities with women's organizations. For example, in her work with survivors of sexual assault Julia Schwendinger identified and debunked five rape myths in legal, theoretical and everyday practice (Schwendinger and Schwendinger, 1974). These were: rape is impossible; a woman who gets raped was asking for it; men rape because of uncontrollable passions; an imbalance in the sex ratio causes rape; and legalizing prostitution will reduce rape.

These myths clearly frame rape in terms of sex rather than recognizing it as an act of domination and control. They also deny the reality of sexual violence while simultaneously suggesting that women are the guardians of morality and men are not responsible for their own sexual behaviour. The misconceptions imply that rape is the response of overwhelming passion which a woman 'invites' by her provocative presence. Consequently, the myths suggest that women, not men, are to blame for sexual assault.

Offering a perspective from the medical profession, Elaine Hilberman (1977) described her experiences and impressions of sexual violence from the viewpoint of project director of an emergency room rape crisis counselling programme. In her work with victims of sexual abuse she identified several myths which were widespread in society and apparent in medical institutions: women get raped because they ask for it by dressing seductively or behaving provocatively; women cannot be raped unless they want to be; victims are floozies, malicious and deceitful. She also described an allied misperception that rape is a sexual crime.

Pamela Lakes Wood (1973) added a perspective from the legal profession by cataloguing rape myths found in the criminal justice system. Not surprisingly, the misconceptions were strikingly similar to those found in the medical setting: women make false accusations of rape because they have consented to intercourse and have changed their minds, because they are mentally sick, because they are pregnant, because they are malicious or fantasizing. Along these lines Wood further argued that the law was designed to afford primary protection to men who may be the victims of false accusations.

About the same time reference to rape myths was beginning to creep into the academic literature. Martha Burt and Rhoda Estep (1977) identified several myths which affected the definition of sexual victimization. They stressed that these pervading misconceptions undermined the reality of sexual assault. Myths included: victims are lying; victims are malicious; sex was consensual; and rape is not damaging. They also pointed out that the underlying assumptions about rape suggested that women are essentially responsible for male sexual behaviour.

In the 1970s, then, feminists had begun to identify prominent misconceptions about sexual violence. There were many sources for identifying these myths. Much of the literature on rape myths emerged from direct interaction with victims of sexual abuse. As such, ethnographic observations and interviews provided considerable information about perceptions of sexual assault. However, feminists drew on varied sources to extract and elaborate popular conceptualizations of sexual violence. These included the description of rape in popular journalism and the professional literature as well as analysis of rape legislation.

Feminist Ethnography and Archival Research

Victims' Experiences with Social Institutions
As a substantial portion of the feminist literature on sexual violence
arose from providing support for rape recovery, there was ample
opportunity to observe and document victims' interactions with the
police, hospitals and courts. There was also the occasion to rely on
archival sources to assess the institutional management of rape
cases. Both observational and archival data suggested that the
policies and practices in legal and medical institutions are guided by
popular misconceptions of sexual violence. The most basic and
consequential myth is that 'there is no rape'. Of course, denial of
rape by legal and medical authorities may be based on a number of
premises. One is that unwanted intercourse is easily avoided. As
one judge summarized, 'A hostile vagina does not admit a penis'
(cited in Robin, 1977, p. 52). Another is that the victim is lying.
Both suppositions are implied by one victim's encounter with
hospital staff:

> My experience with the doctor was much worse than with the police. The
> doctor said he didn't believe in rape of a girl who really wanted to resist
> it. He performed a little trick with me holding a cup and showing that if I
> moved it around he couldn't put a stick in it. (cited in Schwendinger and
> Schwendinger, 1974, p. 20)

The beliefs that 'real' rape is easily avoided and that women
fabricate stories of sexual assault are intertwined with the fallacious
assumption that rape is merely sex. Consequently, issues regarding
women's consent arise in the investigation and treatment of sexual
offences. In her earliest writings Griffin (1971) cited the case of a
Berkeley woman who had been raped at knifepoint on the street at
midnight. Despite the 10 inch knife that was held to her throat, the
police commenced with questions such as 'Were you forced? Did he
penetrate you? Are you sure your life was in danger and that you
had no choice?' and persisted even after she had been subjected to a
pelvic examination which corroborated intercourse. Not only did
repeated questioning undermine the reality of rape and the credibility of the victim, but it also impeded the practical management of
the investigation. In this instance the victim was forced to relate the
story to the police at the crime site while the assailant was escaping.
Her response to the situation was: 'The rape was probably the least
traumatic incident of the whole evening. If I'm ever raped again I
wouldn't report to the police because of all of the degradation. . .'
(cited in Griffin, 1971, p. 32). It is also worth noting that similar
criticisms of police scepticism regarding sexual assault were being
voiced by feminists in the Netherlands, Scandinavia and France in

their International Tribunal on Crimes against Women (Russell and Van de Ven, 1976).

A further consequence of the tendency to equate rape with sex is to assume that the victim might as well relax and enjoy it. In her feminist analysis of forcible rape Pamela Lakes Wood (1973, pp. 209–10) incorporated material from interviews with victims of sexual assault in the Washington, DC, area. Many complained about derogatory remarks made by police investigators: 'How many orgasms did you have?' 'How big was he?' One victim indicated that although rape was extremely traumatic, the police interrogation was six times as horrible. Similar responses were observed in courtroom procedures. Cross-examination tactics such as those cited in Berger's analysis of the prosecution of rape cases illustrate this point.

> Isn't it a fact that at the point when your girdle came off, you assisted in taking that girdle off? Did you in any way pull that girdle down? Isn't it a fact that you helped those men take that girdle off your body? Isn't it a fact, further that you did not resist their taking off those underpants from your body? Is it not a fact that on the third intercourse you said to the man, 'come on, come on'? (1977, p. 13)

When the reality of rape can no longer be denied, patriarchal visions attribute blame to the woman. The prevailing attitude is that she essentially got what she deserved. In short, women are believed to provoke rape by their appearance or behaviour. The attitudes are apparent in police investigation of sexual crimes: 'Weren't you a little cold in that miniskirt, sweetie?'; 'Well, why were you out so late?'; 'Don't you ever wear a bra?' (cited in Robin, 1977, p. 140). They are also broadly manifested in the criminal justice system. A particularly graphic case of victim blame was presented by Sandy Boucher and Susan Griffin in their Power of Consciousness collage. In this 1977 case Judge Archie Simonson of Madison, Wisconsin, ruled that a 15-year-old boy who raped a fellow student in a high-school stairwell was reacting normally to prevalent permissiveness and woman's provocative clothing: 'This community is well known to be sexually permissive. Should we punish a 15- or 16-year-old boy who reacts to it normally?' The judge claimed nationwide support for his advice that women should stop being provocative and teasing men. Simonson stated that: 'Even in open court we have people appearing – women appearing without bras and with the nipples fully exposed, and they think it is smart, and they sit here on the witness stand with their dresses up over the cheeks of their butts, and we have this type of thing in the schools.' When challenged by the prosecutor that this reflects an unacceptable idea that women provoke assault, Judge Simonson replied, 'It sure raises a lot of interest in my mind from time to time' (cited in Griffin, 1979, pp. 86–7).

Although women are largely perceived as being blameworthy in the dynamics of sexual violence, there is also an underlying notion that men are routinely permitted to achieve sexual gratification and are entitled to use women as sexual commodities. A number of rape myths are predicated on the belief that women are essentially the property of men. As illustrated in this description of attempted rape:

> She stopped resisting and she said, 'all right, just don't hurt me.' And I think when she said that . . . all of a sudden a thought came into my head: 'My God, this is a human being . . .' It was difficult for me to admit that I was talking to a woman, I was dealing with a human being, because if you read men's magazines, you hear about your stereo, your car, your chick. (cited in Griffin, 1979, p. 74)

While feminists have been quick to identify rape myths and misconceptions, in particular the stereotyped and inaccurate beliefs that women provoke sexual violence and should accept blame for sexual abuse, they have also emphasized the negative consequences that these myths have for survivors of sexual assault. More specifically, it has been noted that victims themselves often internalize popular misconceptions of rape and subsequently blame themselves for sexual abuse.

> I was raped by my father's best friend when I was 14. . . . Afterwards, I was made to feel dreadfully guilty. This man blamed me. The next morning he told me I was a bitch, a whore, a little slut, etc. etc. And when I tried to talk about it, when I tried to say what had happened to me, people threw the same accusations at me. (cited in Griffin, 1979, p. 73)

Working with victims of sexual violence, feminist scholars were the first to identify the widespread operation of rape myths in the institutional treatment of rape. Although relying on diverse data sources, they discovered considerable overlap in rape myths apparent in medical and legal practices. In addition to this line of investigation, however, feminists expanded their research base and began to survey the professional and popular literature and to consider what messages these media conveyed about sexual violence.

Rape Myths in the Popular Press

The press and the popular media provided feminists with ample archival material on pervading rape myths in society. Brownmiller's (1975) study of news tabloids and true confession magazines unearthed substantial gratuitous sex and violence in rape portrayals. In her first sojourn into the popular press Brownmiller monitored the daily editions of the 1971 New York *Daily News*, which, at that time, had a wider circulation than any other newspaper in the United States. She concluded that selected rapes were featured and 'dressed up' to fit male sexual fantasies. Although rape statistics documented a wide age range among sexually assaulted females and indicated that blacks were raped more frequently than whites, the newspaper was preoccupied with young, white, middle-class and attractive victims. In fact, over a one-year period Brownmiller found only two instances in which the rape victim was not described as attractive; in one of these cases the victim was 8 years old.

Subjecting the press releases to content analysis, Brownmiller noted that rape victims were not described as real, flesh and blood women in the newspaper reports; instead, they were presented in superficial, stereotyped terms as cardboard cut-out figures. Victims were frequently objectified and glamorized, often on the basis of something as trivial as hair colour: 'Blonde tied to bed, strangled': 'Brunette, 26, found slain in village flat.' Little substantial information was actually provided about their identities, who they really were, or what they were really like. For example, victims' occupations were included in press releases only if they reeked of sexual innuendo: model, stewardess, heiress. Yet superficial descriptions linking beauty, vulnerability and sexual destruction were routinely found. In this sense Brownmiller strongly argued that: 'The myth that rape is a crime of passion touched off by female beauty is given great credence, and women are influenced to believe that to be raped, and even murdered, is a testament to beauty' (1975, p. 41.

In addition to tabloid journalism Brownmiller examined a range of true confession magazines in early 1972. She found frequent features on rape, near rape and rape fantasy, often in conjunction with themes of punishment and control. The magazines promulgated a philosophy of male dominance–female submission and made prominent reference to women's wish to be overpowered: 'I thought nobody had rape dreams like mine'; 'I made him do it to me.' In a number of incidences women were punished by rape for being too smart, daring or liberated, again highlighting the social control of 'uppity' or obstreperous women. One example cited was the story of a young woman who felt a little guilty after she was almost gang raped: 'I am grateful that I got out of it without being assaulted, that my sharp tongue and know-it-all attitude didn't wreck my life as it could have so easily done.' The theme was more forcefully illustrated by another title: 'Gang raped by seven boys because I led their girls into a women's lib club.'

Brownmiller's analysis of rape portrayals in news reports and confession magazines demonstrated that selected and stereotypic features of sexual violence were typically highlighted in the media. The emphasis on victims' attractiveness in the description of sexual violence implicitly supports the misconception that rape is a crime of sexual passion unleashed by an attractive or provocative woman. Attribution of responsibility to the victim in rape precipitation is also implicit in true confession magazines in connection with the theme that women desire to be ravished and overpowered. Similar themes, of course, are widely found in popular literature. Kate Millett's *Sexual Politics* (1969), for example, has documented similar rape imagery in modern fiction.

Rape Myths in the Professional Literature

As the popular press did much to reflect and perpetuate rape myths in society, feminists of the 1970s turned to the professional literature in hopes of finding more insightful writings on sexual assault. Unfortunately it became quickly apparent that relatively little existed on this topic (Griffin, 1971). Although scarce, the available psychological, sociological, legal and medical literature conveyed a fundamental scepticism toward rape and a prevailing tendency to blame the victim. The professional writings were clearly underpinned by and contributed to popular rape myths.

Nowhere were rape myths more apparent than in the psychoanalytic literature on female development (as cited and discussed by Brownmiller, 1975). Freud initially propagated the notion that females are unable to distinguish fact from fiction; cases of incestuous sexual abuse reported by his patients in clinical practice were routinely attributed to unconscious sexual desires and fantasies. In addition, Freud postulated that women have an inherently masochistic nature and that they crave the 'lust of pain'. Later psychoanalysts embraced the notion of female masochism and highlighted the significance of these unconscious motives as defining the mature feminine personality. Helene Deutsch, for example, argued that women have the need to be overpowered and that rape fantasies can satisfy these masochistic cravings. It is important to note that the psychoanalytic literature, by and large, did not distinguish rape from consensual sexual intercourse. Deutsch stated that women's ideas of coitus were 'closely associated with the act of defloration, and defloration with rape and a painful penetration of the body. . . . The rape fantasy reveals itself only as an exaggeration of reality' (cited in Brownmiller, 1975, p. 353).

In interpreting the psychoanalytic literature in a later paper Rochelle Albin (1977) acknowledged that Freud bequeathed us the notion of victim-precipitated rape. Emphasizing again both the denial of rape and the attribution of victim blame, she maintained that psychoanalytic theory and practice perpetuated the belief that rape is the result of female fantasy or invitation. In any event, psychoanalytic writings had significant ramifications not only for popular views of female sexuality but also for institutional processing of rape cases. In her analysis of rape legislation and prosecution practices Camille LeGrand (1973) cited psychoanalytic theorizing as a major factor affecting conviction rates in rape cases. This was to be expected in light of Helene Deutsch's (1944) explicit advice: 'Even the most experienced judges are misled in trials of innocent men accused of rape by hysterical women' (cited in Albin, 1977, p. 424).

The expert sociological literature on rape in the 1970s mirrored psychoanalytic thought and reiterated the conception of victim precipitation. Feminists were particularly critical of work by Menachim Amir (1971), who advanced the concept of 'victim-precipitated forcible rape'. Amir's all-embracing definition of precipitation included a range of situations in which the victim had (from the assailant's point of view) implicitly agreed to intercourse or had allowed herself to be placed in a dangerous or vulnerable situation. Consuming alcohol, accepting a lift from a stranger, entering a man's apartment, allowing any form of sexual intimacy and not resisting strongly enough all constituted examples of victim precipitation. Based on his research with Philadelphia rape cases Amir concluded that: 'In a way, the victim is always the cause of the crime' (1971, p. 258). The effect of his theorizing was to make the victim partly responsible for sexual assault and to mitigate guilt of the assailant.

Feminists recognized the operation of rape myths and the misplaced blame attributed to sexually assaulted women and sought to undermine the concept of victim precipitation. In Pamela Lake Wood's (1973) analysis of forcible rape she argued that the only way a woman could remain 'blameless' was to live in a constant state of fear that every man was a potential rapist. Similar criticisms were made by Kurt Weis and Sandra Borges who maintained that according to Amir's conceptualization of rape the 'only ingredient necessary for constituting a victim precipitated rape is the offender's imagination' (1973, p. 80). They also sadly noted that in the absence of any scholarly criticism of victim-precipitated rape they could only conclude that Amir's views were widely accepted. They summarized his theorizing as 'the personification and embodiment of the rape mythology cleverly stated in academic-scientific terms' (1973, p. 87).

The influence of the sociological and psychoanalytic literature was also reflected in medical and in legal practice. Elaine Hilberman (1977) strongly criticized early medical papers for the assumption of victim blame. Physicians were often cautioned that the major objectives in the management of sexual assault cases were the determination of rape and victim provocation (Halleck, 1962). Similar myths pertaining to victims' behaviours were found in commentaries by legal experts. A 1975 treatise condensed a number of rape myths into the description of a *real* rape victim.

> The true victim of rape exercises due care and caution for her own safety. She possesses a reputation for chastity in her community. Additionally, she copes well with aggression, usually meeting force with force. Should she fail to overpower her aggressor and rape occurs, she will make an immediate complaint in a hysterical state. (cited in Berger, 1977, pp. 23–4)

An overarching theme of the expert legal writings on the topic of rape was centred on the obsessive belief that women habitually make false accusations. A 1967 commentary in the *Columbia Law Review* (cited in LeGrand, 1973, p. 936) expressedly stated that 'stories of rape are frequently lies or fantasies'.

Recognizing the operation of rape myths in professional 'theory', feminists went on to reconsider practice. Rather than concentrating on individuals' experiences with social institutions, in this instance feminists reinterpreted rape legislation and its implementation in the courtroom. The following section presents a feminist analysis of law and its relationship to rape myths in society.

Rape Myths and Legal Practices

Feminist writers in the 1970s concerned themselves both with the legal definition of rape and with the application of the penal code in the criminal justice system. Analysing rape legislation, legal commentaries, case precedents and patterns of conviction in sexual assault cases, feminists initially argued that rape laws were framed in terms of property crimes. Rape, essentially, was recognized as illegal, rather than unwanted sex; it was defined as forced intercourse against a woman's will and without her consent – provided that the woman was not the wife of the perpetrator. Secondly, feminists pointed out that even if the specified criteria for rape were met, legal practice was based on the underlying assumption that innocent men are easily convicted of sexual offences due to the false accusations of unstable or malicious women. They also noted that, contrary to the widely cited Matthew Hale adage that charges of rape are easy to make and hard to disprove, the conviction rate for rape was considerably lower than for other felonies (Berger, 1977).

The most powerful rape myth to operate in the legal arena is that women fabricate rape accusations. Their motives are assumed to be varied but include malice, guilt and revenge. Secondary myths derive from this supposition and function to undermine victim credibility:

many alleged sexual offences are merely sexual fantasies; most alleged rapes are actually cases of consensual intercourse; only women with impeccable characters and behaviours can be real rape victims; lack of utmost physical resistance constitutes consent. If forced sex cannot be ultimately refuted, and in the end rape must be acknowledged, then women are held largely accountable.

What evidence did feminist commentators have that rape myths underpin legislation and legal precedent? What evidence is there that rape is perceived as improbable and victims' stories as incredible? The supposition that innocent men must be protected from lying and vindictive women may be examined in relation to issues of credibility, character and consent.

Fundamentally, legal practices and precedents of the 1970s guarded against false rape accusations by critically scrutinizing victim credibility and by demanding corroboration of allegations. Corroboration beyond a victim's statement was generally required in rape trials although this was not the case in other crimes such as assault and robbery (Wood, 1973). In addition, a victim's psychiatric state was considered pertinent to her credibility. Some legal commentators argued in favour of compulsory psychiatric examinations of victims (see Wigmore, cited in Wood, 1973). Others recommended that complainants be subjected to lie detector tests because they are prone to false accusations prompted by neuroses, fantasy, jealousy, spite and refusal to admit consent. Furthermore, cautionary charges were frequently injected into courtroom proceedings with jurors receiving instructions about the careful consideration of the victim's testimony (Berger, 1977).

In addition to the controversy surrounding victim credibility, the question of consent was also a contentious issue in the prosecution of sexual offences. In most cases consent was implicitly assumed unless evidence to the contrary could be provided. In the more stringent statutes and case laws there were requirements that the victim prove she risked injury or sustained injury resisting an attack which placed her in fear of immediate death or serious bodily harm. For example, utmost resistance was defined by the Wisconsin Supreme Court as: 'The most vehement exercise of every physical means or faculty within the woman's power to resist the penetration of her person, and this must be shown to persist until the offence is consummated' (cited in Robin, 1977, p. 144). In practical terms feminist analysts maintained that anything less than sustained physical resistance implied intercourse was consensual.

The issues of credibility and consent were also bound up with perceptions of victim character. Feminists found that establishment of consent in the courtroom was often based more readily on perceptions of the victim's sexual conduct than on features of the crime itself. The underlying rationale was apparent. A woman who has consented to sexual intercourse once was believed to be more likely to do so again. Consequently, evidence about the complainant's reputation was generally admissible in a court of law. Indeed, the law reflected a double standard about the admissibility of information regarding sexual activities. Previous sexual activity could be used to impeach the character and credibility of the female but not the male; past sexual offences were not admissible in rape trials. Camille LeGrand described the inequities as such: 'Legally, a man's previous sexual attacks, even if criminal, are of no relevance to his credibility, but once a woman has had sexual relations with one man, a legal presumption exists that she has consented to sexual relations with all men' (1973, p. 973).

The demands for impeccable character and utmost resistance reflect the assumption that rape is just sex and that most women (save the inexperienced or most violent resisters) consciously or unconsciously desire it. However, feminists were quick to point out that female sexuality and desires were inaccurately defined from a male perspective. In a court of law consent was often implied by normal social activities such as sharing a drink or having a date. Other behaviours which may be regarded as less prudent such as hitch-hiking or walking alone at night were also assumed to be some form of a sexual invitation. In effect, both written and unwritten law presumed consent; the burden of proof of resistance was placed on the victim.

Although feminists concentrated on the law and its implementation in the courtroom, they also commented on extra-legal factors. Along these lines they paid particular attention to the notion of victim blame and precipitation. While victim precipitation was not technically recognized under the law, it was acknowledged that jurors perceive certain circumstances as grounds for defence and as mitigating factors. Commentators noted that the likelihood of obtaining a conviction for rape was enhanced if the features of the case, including characteristics of the victim, fitted more conventional stereotypes of rape. It was also helpful if complainants were chaste, mentally healthy, reported the crime immediately and were willing to undergo the horror of a trial.

Consistent with feminist critiques of psychology, sociology and medicine, commentaries on rape laws and courtroom procedures identified blatant rape myths and their consequences for processing sexual offences in the criminal justice system. Feminists situated these phenomena in a broader context of patriarchal oppression and reiterated the relationship between law and society. LeGrand, for example, commented 'that law both influenced and is influenced by the relationship between men and women in society' (1973, p. 919). Feminists also argued that rape legislation of the 1970s restricted rather than protected women and served to reinforce traditional sexist attitudes. Their early work had much influence on the changes in rape legislation and the subsequent introduction of rape shield laws in the last two decades.

Evaluating Feminist Theory and Method

Theories represent abstract and speculative systems of ideas which attempt to explain phenomena. While all theories share these functional properties, theories may be developed in different ways and allied to different research strategies. In psychology, as in most natural and social sciences, we tend to adopt a *deductive* approach to theory and research. In essence, we assess the validity of an existing theory by empirically testing specific hypotheses and by gathering research data. Of course a theory can never be proven, as such. It may receive support or it can be invalidated through the research process. It may also be revised, refined and reformulated in light of research data.

Deductive approaches are not the only route to theory formulation. Researchers may also rely on *inductive* techniques. In this instance, data are accumulated and examined, patterns are sought, regularities emerge and theories are subsequently induced. While there are those who have called for more data-generative research in psychology (Manicas and Secord, 1983), for the most part inductive theorizing has been criticized by social scientists as atheoretical. Indeed, Milton Blum and Paul Foos (1986) in their book on data gathering maintain that there are few, if any, acceptable inductive theories in the social sciences at present. Despite the views of mainstream social psychologists, feminist scholars have relied heavily on inductivist approaches in their theory and research (Stanley and Wise, 1983). Women's experiences assume priority in the research process; theory is subsequently derived from overviewing and synthesizing experiential data, ensuring a consistency between feminist theory and data.

The appraisal of feminist theory and method, therefore, depends very much on the values and perspective of the critic. Feminists Liz Stanley and Sue Wise (1983) maintain that there are three fundamental and distinctive features of feminist theory and research which may guide evaluation: (1) the core assumption that women are oppressed; (2) the acknowledgement that the personal is political; and (3) the reconstruction of reality through feminist visions and feminist consciousness-raising. In short, feminist theory and research should be concerned with the basic principles and implications of feminism itself.

In these terms feminist theory and research on rape and rape myths are exemplary. Theory derived from direct work with sexually assaulted women and was often developed in conjunction with grassroots consciousness-raising activities. In addition, pioneering scholars often emphasized the reflexive influence that the consciousness-raising experiences had on their lives and then shared their evolving visions with others. The theory and research commenced with the acknowledgement that women are oppressed, highlighted political elements in the perceptions and treatment of rape victims, and, more importantly, was almost solely responsible for creating social and political awareness about rape. In addition, this feminist literature was widely recognized as underpinning psychological theorizing on rape (Sorenson and White, 1992) and as prompting psychological research on the topic (Donat and D'Emilio, 1992).

In methodological terms feminists have adopted a variety of strategies, but have heavily relied upon participant observation techniques in their study of rape myths and attitudes. In many cases their observations were part of a larger action-oriented research programme designed to empower women and to precipitate social change. This line of research is generally favoured by feminists as it is grounded in real world experiences, shares power between the researcher and the researched, relies on qualitative rather than quantitative data, and is explicitly linked to feminist theory.

Despite this favourable appraisal, the evaluation of feminist literature from the perspective of a deductive social psychologist would look somewhat different. While acknowledging the significance of feminist theory, most would argue that these theoretical speculations require more empirical grounding. Psychologists would prefer to supplement qualitative data from ethnographic and archival research with quantitative investigations. Case studies, used in ethnographic research, would be subject to particular criticism as their reporting appears more anecdotal than systematic. This is not surprising given that the pioneering feminists were more likely to collect this material in the process of rendering social support than in the process of theory-testing.

Archival studies and action-oriented research could also be subject to criticism. In the first instance psychologists would be quick to point out the limitations of qualitative interpretations and deficient sampling of archival materials. With respect to action-oriented projects, more conservative psychologists would argue that science and politics should not be mixed and would criticize the value-laden nature of feminist research.

Despite these criticisms many social psychologists have been able to recognize the contributions of inductive feminist scholarship and have used it as a springboard for their own research on rape myths and attitudes. In short, they have tentatively embraced feminist theory and have chosen to investigate it in more depth. Feminist observations have provided a preliminary description of rape and rape attitudes; later psychological research has attempted to add substance to these descriptions and to go on to explanatory and predictive research.

In Conclusion

All in all, the feminist scholarship of the 1970s was responsible for demystifying the topic of rape. It was also the first literature to identify popular misconceptions about sexual violence and to contextualize these myths in a theoretical framework of male oppression and domination of women. What are the myths? Rape is impossible; women want to be overpowered and ravished; women provoke rape and get what they deserve; rape is a crime of sexual passion; women often make false accusations of rape. Feminists argued that these misconceptions are widespread, subversive, ingrained and uncritically accepted. They also maintained that rape myths directly affect the perception and treatment of rape victims. This occurs on both a personal and an institutional level, and ultimately the myths affect the way victimized women view themselves.

Feminist writings on rape myths went on to inspire psychological research on the topic. The next chapter considers social psychological responses to feminist theory and reviews studies of attitudes toward rape and rape victims. This research reflects attempts by social scientists to bring the topic of rape into the psychological domain and focuses on the identification, quantification and prediction of rape attitudes.

2

Attitudes toward Rape and Rape Victims: Survey Research

Do you agree or disagree?

- If a woman is going to be raped, she might as well relax and enjoy it.
- It would do some women good to be raped.
- In most cases when a woman was raped she was asking for it.
- Women do not provoke rape by their appearance or behaviour.
- A woman who goes out alone at night puts herself in a position to be raped.
- A healthy woman can successfully resist a rapist if she really tries.
- Men, not women, are responsible for rape.

And how would you expect others to respond to these statements?

Feminists have long argued that rape myths – prejudicial, stereotyped and inaccurate perceptions of sexual violence – are prevalent in patriarchal societies and that the tendencies to blame and denigrate women are at the core of these misperceptions. The first serious and systematic examination of these feminist claims was undertaken in the mid-1970s by Herbert Feild, who assessed attitudes toward rape and rape victims (Barnett and Feild, 1977; Feild, 1978a). The results of his studies lent substantial support to feminist perspectives on rape victimology. What were his findings? A study of 400 students at a large southeastern university in the United States revealed that 7 per cent of women and 17 per cent of men concurred that if a woman were going to be raped, she might as well try to enjoy it. In addition, 8 per cent of females and almost one in three males (32 per cent) agreed that 'It would do some women good to be raped', and 4 per cent of females and 17 per cent of males agreed that most rape victims were 'asking for it'. Clearly these attitudes, although held by a minority of respondents, trivialize sexual violence by implying that rape is merely sex and suggesting that women are responsible for sexual abuse.

Have attitudes improved since then? Not as much as we might hope. My own research with Betty Newlon at the University of Arizona in the mid-1980s indicated that the percentage of students agreeing that 'it would do some women good to be raped' had dropped to 5 per cent. In addition, only 3 per cent agreed that 'In most cases when a woman was raped, she deserved it'. However, attitudes toward victims were still very unsupportive. Only 36 per cent disagreed that rape is provoked by women's appearance and behaviour, and 60 per cent maintained that women who go out alone put themselves in a position to be raped.

Of course, attitudes toward rape and rape victims are affected by many factors and may vary not only over time, but also across cultures. Undermining the reality of the sexual violence and implicitly ignoring the variety of coercive techniques used to gain sexual compliance, 20 per cent of American students in our research believed that healthy women could successfully resist rape; however, only 7 per cent of German students and 8 per cent of English students held this position. Fifteen per cent of students in Barbados and 22 per cent of Israeli students endorsed the view, but the percentages of agreement were much higher in Turkey (45 per cent), India (50 per cent) and Malaysia (56 per cent). One of the most striking findings of our research is that less than half of the students in the United States, Canada, Barbados, Israel, Turkey, Singapore, Malaysia, Zimbabwe and Mexico believed that men, not women, are responsible for rape (Ward et al., 1988)!

The findings above suggest that misconceptions about sexual violence are still prevalent and that individuals cling to stereotyped, prejudicial views of victims of sexual assault. These attitudes illustrate the common rape myths cited by feminists which pertain to issues of credibility – women falsely accuse men of rape; blame – victims provoke rape by their mode of dress; responsibility – men are not responsible for sexual violence; deservingness – women are 'asking for it'; and trivialization – women might as well relax and enjoy it. But while these findings describe the general pattern of rape attitudes, a finer grain analysis is required.

Along these lines psychologists have become interested in the description and measurement of attitudes toward rape victims. In this context they have posed a number of important questions: what are prevalent attitudes toward victims of sexual violence? What are the best ways to assess these attitudes? Which factors predict attitudes toward rape victims? Do they vary between men and women? Across cultures? Are attitudes associated with certain experiences or personality traits? Survey research has provided the methods for investigation of these phenomena, and social psychological theory on attitude measurement, formation and change has provided the conceptual framework for analysis of the data.

Attitude Theory

Although attitudes have been a central area of social psychological research, have been frequently debated by feminists, and are commonly discussed by laypeople, there is surprisingly little agreement on what attitudes actually are. Robert Dawes and Tom Smith (1985) reported that over 20,000 books and articles on attitudes were published in the 1970s, and during the same period Martin Fishbein and Icek Ajzen (1972) found 500 different operational definitions of the construct! Despite the variations in definitions, attitudes may be described as general, relatively stable and enduring cognitive tendencies to respond in a certain way to a variety of social stimuli. This definition smacks of the scientific jargon of which psychologists are so fond; however, this social psychological description of attitudes can be broken down into a more readily accessible explanation which is provided below.

1)   Attitudes are general or global rather than narrow or specific. For example, you may hold liberal or conservative political or social attitudes. It is important to note that general attitudes may differ from views on specific issues. A person may typically endorse liberal attitudes toward women but may simultaneously support right to life groups.

2)   The 'social stimuli' in the definition of attitudes may refer to people, objects or abstract ideas. You may admire Norwegians, like Asian food or be committed to the principle that all people are created equal.

3)   Attitudes are enduring and remain largely unchanged over time and circumstance. In this sense they constitute psychological dispositions.

4)   Most psychologists distinguish three components of attitudes: (a) cognitive, (b) evaluative and (c) conative. The cognitive dimension refers to the actual attitudinal belief. For example, I may believe that rape victims generally provoke sexual assault by their appearance. The evaluative or affective dimension refers to the appraisal of the belief, the evaluation of the 'social stimulus' in positive or negative terms. If I believe that victims generally precipitate rape, I am likely to hold a negative opinion of them and consider them deserving of their abuse. The third component is linked to behavioural implications. The conative dimension is often referred to as the 'ought' of attitudes. Having a negative attitude toward rape victims who are perceived as responsible for their assault, I am likely to maintain that women ought to dress more modestly to reduce the incidence of sexual violence.

5)   Despite the cognitive and evaluative components of atti-

tudes, social psychologists tend to distinguish attitudes from related concepts such as beliefs, which lack evaluative dimensions, values, which are more abstract, and opinions, which are treated as more specific manifestations of attitudes (Saks and Krupat, 1988).

6)   Attitudes are hypothetical constructs. That is, no one has ever seen an attitude. However, as a hypothetical construct, attitudes have explanatory power in psychological theorizing. As psychologists cannot directly access attitudes, they make inferences about them by observing behaviours or relying on self-report.

7)   Most psychologists assume that attitudes are also mediational constructs; that is, they are linked to response patterns of thoughts, feelings and actions (McGuire, 1985). More specifically, attitudes organize the way we respond to our environments. For example, if we are prejudiced against Asians, we are less likely to have Chinese friends. However, the link between attitudes and behaviours has been one of the more contentious areas in social psychology, and it is widely recognized that behaviours are influenced by multiple factors.

8)   Attitudes are formed through a variety of social influences. On the most basic level they are moulded through learning processes – classical conditioning, operant conditioning and modelling. Positive attitudes toward initially neutral stimuli may also be prompted merely by repeated exposure (Zajonc, 1968). Agents of socialization such as parents, peers, the media, schools and other social institutions have a strong impact on attitude formation.

9)   Attitudes can be measured. Psychologists assess attitudes in a number of ways. Attitudes are sometimes inferred from direct behavioural observations. More commonly, psychologists rely on scalar measurement, carefully constructed questionnaires which quantify attitudinal responses.

10)   Attitudes can be changed. Decades of persuasion research in social psychology have demonstrated that the basic components of the communication process can affect and alter attitudes. This includes the source of the persuasive message, the medium through which the message is conveyed and the actual content of the message. These will be discussed in greater detail in Chapter 6.

Survey Research and Attitudes toward Rape Victims

Survey research is a descriptive method which relies on the sampling of large numbers of respondents. There are various ways to conduct surveys – as interviews, both in person and over the telephone – and by questionnaires – sent by mail or administered face to face. Most of the survey research on attitudes toward rape victims has been conducted with university students and has been undertaken in classrooms; however, there are also studies which have randomly sampled urban populations using both postal questionnaires and telephone interviews.

A portion of survey research focuses on a single question; for example, Charles Jeffords and Thomas Dull (1982) queried 2000 Texas residents on their support for legislation which allows a wife to accuse her husband of rape (and they found that only 35 per cent supported such a law). Most survey research in social psychology, however, uses more complex measurements of attitudes. These measurement scales are generally composed of a number of related statements, worded in both positive and negative terms, which tap attitudes toward rape or rape victims. In response to these statements research subjects are typically asked to indicate their agreement or disagreement. The statements presented at the beginning of this chapter, for example, are items taken from scales designed to measure attitudes toward rape or rape victims. Some of the best known attitude scales in this area include Feild's (1978a) Attitudes toward Rape Scale, Burt's (1980) Rape Myth Acceptance Scale and my own Attitudes toward Rape Victims Scale (Ward, 1988a).

A major concern in survey research centres on the reliability and validity of the attitude scales. Reliability refers to consistency; that is, all items on an attitude scale must 'hang together' and measure the same thing. If the items on an attitude scale are sufficiently interrelated, the total scale may be scored by summing item responses to produce a quantitative index of a general attitude. Depending on the instrument, these scores may be described as favourable/unfavourable or supportive/unsupportive attitudes toward victims or as high/low in rape myth acceptance.

In contrast to reliability, or the 'how' of measurement, validity refers to the 'what' in assessment. Does the scale actually measure what it purports to assess? In this case, it is important that the measurement actually taps attitudes toward rape or rape victims, as opposed to some other, related attitude domain. Of course there are specific techniques for testing the reliability and validity of attitude measurements, and these are considered along with the appraisal of popular instruments in Appendix B.

Once it has been ensured that the measurement instruments are both reliable and valid, they may be employed to examine attitudes toward rape victims in various contexts. Psychologists are particularly interested in variations in attitudes in relation to demographic characteristics. For example, what are the differences in perceptions of rape victims as held by men and by women? Survey research allows the comparison of attitudes among these and other groups.

Social psychologists are also interested in the pattern of relationships between rape attitudes and other attitudes and personality dimensions. For example, are perceptions of victims of sexual violence related to attitudes toward women in general? Is a traditional gender role orientation associated with more negative attitudes toward rape victims? In these instances psychologists are able to examine the relationship among variables through correlational techniques. Of course, this does not suggest cause and effect relationships between personality and attitudes, but the research may demonstrate an association between two or more personality or attitudinal domains.

The usefulness of survey research depends substantially on the sample under study and the extent to which the findings can be generalized. Most research has been undertaken with university students and tells us little about what the 'average' person on the street thinks or feels about rape or rape victims. University students are better educated than the general population, and education has typically been associated with more liberal or supportive attitudes toward victims of sexual assault. Nevertheless, university-based studies may still be used effectively to inform us about the relationship between rape attitudes and other personality or attitude domains.

In terms of survey research on perceptions of rape victims, the most common approach has been to administer standard attitude scales to large numbers of subjects and to compare the responses among various groups within the sample or to correlate scores on attitudes toward rape victims scales with other personality or attitude dimensions. The advantages of survey research are that broad descriptions of general attitudes may be obtained and large numbers of people may be sampled with relative ease. However, there are also certain limitations. First, the sampling issue mentioned above restricts the findings on attitudes toward sexual violence. Secondly, responses to survey research are often contaminated by distortion, in particular social desirability influences. Finally, there has been a problem linking attitudes and behaviour. The fact that one may believe rape victims are generally to blame for their abuse does not tell us how that individual will react to a particular rape victim. More specifically, what does attitude research tell us about rape in the real world?

Empirical Research

Attitudes toward Victims of Sexual Violence:
What Are They?
Early research by Feild (Feild and Barnett, 1978) and more recent studies in social psychology have given considerable support to

feminist claims of widespread rape myths and victim-blaming ideologies. Brownmiller's (1975) description of rape-related attitudes, which maintain that women really want to be raped, that they provoke sexual violence by their physical appearance and that they falsely accuse innocent men, is clearly confirmed by psychological research. Pervading attitudes suggest rape is rare – after all, it must be difficult to commit since women are generally capable of resisting. If it occurs, raped women are in some way to blame for their abuse, probably because of their provocative appearance, but possibly by their daring behaviours. Popular conceptions also reflect the belief that rape is a sexual crime committed by deviant men. This ignores the fact that the majority of men admit to some form of sexual coercion and that date rape is particularly common. There also appears to be little recognition of the role that society plays in shaping rape prevalence.

What are common perceptions of rape and rape victims? Tables 2.1–2.4 are extracted from survey research with university students

Table 2.1   *Attitudes toward rape (Barnett and Feild, 1977)*

Women provoke rape by their appearance or behaviour	49
Most women secretly desire to be raped	13
A raped woman is a less desirable woman	9
A woman cannot be raped against her will	7
During a rape a woman should do everything she can to resist	54
Rape is a sex crime	88
A woman should be responsible for preventing her victimization in a rape	34
All rapists are mentally sick	64

Note: Figures represent percentage of agreement.

Table 2.2   *Attitudes toward rape (Giacopassi and Dull, 1986)*

A female cannot be forced to have intercourse against her will	17
The victims of rape are usually a little to blame for the crime	18
Normal males do not commit rape	32
Women often falsely accuse men of rape	30

Note: Figures represent percentage of agreement

Table 2.3   *Attitudes toward rape victims (Ward, 1988a)*

Even women who feel guilty about engaging in premarital sex are not likely to falsely claim rape	55
A healthy woman can successfully resist a rapist if she really tries	20
Men, not women, are responsible for rape	46
A woman who goes out alone at night puts herself in a position to be raped	60

Note: Figures represent percentage of agreement.

Table 2.4   *Attitudes toward rape (Holcomb et al., 1991)*

Women frequently cry rape falsely	24
Rape is often provoked by the victim	22
Any woman could prevent rape if she really wanted to	22
Some women ask to be raped and may enjoy it	32
If a woman says 'no' to having sex, she means 'maybe' or even 'yes'	29

Note: Figures represent percentage of agreement.

in the United States. Although there is considerable variation in attitudes toward rape, a noticeable proportion of university students hold inaccurate perceptions of sexual violence and maintain substantially prejudicial attitudes toward victims of sexual assault.

Despite the recognition of rape myths in surveys with university students, recent research with urban populations suggests that feminist conceptualizations of rape may be becoming more widespread and familiar. Rich and Sampson (1990) examined rape attitudes in a representative sample of 450 Chicago residents. They found that 75 per cent of the respondents disagreed with the statement that rape is often caused by the way women act and dress. In addition, 89 per cent agreed that most rapes are crimes of violence, and 51 per cent agreed that husbands should be prosecuted for marital rape. Despite the varying levels of education in the sample, these attitudes appear to be more in line with feminist perceptions of the nature and causality of sexual violence.

Sex Differences
Feminists have argued that rape myths in patriarchal societies underpin sexual violence and are responsible for the unjust treatment of women who have been victims of sexual assault. Men, as oppressors of women, are more likely to cling to rape myths and are more likely to blame and denigrate victims of sexual abuse. This allows men to retain authority and control and constrains women to positions of powerlessness in society. Social psychologists, like feminists, would predict a greater likelihood for men to accept rape myths and to hold less supportive attitudes toward victims of sexual assault. This prediction derives from a solid tradition of intergroup research. Studies on social identity and social comparison have revealed that individuals tend to hold favourable attitudes toward members of their own group and unfavourable attitudes toward members of outgroups. Consequently, men should be more likely to identify with the perpetrators of sexual offences whereas women

should be more likely to empathize with rape victims. Are feminists and social psychologists correct? Standard survey instruments have demonstrated that men are more accepting of rape myths (Margolin et al., 1989), have less supportive attitudes toward rape victims (Ward, 1988a), are more tolerant of rape (Hall et al., 1986), have less empathy toward victims (Brady et al., 1991; Deitz et al., 1982), are less intensely concerned about rape (Young and Thiessen, 1992), and are more blaming and denigrating of sexual assault victims (Feild, 1978a).

These trends may be examined in more detail with item-level analysis in survey research. Giacopassi and Dull (1986), who acknowledge substantial evidence of rape myths in their own research, are also quick to point out that rape attitudes vary between men and women. As might be expected, women are specifically more likely to reject the notion that men are falsely accused of rape and that women have rape fantasies. Men, on the other hand, are more likely to agree that normal men do not commit rape. This last finding is particularly significant given the high proportion of men who actually engage in sexually coercive behaviours.

Dull and Giacopassi's (1987) later research focused more specifically on the issue of date rape. In this context, 44 per cent of students agreed that date rape is a common occurrence. However, there were sex differences in attitudes toward dating and sexual violence. Females were more likely to disagree that women who ask men out are probably looking for sex, that women say no but mean yes, and that date rape should not be considered as serious as stranger rape. Again, the sensitive issue of coercive sex between people who know each other – the most common form of sexual violence – appears to be trivialized more frequently by men.

Our own research with the Attitudes toward Rape Victims Scale (ARVS), which taps favourable and unfavourable attitudes toward victims of sexual assault, has demonstrated consistent sex differences, with men being less supportive than women. The scale items reflect issues pertaining to blame (for example, 'A woman should not blame herself for rape'), credibility (for example, 'Many women who report rape are lying because they are angry or want revenge on the accused'), responsibility ('Men, not women are responsible for rape'), trivialization ('Sexually experienced women are not really damaged by rape') and deservingness ('In most cases when a woman was raped she deserved it'). Research has shown that both in Singapore, where the ARVS was originated, and in the United States, where it was subsequently tested, men are significantly more likely to endorse negative attitudes toward victims in all of the above domains.

Research by James Selby and colleagues (1977), however, demonstrated that not all rape-related issues divide men and women. Their study of rape attitudes focused on two themes: (1) rape causality and (2) rape severity. In the first instance, men attributed rape more to both the victim's personality and behaviour than did women. They also ascribed victims more overall blame whereas women perceived rapists as more at fault. Interestingly enough, however, there were no sex differences in attitudes about the severity of sexual assault.

Age and Educational Differences
Feminist scholars and advocates for other oppressed groups have highlighted the significance of education in effecting social change (for example, Friere, 1970). In the area of sexual violence feminists have recommended consciousness-raising as a means of eliminating rape myths and improving attitudes toward victims of sexual assault. Consciousness-raising may be implemented directly or indirectly and may occur on a general or specific level. For example, my own research has indicated that specific knowledge about the nature of sexual offences is associated with more supportive attitudes toward rape victims. In general, however, exposure to broad educational influences may also affect attitudes toward sexual assault. Social psychological research, for example, has corroborated the liberalizing impact of education on a variety of social attitudes and has emphasized its influence on the reduction of prejudice. Both feminists and social psychologists, then, would predict that higher levels of education should be associated with greater rejection of rape myths.

This prediction was borne out in early survey research on rape myth acceptance. Martha Burt (1980) sampled approximately 600 adults in Minnesota and found that education exerted a direct effect on the rejection of stereotyped, prejudicial views of rape. Better-educated respondents were less willing to endorse such statements as 'A woman who goes to the home or apartment of a man on their first date implies that she is willing to have sex', 'A woman who is stuck-up and thinks she is too good to talk to guys on the street deserves to be taught a lesson', and 'In the majority of rapes, the victim is promiscuous or has a bad reputation.'

Along similar lines, and from both feminist and social psychological perspectives, it has been argued that younger adults are more concerned about changing social attitudes, demonstrate greater rape awareness and maintain more liberal attitudes toward rape victims. This has been corroborated by public opinion polls in the United States which examined perceptions of rape causality and support for proposed legislation for the prosecution of marital rape. When Robert Rich and Robert Sampson (1990) queried 450 Chicago residents about conceptions of rape, they found that older subjects were twice as likely to believe that rape was caused by the way women dress and act. Younger respondents were more likely to see rape as an act of violence. Both younger and better-educated respondents endorsed feminist interpretations of rape. Higher levels of education were associated with rejection of the notion that women precipitate rape and acknowledgement that rape is an act of violence.

Age and education also predicted support for legislation against marital rape. As expected, younger and better-educated respondents favoured such legislation (Rich and Sampson, 1990). The same pattern of results was reported by Charles Jeffords and Thomas Dull (1982) in their Texas poll. In this instance, supporters of marital rape legislation were more likely to be female, single, young and well educated.

Ethnic Differences
Rape does not exist in a cultural vacuum; the patterns, prevalence and explanations for sexual violence are influenced by a wide variety of socio-cultural factors and vary across ethnic groups. Along these lines McDermott (1979) studied rape in 26 American cities and reported that 70 per cent of offenders who committed rape were minority men. She also estimated that victimization rates for black and other minority women were 1.7 times higher than for white women. Although these figures are undoubtedly influenced by the methods of handling sexual offences in the criminal justice system, attitudes toward sexual abuse are likely to vary with differential perceptions and patterns of sexual violence and victimization rates.

One of the most comprehensive studies of white, black and Hispanic attitudes toward rape was undertaken by Joyce Williams (1979), who sampled over 1000 San Antonio residents. Informants were exposed to a series of descriptions of sexual violence and were asked about their definitions of the situations, women's contributory fault and willingness to prosecute the offences. They were also questioned about their demographic characteristics. Results revealed that whites were more likely to define a situation as rape and were less likely to attribute fault to the victim than either blacks or Hispanics. Overall, education was the most powerful predictor of rape attitudes; however, this varied across groups. For whites education and sex were the most significant predictors of rape attitudes; for blacks income and sex were the most powerful predictors of rape attitudes, but for Mexican-Americans age was the most salient predictor of attitudes toward rape. Surprisingly, in the Hispanic sample, older adults were more likely to evince a willingness to prosecute rape and less likely to attribute fault to the victims. This study demonstrates the limitations of the bulk of contemporary research on rape attitudes which is primarily undertaken with white, middle-class Americans. Ethnic differences in attitudes to sexual violence exist, and attitude predictors vary across ethnic groups. Consequently, attempts to generalize from limited sample bases can have dangerous and inaccurate repercussions.

When ethnic differences in perceptions of rape occur, black and Hispanic minorities in the United States are generally found to hold more stereotyped and victim-blaming attitudes. Thomas Dull and David Giacopassi (1987) conducted a survey on sexual and dating attitudes in university students and found that blacks were more likely to expect the man to be the aggressor in dating relationships and more likely to see the man as predator and the woman as prey; blacks were also more likely to agree that men would rape if given the assurance that no one would know about it. In a previous study the researchers had also reported that blacks tend to be more accepting of conventional rape myths – that rapes are unplanned acts of passion and that a woman cannot be forced against her will (Giacopassi and Dull, 1986). Furthermore, black women were more likely to blame victims than were white women.

Gloria Fischer's (1987) work with Anglo and Hispanic students also found more prejudicial attitudes toward forcible date rape in the minority sample. Hispanics had more conservative attitudes toward women in general and were more tolerant of date rape than were whites. There were, however, differences among Hispanics which related to bilingual and bicultural identity.

It should not be construed from the above findings that minority groups have intrinsically more stereotyped and conservative attitudes toward sexual violence. Indeed, it may be the case that the factors which most strongly influence rape stereotyping in Hispanics are quite different from the factors which underpin such attitudes in blacks. Conservative attitudes toward women more generally have been emphasized as a salient characteristic of Hispanic groups (Fischer, 1987). In contrast, Judith Howard's (1988) work on rape attitudes in blacks and whites emphasized cultural and structural differences in black and white patterns of education, consensual sexual activities, rape prevalence and victimization, attitudes toward marriage and child-bearing, experience of violence and differential treatment by social institutions. Howard's research relied on a random sample of 14- to 17-year-olds in the Milwaukee area. She found that there were no racial differences in responses to a standardized attitudes toward rape questionnaire; however, when respondents provided spontaneous replies about possible outcomes of sexual assault, young black women were more likely to anticipate blaming themselves in response to acquaintance rape and worrying more about venereal disease, whereas young white women were more likely to express concern over what others would think, getting a bad reputation and feeling guilty. Overall blacks expected more negative reactions from the police and other institutional supports such as rape crisis centres, very likely a realistic appraisal of actual differences in treatment by the criminal justice system. Howard also noted that most racial differences in attitudes toward rape disappeared when education and socio-economic status were controlled, and she concluded that it was these structural factors, rather than cultural ones, which were primarily responsible for attitudinal discrepancies.

Individual Differences: Personality and Attitudes
Feminists have long claimed that rape is a crime of violence, only one of many examples of men's power and control over women. This contrasts with a more traditional viewpoint on rape which suggests that sexual assault is primarily motivated by uncontrollable lust or passion. Social psychological research on rape-related attitudes provides one avenue for testing these competing theories of sexual abuse. If feminist theorizing is correct, we should anticipate that attitudes toward rape victims are strongly linked to attitudes toward women in general; the tendency to blame and denigrate victims of sexual assault is a specific example of a more general tendency to restrict and constrain women in society. Furthermore, if rape is a crime of violence, attitudes toward rape should be strongly associated with beliefs and opinions about interpersonal violence. If the more traditional interpretation of rape is accurate, however, we might expect a more salient connection between rape attitudes and attitudes about human sexual behaviour.

Feminists have not only argued that rape is a crime of domination and control, but they have also been quick to point out that rape is merely an extension of commonplace male sexual behaviours which involve the conquest, domination and exploitation of female partners. Andra Medea and Kathleen Thompson have succinctly summarized this argument: 'Rape is simply at the endpoint of the continuum of male aggressive, female passive patterns and an arbitrary line has been drawn to mark it off from the rest of such relationships' (1974, p. 11). If this is the case, two additional elements become relevant to feminist theorizing about rape attitudes and behaviours. First, what are the attitudes toward male–female relationships? Are they mutually enhancing or fundamentally exploitative and adversarial? Feminist scholarship suggests that tolerance of rape should be associated with exploitative attitudes toward male–female interactions. Secondly, given the emphasis on traditional masculine and feminine modes of behaviour, personality (more specifically psychological masculinity and femininity) should relate to attitudes toward rape victims. Feminists would predict that conventional, gender-typed personality profiles are linked to more conservative attitudes toward rape and rape victims.

The earliest and still in many ways the most impressive examination of these feminist claims was undertaken by Martha Burt, who devised a Rape Myth Acceptance Scale to assess 'prejudicial, stereotyped or false beliefs about rape, rape victims and rapists' (1980, p. 217) and then examined rape ideology in relation to gender role stereotyping, adversarial sexual beliefs, sexual liberalism/conservatism, and attitudes toward interpersonal violence. Her findings lent substantial support to feminist theorizing. Burt reported that tolerance of interpersonal violence was the strongest predictor of rape myth acceptance. Gender-role stereotyping and endorsement of adversarial sexual beliefs were also predictive of prejudicial attitudes, but contrary to popular notions, sexual liberalism/conservatism was unrelated to rape myth acceptance. These findings have been replicated and extended in a number of studies. My own research in Singapore with the Attitudes toward Rape Victims Scale similarly demonstrated that unfavourable attitudes toward rape victims were associated with acceptance of interpersonal violence, adversarial sexual beliefs and traditional attitudes toward women's roles – but not sexual ideology. Along the same lines rape tolerance and rape myth acceptance have been linked with condoning male dominance in sex, the perception of women as sex objects, and the reported likelihood of raping, further evidence of power and control and the exploitation of women in male–female relations (Hall et al., 1986; Hamilton and Yee, 1990; Reilly et al., 1992).

More recently Robert Quackenbush (1989) also reported an association between tolerance of interpersonal violence, adversarial sexual beliefs and rape myth acceptance in university men; however, he additionally investigated gender-specific personality domains in relation to these attitudinal measurements. Of particular interest were psychological masculinity, defined in terms of agentic-instrumental traits, and psychological femininity, described in terms of expressive-nurturant qualities. As he expected and feminists would have predicted, those men who incorporated more masculine traits into their self-concepts were more likely to accept rape myths, tolerate interpersonal violence and endorse adversarial sexual beliefs. In contrast, psychological femininity was associated with a reduction in rape myths, acceptance of violence and adversarial sexual beliefs.

Traditional gender roles or traditional attitudes toward gender roles have been consistently linked to conservative and victim-blaming rape attitudes. Alyce Bunting and Joy Reeves (1983) reported that a 'macho' orientation was related to greater rape myth acceptance. Likewise, Frank Costin (1985) found that acceptance of rape myths was associated with conservative attitudes toward women's roles, Gloria Fischer (1986) noted that tolerant attitudes toward forcible rape were linked to traditional attitudes toward women, and Ilsa Lottes (1991) reported a correlation between callous attitudes toward victims and traditional gender role beliefs. Interestingly enough, this association between victim-blaming attitudes and attitudes toward women's roles has held up in multiple cultural contexts – including Israel, the United Kingdom, Germany, Hong Kong and Singapore (Costin and Schwarz, 1987; Lee and Cheung, 1991; Ward, 1988a). In their Hong Kong study Betty Lee and Fanny Cheung also reported that negative attitudes toward rape victims were associated with traditionalism more generally.

An especially interesting exploration of rape attitudes was undertaken by Leslie Margolin and colleagues (1989), who critically assessed the feminist proposition that rape is merely the end of a continuum of men's exploitation and violation of women. In this context, they considered reactions to 'kissing violations' and their relationship to rape myth acceptance. In this research students were presented with a scenario of a dating situation in which a man and a woman were watching a movie. During the film the man began feeling 'romantic' and turned to kiss his partner. The partner indicated that she did not wish to be kissed because of embarrassment at public display of affection. Nevertheless, in the scenario the man persisted and kissed the woman. Respondents were then asked to indicate the acceptability of the male's behaviour and to explain their evaluations. Finally, subjects completed Burt's Rape Myth Acceptance Scale. As expected, men were more likely to accept rape myths, to excuse the man of any wrongdoing, and to accept the 'kissing violation'. In addition, acceptance of the male behaviour in the research scenario was related to rape myth acceptance, supporting Medea and Thompson's (1974) analysis of male sexual behaviour.

Studies by Sandra Byers and Raymond Eno (1991) and by Gloria Fischer (1992) extended the research on rape-related attitudes to include actual sexual behaviours. The researchers found that rape-supportive and victim-callous attitudes predicted the use of verbal and physical coercion of sexual intercourse. In a parallel study Karen Rapaport and Barry Burkhart (1984) found acceptance of interpersonal violence and adversarial sexual beliefs to be associated with both endorsement of force in sexual relations and coercive behaviours. Charlene Muehlenhard and Polly Falcon (1990) also reported that men who adopted traditional gender roles were more likely to engage in verbal coercion and forcible rape. A series of investigations, then, have reported that attitudinal variables predict not only men's rape-related attitudes but also their sexually coercive behaviours.

Other studies have examined rape-related attitudes in conjunction with dating and general sexual behaviours. One factor which has received particular attention has been sexual activities. People who are sexually permissive in their behaviours are more likely to be tolerant of forcible date rape (Fischer, 1986) and to see rape as a less serious offence (Kanin et al., 1987). This suggests an underpinning of the 'rape=sex' myth. Despite this link, it has also been demonstrated that accurate sexual knowledge reduces rape myth acceptance (Fischer, 1986).

How do these attitudes relate to beliefs about rape causation and prevention? Again, rape attitudes appear to be linked to general attitudes toward women. Feminists are likely to cite societal reinforcement of male violence as a cause of rape and to acknowledge the impact of society's encouragement of passive behaviour in women (Krulewitz and Payne, 1978). In addition, feminists perceive strategies which require men or society to change (such as more efficient police intervention or enhancing male acceptance that a woman's body is her own) as more effective preventions than strategies which require women to change (such as avoiding dangerous situations or learning self-defence), whereas others are more likely to favour strategies which require women to modify their behaviours (Krulewitz and Kahn, 1983).

Finally, there have been attempts to relate rape attitudes to miscellaneous personality characteristics, although on the whole these studies have not been motivated by feminist theorizing. Stereotyped or tolerant attitudes toward rape are associated with an internal locus of control (tendency to perceive situations and behaviours as under an individual's control), extrinsic (orthodox and dogmatic) religious orientation, machiavellianism (the propensity to manipulate others to obtain desired ends), anomie (normlessness or social alienation), dogmatism, untrustworthiness and antisocial personality profiles (Ashton, 1982; Hall et al., 1986; Larsen and Long, 1988; St Lawrence and Joyner, 1991). These results appear to suggest that rape myth accepters are generally unpleasant people!

A Cross-cultural Perspective on Psychological and Social
Correlates of Attitudes toward Rape Victims

Over the past years I have had the good fortune to be involved with an international network of researchers who have examined cross-cultural differences in attitudes toward rape victims. The network includes Betty Newlon (United States), Barbara Krahé (United Kingdom and Germany), Kathleen Myambo (Zimbabwe), Yildiz Taştaban and Şahika Yuksel (Turkey), Rehana Ghadially and Usha Kumar (India), Betty Lee and Fanny Cheung (Hong Kong), Shripati Upadhyaya (Malaysia), Jerry Patnoe (Israel), Carol Kirby (Canada), Antonio Vasquez Gomez, Elena Parra and Laura Colosio (Mexico), Monica Payne (Barbados), Jennifer Boldero and Danyelle Guiliano (Australia). I have contributed additional data from Singapore and New Zealand. The research has spanned several years, employed the Attitudes toward Rape Victims Scale and sampled university students in 15 countries. The psychometric details of the ARVS, including its reliability and validity, are reported in Ward et al. (1988).[1] Of course the research is not based on a representative sample of the world's societies, but to date it is the most extensive cross-cultural project on rape attitudes.

The survey has revealed that there is considerable variation in cross-cultural attitudes toward rape victims. Mean scores on the ARVS range from a low of 18.3 (United Kingdom) to a high of 51.6 (Malaysia) within a possible range of 0–100. The mean scores of students from 15 countries are presented in Table 2.5 and listed in rank order from most to least favourable attitudes.

Survey data have shown that attitudes toward rape victims mirror attitudes toward women more generally. It has also been argued that rape myths function to sustain the oppression of women in patriarchal societies. A fundamental question, then, is: Do attitudes toward rape victims relate to the status of women across cultures? To address this issue we examined the association between ARVS scores and female–male ratios of labour force participation, literacy and enrolment in higher education (Sivard, 1985). Results indicated that rape attitudes were significantly related to the status variables: employment ($r = -.49, p < .04$) and literacy ($r = -.68, p < .005$); less supportive attitudes toward rape victims were found in those countries with lower percentages of female labour force participation and lower literacy rates. There was a similar trend for the association with female higher education ($r = -.39$); however, this was not statistically significant. Various studies, then, have clearly supported the feminist claims that rape myths (Burt, 1980) and rape prevalence (Sanday, 1981) reflect the status of women in society.

Table 2.5   *ARVS scores in 15 countries*

United Kingdom	18.3
Germany	20.9
New Zealand	21.8
United States	26.2
Australia	27.5
Canada	29.5
Barbados	30.0
Israel	32.0
Hong Kong	32.9
Singapore	36.2
Turkey	39.2
Mexico	39.7
Zimbabwe	39.8
India	40.6
Malaysia	51.6

Note: The ARVS scores are weighted by subject sex in those samples which had unequal numbers of men and women.

Continuing along similar lines, we also investigated rape attitudes in relation to value domains. Here we relied on previous research by Geert Hofstede (1984), who conducted survey research on work values in 40 countries. In a massive factor analytic study Hofstede isolated four value domains: masculinity, individualism, power distance and uncertainty avoidance. Of prime interest to feminist theory are the masculinity and power distance domains. It would be predicted that societies which value masculinity and have high power distance (that is, are structured in terms of clearly defined hierarchies and status differentials) would also have more negative attitudes toward rape victims. Analysis revealed that there was no significant relationship between masculinity and attitudes toward rape victims ($r = -.40$) in the 11 of our countries which were included in Hofstede's study; however, there was a strong positive correlation between power distance and attitudes toward rape ($r = .76, p < .003$); that is, students in cultures which evidenced high power distance were more likely to have negative attitudes toward rape victims.

The cross-cultural data are impressive in that they extend the range of variation in rape attitudes and examine broader links among macro-level factors. Despite these findings, however, there was no significant relationship between attitudes toward rape victims and actual reported incidence of rape ($r = -.27$.; Interpol, 1988).

Attitudes in Field Research

Professional Groups   Research with university students has provided us with basic information about rape myths and associated attitudes and values. Of far greater practical significance, however, are the attitudes toward sexual violence that are held by those professionals and paraprofessionals who work directly with victims of sexual assault. These individuals are likely to exert substantial influence on rape and incest survivors and have the capacity to facilitate or impede their recovery from sexual abuse. In this domain police, doctors, nurses, lawyers, social workers, psychologists, counsellors and volunteer crisis workers have received special attention.

The police have consistently come under fire for negative and prejudicial attitudes toward victims of sexual offences. There have been numerous anecdotal reports of police mistreatment of rape complainants, and comparative studies have generally demonstrated that police have more negative perceptions of victims than other professionals. Feminists have been particularly scathing of police attitudes. Brownmiller, for example, charged that: 'Despite their knowledge of law they are supposed to enforce, the male police mentality is often identical to the stereotypic views of rape that are shared by the rest of male culture' (1975, p. 366). While empirical evidence on police attitudes has been mixed, Brownmiller was apparently mistaken to limit her accusations to male officers. Female police recruits tend to see the victim as playing a significant part in victimization and expect substantial evidence of rape resistance in their investigations (Lester et al., 1982). Furthermore, the police may hold even more biased and stereotyped attitudes than those who are unfamiliar with law enforcement policies and procedures. When compared with a student sample, for instance, police recruits are more likely to perceive rape as a sex crime and more likely to point to victim causality in sexual offences.

A more recent and comprehensive study of police attitudes was undertaken by John LeDoux and Robert Hazelwood (1985), who conducted a survey of over 2000 American police officers. Their research revealed a general unwillingness to blame victims or to trivialize sexual assault; however, police were inclined to agree that women provoke rape by their appearance. The officers also adopted a conventional and stereotyped view of rape as a sexual crime and tended to perceive rapists as psychologically disturbed. While the police in this survey favoured strong punishments for sex offenders, they also acknowledged that victims' age, appearance and history influenced trial outcomes.

In terms of rape definition, Krahé's (1991) work in Germany

demonstrated that police continue to hold inaccurate, stereotyped notions of sexual violence. One hundred and fifty German police officers were asked to describe typical, credible and dubious rape incidents. A *typical* rape was described as a public attack, occurring between strangers after dark, and perpetrated by an assailant who is psychologically disturbed. A *credible* rape was depicted in the same terms, although the police additionally expected an escape attempt by the victim. A *dubious* rape, by contrast, occurred between friends and indoors, generally in the home of the victim or the perpetrator. These findings are striking in that police perceptions of 'dubious' sexual offences mirror the most common form of sexual assault!

Stereotyped and inaccurate expectations about sexual violence are shared by other professional groups. Both doctors and nurses tend to believe that stranger rape is more common, and there is some evidence that they, as well as medical students, respond more positively to cases which fit this stereotyped pattern of sexual violence (Best, 1983; Best et al., 1992; Cochrane, 1987). Physicians are also fairly likely to endorse the belief that women contribute to sexual assault by wearing provocative clothing or by behaving in a seductive manner. Sixteen per cent of the doctors in L.S. McGuire and Michael Stern's (1976) study estimated that this is the case in at least 60 per cent of rapes, and approximately one third of the respondents (32 per cent) agreed that this was true 40–60 per cent of the time. In my own research the majority of physicians believed that healthy women can resist rape, that resistance should be the primary determinant of rape, and that women cry rape if they have consented to sex and changed their minds (Ward, 1988a). Physicians are also likely to perceive rape as precipitated by victims' personality and behaviour – at least when comparisons are made between their perceptions and those of counsellors (King et al., 1978). However, experience with sexual assault victims may reduce rape myths and stereotypes. A study of British police surgeons found that the more rape cases encountered in professional practice, the lower the estimate of false rape reporting (Geis et al., 1984).

On the whole mental health professionals appear to be well informed and have positive attitudes toward survivors of sexual abuse. A recent study by Ellen Dye and Susan Roth (1990) found that rape myth acceptance was very low in a sample of psychologists, social workers and psychiatrists; they did note, however, that females had more favourable attitudes toward survivors of sexual abuse than their male counterparts and that psychiatrists were more likely to accept rape myths than other professionals. Similarly, Patricia Resick and Thomas Jackson (1981) found little evidence of victim blame in a sample of mental health workers. They reported that societal influence on sexual violence was recognized and that there was a moderate amount of rapist blame, with particular emphasis on the consequences of disturbed personality.

Some of the best research on perceptions of sexual violence has entailed comparisons among various professional groups. Feild (1978a) examined the attitudes toward rape held by counsellors, citizens, police officers and sexual offenders. As might be expected, counsellors maintained the most supportive attitudes toward victims. The most striking finding of the research, however, was that police were more similar to rapists in their attitudes than to other experienced professionals. In particular, they agreed with sexual offenders about motivation for rape, normality of rapists and the attractiveness of victims after sexual abuse. In contrast, counsellors were distinguished from sexual offenders in being less likely to endorse the position that rape prevention is a woman's responsibility, that victims precipitate sexual violence by their appearance, and that a raped woman is less desirable.

In contrast, Shirley Feldman-Summers and Gayle Palmer (1980) investigated the definitions of 'genuine' rape, perceptions of rape causality and recommended prevention strategies in their study of rape crisis counsellors, judges, prosecutors and police officers. In the main, 'false' rape complaints were distinguished from 'true' complaints along stereotyped lines, for example, failure to display physical injuries, waiting more than 48 hours to report the offence, willingness to engage in non-marital sex, and prior social contact with the assailant; however, counsellors were more likely than criminal justice system personnel to believe that most reported cases of rape are true. Rape crisis workers and members of the criminal justice system also differed in their attitudes about perceived causes of rape and prevention strategies. Counsellors were more likely to view the causes of sexual violence as rooted in the socialization process whereas police, prosecutors and judges were more likely to endorse the position that rape is contingent on women's behaviour. Consequently, social service providers were more likely to advocate changing social norms whereas criminal justice system personnel were more likely to recommend changing victim behaviours as strategies for rape reduction.

My own research on attitudes toward rape victims as held by police, lawyers, doctors and counsellors has been one of the most comprehensive studies in this area. Over 500 professionals in Singapore participated in the survey, which included both a test of knowledge about sexual assault and the Attitudes toward Rape

Table 2.6 *Knowledge about sexual offences*

	Lawyers	Counsellors	Doctors	Police
1 The majority of rapes occur in residences (T)	23	27	28	23
2 Most rape victims do not dress provocatively (T)	72	86	78	59
3 Most rape victims are acquainted with their rapists (T)	44	50	50	49
4 Most rape trials result in conviction (F)	26	49	61	32
5 Most alleged rapes involve extensive physical injury (F)	83	71	85	57

Note: Figures indicate percentage of correct responses.

Victims Scale. On the whole doctors, police, lawyers and counsellors were not well informed about rape; they often held stereotyped and inaccurate expectations about sexual violence. Table 2.6 presents items extracted from the test and indicates that a majority of professionals believe that most rapes occur between strangers and in public places. It is also interesting to note that professionals who work in the criminal justice system mistakenly believe that the majority of rape trials result in conviction.

Table 2.7 summarizes attitudes toward rape victims. It can be seen that only a minority believe that women do not provoke rape by their appearance, dress or behaviour, that there is considerable ambivalence about victims' innocence and the credibility of rape accusations, and that less than half of the professionals regard men as responsible for rape.

The study also revealed that rape knowledge and attitudes were related; specifically, the more knowledgeable individuals are about the actual characteristics of rape, the more supportive their attitudes toward victims of sexual violence. As would be expected, female professionals had more favourable attitudes than males; however, there were also differences among the professional groups. Police had the most negative attitudes toward victims of sexual assault, counsellors had the most positive attitudes toward victims, and doctors and lawyers fell between the two extremes. A similar pattern of findings was later reported by Betty Lee and Fanny Cheung (1991), who used the Attitudes toward Rape Victims Scale to examine attitudes held by clinical psychologists, social workers, nurses and police officers in Hong Kong. They reported that psychologists and social workers held the most favourable attitudes toward victims, police maintained the least favourable attitudes, and that nurses fell between these extremes.

Table 2.7   *Attitudes toward rape victims*

		Lawyers	Counsellors	Doctors	Police
1	A raped woman is a less desirable woman	21	11	14	22
2	The extent of a woman's resistance should be the major factor in determining if a rape has occurred	30	17	35	57
3	A raped woman is usually an innocent victim	54	62	53	56
4	Women often claim rape to protect their reputations	25	10	30	33
5	'Good' girls are as likely to be raped as 'bad' girls	82	83	77	63
6	Women who have had prior sexual relations should not complain about rape	3	4	7	11
7	Women do not provoke rape by their appearance or behaviour	36	42	26	34
8	Intoxicated women are usually willing to have sexual relations	51	37	53	37
9	It would do some women good to be raped	5	4	6	12
10	Even women who feel guilty about engaging in premarital sex are not likely to falsely claim rape	52	55	46	44
11	Most women secretly desire to be raped	5	3	4	8
12	Any female may be raped	71	85	80	70
13	Women who are raped while accepting rides from strangers get what they deserve	21	23	38	35
14	Many women invent rape stories if they learn they are pregnant	14	9	33	42
15	Men, not women, are responsible for rape	50	45	47	39
16	A woman who goes out alone at night puts herself in a position to be raped	39	45	67	49
17	Many women claim rape if they have consented to sexual relations but changed their minds afterwards	37	27	51	51
18	Accusations of rape by bar girls, dance hostesses and prostitutes should be viewed with suspicion	63	27	58	57
19	A woman should not blame herself for rape	62	65	69	54
20	A healthy woman can successfully resist rape if she really tries	22	19	27	52

Table 2.7   *Continued*

		Lawyers	Counsellors	Doctors	Police
21	Many women who report rape are lying because they are angry or want revenge on the accused	14	8	18	20
22	Women who wear short skirts or tight blouses are not inviting rape	24	28	20	16
23	Women put themselves in situations in which they are likely to be sexually assaulted because they have an unconscious wish to be raped	9	9	8	18
24	Sexually experienced women are not really damaged by rape	11	3	6	24
25	In most cases when a woman was raped, she enjoyed it	5	0	4	6

Note: Figures indicate percentage of agreement.

Rapists   While there has been extensive research on rapists' personalities and their attitudes toward women, there have been relatively few studies on their perceptions of sexual violence. One example is Feild's (1978a) research cited previously, which noted rapists' tendencies to see women as responsible for rape and as less desirable after a sexual assault. Burt (1982) also studied rapists' attitudes and compared them to opinions held by members of the general public. She found that rapists were more accepting of rape myths and less likely than others to perceive rape as violent. Rapists were twice as likely to offer explanations for woman's contributory fault and more likely to justify brutality in a sexual encounter. Although rapists appear to be more tolerant of rape and to hold more rape myths than the general public, studies have not demonstrated differences in tolerance or myth acceptance when comparisons are made between them and other violent offenders (Buchele, 1985; Hall et al., 1986).

Evaluating Theory and Method

Evaluating Theory
Social psychological theory on attitudes has provided the conceptual base for the understanding of rape myths, and psychological research has clearly documented feminist claims of widespread negative, prejudicial attitudes toward rape victims. In line with feminist contentions, these attitudes reflect elements of blame and

denigration and portray victims as responsible for and deserving of their sexual assault. Findings from social psychological studies are also consistent with feminist theorizing on the nature of rape – that it is a crime of violence, power and control, rather than a narrowly defined sexual offence. In this context rape attitudes are linked broadly to attitudes about male–female relations. They are associated with attitudes toward women in general, the acceptance of interpersonal violence and adversarial sexual beliefs. Attitudes toward rape and rape victims, however, are not influenced by sexual liberalism/conservatism.

Many feminists have argued that rape represents an extreme on a continuum of male oppression and domination of women. The linkage of rape attitudes with adversarial, exploitative sexual beliefs and the tolerance of less violent forms of sexual coercion seems to support this contention. Cross-cultural research has provided further evidence of the association between rape attitudes and socio-political oppression by corroborating that attitudes toward victims of sexual violence are reflective of the actual status of women in society. And as would be expected, men hold more negative and oppressive attitudes toward rape victims than do women. Although psychologists have long debated as to whether attitudes form broader systems and are interwoven into more comprehensive ideologies, research on attitudes toward sexual violence and their association with other attitudinal domains suggests that broader, consistent ideologies are apparent.

Despite the powerful data arising from social psychological studies on attitudes, there has been scant evidence that attitudes predict actual behaviour. This has long been a controversial issue in social psychology, and empirical research has traditionally demonstrated only modest correlations between the two. While it cannot be concluded that attitudes toward rape precipitate sexual violence, research has shown that rape myth acceptance is associated with coercive sexual behaviours in university men and that rapists hold more tolerant attitudes toward rape and cling more readily to rape myths compared to citizens. Research has not demonstrated, however, that rapists' attitudes can be discriminated from those of other incarcerated violent offenders.

The issue concerning the attitude–behaviour link is also pertinent when we consider the attitudes of professionals who are likely to interact with victims of sexual assault. While counsellors are largely supportive of rape victims, similar positive perceptions have not been generally expressed by police, lawyers or doctors. These professionals are more likely to disbelieve victims of sexual assault and hold them responsible for sexual violence. How does this affect the handling of sexual assault cases? This line of empirical research has not directly examined the impact of attitudes on interactions with victims of sexual violence. Although police, for example, readily maintain stereotyped views of sexual violence and believe that both typical and credible rapes occur between strangers, after dark and in public places, the extent to which this affects the manner of their investigations cannot be determined via this line of investigation. Behaviours are affected by multiple factors including personality, motivation and situational variables. Certainly, knowledge and attitudes are interrelated, and the more knowledgeable one is about sexual offences, the more sympathetic the attitudes toward rape victims; however, the actual impact of these attitudes on interactions with rape victims remains a topic for further study.

Evaluating Method
Standard psychological approaches to the investigation of human behaviour involve describing, explaining and predicting behaviour. Survey research is a first step to understanding attitudes toward rape victims. It describes the prejudicial misconceptions about sexual violence and victims of sexual assault. But the survey method has also advanced social psychological research by explaining these attitudes and assessing the association between perceptions of rape and other attitudinal domains.

The strength of survey research on attitudes is based on scalar reliability and validity. In this context there are a number of robust measurement scales for the assessment of attitudes toward rape and rape victims. However, the problem of response bias due to the influences of social desirability and evaluation apprehension remain to be considered. Social psychological research has consistently demonstrated that individuals will distort questionnaire responses in order to present a positive image of themselves. While this can be reduced by anonymous participation in survey research, there is the possibility that genuine attitudes may be even more prejudicial than those reported in social psychological studies. Consequently, the results of survey research should be viewed with at least minimal caution.

The quality of psychological research is also dependent upon samples. A substantial proportion of studies have utilized university students, and the findings may not generalize well across populations. Of greater significance are investigations with random samples of populations and with specific groups which deal with victims of sexual assault. In the first instance, the results have greater external validity. In the latter case, the findings may be more relevant to the real world and more directly impinge upon rape victims. Cross-cultural research has also extended the field and offered important information about rape attitudes.

Unlike experimental research, descriptive survey methods cannot predict cause and effect relationships. There is also the ever-present problem in attitude research about the relationship between general attitudes and specific behaviours. Nevertheless, if evaluated from a psychological perspective, the survey method is reasonably robust and has provided reliable and valid, although limited, information about rape attitudes.

Feminists evaluate methodological concerns from an alternative perspective and rely upon different criteria in their assessment of survey research. In some cases research is viewed as feminist if it serves the aims of the women's movement or works toward changing the status of women in society. In this sense social psychological survey research on attitudes toward rape victims may be viewed as feminist. However, others argue that feminist scholarship is defined by methods which are qualitatively different from those observed in mainstream psychology. This includes power-sharing in the research enterprise, an egalitarian relationship between the reseacher and the 'subjects', an explicit statement of feminist values, observational and non-interventionist research in naturalistic settings, and emphasis on qualitative data and human experience. In those terms survey research may serve the aims of the feminist movement but does not employ the supposedly prescribed means.

In Conclusion

Attitude research has concentrated on individuals' relatively stable dispositions to respond to rape and rape victims in positive or negative fashions. Along these lines, social psychology has corroborated feminist claims that rape myths are widespread and detrimental to victims of sexual violence. In line with feminist theorizing, rape attitudes are linked to general attitudes toward women, attitudes toward violence and exploitative attitudes toward male–female relationships. Attitudes toward rape victims are also reflective of women's status in society. All of this suggests that the feminist positioning of rape in the context of power and control is most appropriate. In the domain of attitude research feminism and social psychology have been sisters in exposing the prejudices against victims of sexual abuse and the nature of sexual violence. However, attitude research has emphasized dispositions or general response tendencies. It is also important to learn more about specific situational factors which affect perceptions of sexual violence. The situational influences on rape perceptions and attitudes are considered in the next chapter on experimental psychology and attribution theory.

Note

1 Neither the monograph nor the correlational analyses include Australian data. See Boldero and Guiliano (1990) for a discussion of Australian findings.

3

Rape Perceptions and Attributions: Experimental Research

Karen and Michael have been dating for two months. Over a holiday weekend they attended a barbecue with a number of mutual friends. Both Karen and Michael consumed large amounts of alcohol during the day. Later that evening Michael drove Karen home, and she invited him in for another drink. After some conversation they began to kiss, and this led to Michael fondling Karen's breasts. Both Karen and Michael were sexually aroused, but Karen did not want to continue with physical intimacy and suggested that they stop. She got up to fix another drink, but Michael pulled her back onto the sofa and continued to kiss her. When she resisted, he became more forceful. Karen tried to push Michael away, but he persisted, trying to coax her into intercourse. When she became uncooperative, he removed her underwear, penetrated her against her will and ejaculated. After the incident, Michael finished his drink, said good-night and went home.

> Was Karen raped?
> Who was responsible for the incident?
> Would you believe this story?
> How serious is the incident?
> Is Karen a 'good' person? Do you like her?

Marybeth was walking home after a church meeting. It was dark, but she had travelled that route many times before and believed that she was safe. When she crossed the street and detoured near a park, she was confronted by a man who pointed a knife at her. He dragged her behind some bushes, holding the blade to her throat. Marybeth struggled, but the man retaliated by pushing her to the ground and ripping her clothes. He removed her underwear, penetrated her against her will and ejaculated. He then ran off, leaving Marybeth lying on the ground.

> Was Marybeth raped?
> Who was responsible for the incident?
> Would you believe this story?
> How serious is the incident?
> Is Marybeth a 'good' person? Do you like her?

Although both of the above cases meet the criteria for a legal definition of rape, most people would respond very differently to Karen and to Marybeth. In many instances there would be some hesitation to define Karen's situation as rape. It would be argued that she had been drinking, that she knew Michael, invited him into her apartment and was willing to engage in some forms of physical intimacy. Although Karen declined to have sexual intercourse, not everyone would agree that her refusal was clear and forceful. To some her behaviour would be interpreted as ambiguous, and others may believe that she was not really unwilling to have intercourse.

This can be contrasted with Marybeth's experience. Marybeth was attending church prior to the incident. She was unacquainted with the assailant, did not engage in any ambiguous or overtly provocative behaviour, and physically resisted the assault even though she was threatened with a weapon. Although her behaviour may be perceived as incautious, her lack of consent undoubtedly appears clear-cut. Most people would readily accept that Marybeth had been the victim of a brutal rape.

If judgements were made about these cases, such salient features as victim behaviour and relationship with the offender would not only affect the definition of rape and the perceived credibility of the victim, but would also influence the attribution of responsibility for the incident. It is less likely that Marybeth, compared to Karen, would be blamed for her sexual assault. She did not behave in a provocative fashion and had no previous relationship with the perpetrator. Karen, on the other hand, is more likely to be perceived as inviting sexual intercourse in a dating situation.

It might also be argued that Marybeth's rape is more serious and that she would suffer more severe psychological consequences. In this instance the forceful violation by a stranger might be distinguished from 'normal' sexual intercourse between heterosexual couples. In addition, given the victims' behaviours before the sexual assault (drinking versus attending church), Marybeth would probably be perceived as more likeable and would evoke a more sympathetic response than Karen.

Would you agree? And what does psychological research tell us?

Certainly there is ample empirical evidence which indicates that situations are defined as rape in relation to the amount of force used on the victim and the ambiguity of the victim's response. In addition, resistant victims are seen as more credible. Furthermore, studies have revealed that forced sex between dating couples is considered justified depending on the man's level of sexual arousal, the amount of money spent on the date, and previous intimacy. Given the case characteristics, then, psychological research would predict that Marybeth is more likely to be believed and that she is more likely to be perceived as a legitimate victim of rape.

Karen, on the whole, would evoke less sympathetic responses. For example, studies have indicated that women who have been raped by acquaintances are seen as more responsible for their assault than women who have been raped by strangers. Research has also demonstrated that stranger rape is perceived as more serious and as precipitating greater psychological distress. Finally, a number of investigations have shown that 'respectable' victims are liked more than 'unrespectable' ones. Given the case characteristics, then, Marybeth is likely to be perceived as less responsible, as suffering greater psychological distress, and as a more attractive and likeable person.

It is clear from the above that individuals take into account a range of factors – victim, assailant and situational characteristics – when they respond to rape-related issues. In the broadest terms cases which more readily conform to the common stereotypes of rape are more likely to be defined as such, to be perceived as serious and to evoke more sympathy for the victims. While this reflects a general trend, a finer grained analysis of the range of factors and the magnitude of their influence on the perception and interpretation of rape is required.

Along these lines psychologists have begun to become interested in the way people process information about sexual violence. In this context they have posed a number of important questions: How is rape defined? Who or what is responsible for the event? How is blame apportioned? Which characteristics of the victim, the assailant and the situation affect our perceptions and interpretations of sexual violence? Experimental social psychology has provided the methods for investigation of these phenomena, and attribution theory has provided the conceptual framework for analysis of the data.

Experimental Social Psychology and Perceptions of Sexual Violence

Unlike descriptive survey methods which assess the static relationships between demographic factors and rape-related attitudes, experimental methods deal with the manipulation of variables and the establishment of cause and effect relationships. In order to establish causal relationships, however, the experimenter must exert considerable control over the research conditions and procedure. In the simplest terms, the logic of an experiment involves creating a situation or an environment in which all factors or variables are identical except for the specific factor under investigation. This factor, variable or 'cause' is manipulated while changes in various outcomes or 'effects' are monitored. In psychological jargon, the manipulated factor, that is, the presumed cause in the cause and effect relationship, is referred to as the independent variable. In contrast, the unconstrained outcome or result, that is, the presumed effect in the relationship, is referred to as the dependent variable.

In addition to the manipulation of independent or causal variables, experimentation demands the control of other factors which may contaminate the cause and effect relationship. There are various techniques for doing this, such as the use of constancy and balancing. For example, the two cases presented above would not make suitable contrasts for an experimental investigation of attribution of responsibility for rape. If, as predicted, subjects attributed more blame to Karen than to Marybeth, the experimenter would be unable to draw conclusions about which factor contributed to the differential outcome. The cases vary on so many features (for example, acquaintanceship, use of weapon, forcefulness of resistance), and any of these factors may have determined the differential blame attributions. To identify the cause of the attribution effect the researcher should hold all case characteristics constant except for the independent variable of interest. To illustrate, two versions of Marybeth's case could be presented. In each case the details would be identical except that in one instance the victim is described as walking home from a bar and in the other as walking home from church. If responses to these two versions resulted in different outcomes, the experimenter could confidently conclude that the effects were due to differences in the victims' pre-rape behaviours.

Of course it is often the case that psychologists are interested in the influence of more than one factor on rape perceptions and interpretations. However, the same rationale applies, and constancy and balancing could be used in tandem to achieve the appropriate level of control in multi-factorial experimental designs. For example, Marybeth may be presented as returning from church or a bar and as being assaulted by a stranger or by an acquaintance. If the experimental conditions are balanced so that four versions of the scenario are utilized (bar/church × acquaintance/stranger), the researcher may draw conclusions about the effects of both pre-rape behaviour and relationship to offender on rape attribution. In addition, the interaction between these factors may be considered.

In terms of experimental research on rape victims the most common approach is to use hypothetical scenarios. These most frequently occur in the form of written vignettes, such as mock newspaper articles, trial transcripts or general descriptions such as those above; they are sometimes accompanied by photographs of the alleged victim. Audio- and videotapes of interviews with model victims of sexual assault are also occasionally employed.

In response to these case descriptions subjects are asked to consider issues such as victim and offender credibility, blame, responsibility, trial verdict or sentencing outcome. Typically they rely on quantitative rating scales to make their evaluations. In the experimental tradition characteristics of the victim (for example, attractiveness, respectability), assailant (for example, social status, race) and encounter (for example, setting, outcome) are varied and sometimes additionally considered in conjunction with observer characteristics (for example, personality, gender) to examine their impact on attitudes toward rape and rape victims. Attribution theory provides the theoretical underpinnings for most of these investigations.

The advantages of the experimental approach are that the researcher can undertake a detailed and comprehensive analysis of the quantity and quality of factors that affect judgements of rape and perceptions of rape victims. A major drawback, however, is that there are limitations as to how much this technique will tell us about how an individual will respond to a particular real life case. This type of research, consequently, is often criticized in terms of its external validity or generalizability.

Attribution Theory

Classic Theories and Victimology Research

Attribution theory is a collection of ideas about the cognitive processes people rely upon to make sense of the world. The theories are concerned with how, when and why causal inferences are established. Early theorists such as Fritz Heider (1958) concentrated on conceptual frameworks for the analysis of attributions. Heider described the types of attributions people rely upon, distinguishing internal (for example, due to one's disposition) and external (for example, due to circumstances or luck) factors. Later work refined the internal–external distinction and elaborated stability controllability and globality dimensions of causal attributions. Harold Kelley (1973), by contrast, emphasized the fundamental elements in the attribution process, highlighting consensus, distinctiveness and consistency as guiding our cognitive processing. In addition to the structure and function of attributions, the literature has also been concerned with the operation of biases in cognitive processing; for example, it has been noted that different attributions are made when explaining one's own behaviour compared to the behaviour of others.

Detailed descriptions of classic attribution theory are beyond the scope of this book; however, an important area of attribution theory as it relates to sexual assault concerns the proposed motivational influences on causal thinking. Theorists have argued that two basic ego-protective processes are at work in understanding and explaining behaviour. The first process has an instrumental objective – to maintain control over one's environment. The second is directed toward an affective aim – to enhance self-esteem. When these attributional motivations are linked to the victimology literature, two conceptual frameworks emerge: (1) the 'just world' hypothesis and (2) the theory of defensive attribution styles.

Pioneering work by Milton Lerner, Elaine Walster and Elliot Aronson has been synthesized into what is now known as the 'just world' hypothesis. The basic assumption behind the 'just world' phenomenon is that attributions are predicated on the belief that individuals get what they deserve and deserve what they get. Influenced by earlier work by Heider, the theorists acknowledged that both behavioural and dispositional factors are evoked in explaining events. However, in cases where individuals suffer misfortune but appear behaviourally blameless, there is a tendency to derogate and denigrate them, suggesting that they are in some way deserving of their fates. This tendency was apparent in studies by Lerner and Simmons (1966) which found that observers derogated victims when they were unable to compensate them for their suffering. Jones and Aronson (1973), who later referred to this as the 'just world' phenomenon, lent further credence to the notion of victim deservingness. Approaching the phenomena from the opposite perspective (that is, when victims' characters are beyond reproach, their behaviours must be blamed for precipitating the misfortune), the researchers demonstrated that individuals of good moral character were seen more at fault in their criminal victimization. Walster's (1966) research with accident victims contributed further to the theory by postulating the motivational elements in the attributional process and highlighting the need for control. In short, psychologists concur that observers feel less vulnerable and more in control of their own fates if they can either generate explanations based on blameworthy behaviours or can distinguish themselves from deserving victims.

Despite the popularity of this theory, it appears to have some limitations. In particular, empathy with victims has been suggested to affect the motivational biases in cognitive processing and to decrease victim blame and denigration. In this context an alternative theory of defensive attribution styles was generated by Kelly Shaver's (1970) work with accident victims. Shaver noted that as victims become more similar to observers, there is a decrement in the attribution of responsibility. Two prerequisites are necessary for the emergence of the defensive style: (1) perceived similarity with the victim and (2) recognition that a similar fate may befall the observer. As we will see later, the defensive attribution theory has been used to explain sex differences in perceptions of rape victims and attributions of blame, fault and responsibility.

As can be observed from the above description, attribution theory is especially relevant to understanding and interpreting perceptions of victims of sexual violence. Its emphasis on issues of blame and responsibility as well as its consideration of victim denigration reflect feminist concerns for victims of sexual assault. For example, Ward (1988a) identified and elaborated salient themes in the rape victimology literature, adding to issues of blame and denigration, trivialization, victim credibility and victim deservingness. These themes have also been investigated in attribution research in contemporary experimental psychology.

Models of Blame in Rape Victimology Research

While emphasis here is placed specifically on perceptions of and attitudes toward rape *victims*, sexual violence can be viewed from a broader perspective. Rape occurs in a social context which brings together an offender and a victim in a particular situation and in a specific society. As such, multiple factors should be considered in predicting, explaining and interpreting sexual violence. Attribution research has certainly demonstrated that victim, offender and situational factors are important in defining rape and apportioning responsibility and blame.

Stanley Brodsky (1976) identified four primary factors – the victim, offender, situation and society – and lucidly discussed what he termed 'blame models' in his analysis of strategies for the prevention of sexual violence. He first noted the widespread existence of victim-blame models which highlight victim behaviour (for example, provocative, incautious) and victim character (for example, immoral) and their role in precipitating sexual abuse. This was contrasted with models of offender blame. Again either offender behaviour or character might be considered, although in most cases sexually deviant or aggressive traits are more likely to be stressed. Situational features of sexual violence which are frequently emphasized relate to location (for example, dark alleys) and context (for example, high alcohol consumption). Finally, societal blame is elaborated, where elements of social values and customs which contribute to the abuse of women are highlighted. Along these lines experimental attribution research has pursued the investigation of the effects of victim, offender and situational influences on perceptions of sexual violence.

Experimental Research on Attribution

The following sections review the results of experimental research on the perceptions of rape victims. The methodology employed has been described above, and typically involves the use of hypothetical scenarios with manipulated variations of victim, offender and situational characteristics. Various outcome measures are utilized in the experimental research: responsibility, blame, victim and offender likeability, likelihood of sexual assault, and credibility. In addition to defining rape the following sections highlight the outcome measures consistent with Ward's (1988a) emphasis on credibility, trivialization, denigration, blame and deservingness.

Definitions of Rape

Definitions of rape emerging from experimental attribution research reflect the same rape myths disparaged by feminists and typically observed in attitude surveys. Hypothetical scenarios that correspond to stereotyped misconceptions, such as provocative female behaviour, are more readily labelled as rape. In contrast, the more common pattern of sexual assault, such as forced sex between dating couples, is often considered normal behaviour and is recognized neither as sexually abusive nor as criminal.

Characteristics of both the victim and offender affect the perception and definition of rape. For example, a sexual encounter is more likely to be defined as rape with: the increasing use of male force, including weapons; strong and early onset of female resistance; and sustained physical injuries (Krulewitz and Nash, 1979; Krulewitz and Payne, 1978; Shotland and Goodstein, 1983). Identifiable provocation augments the perceived likelihood of rape (Kanekar et al., 1981), and victims' physical attractiveness increases the acknowledgement that rape has occurred (Seligman et al., 1977). Any ambiguity in female behaviour which might suggest sexual desire diminishes the probability that intercourse will be labelled as rape (Johnson and Jackson, 1988). Although relatively little experimental work has been done explicitly on victim credibility in relation to rape definitions, two findings merit specific attention: emotionally expressive victims are seen as more believable than emotionally repressed ones (Calhoun et al., 1981); and resistant victims are also seen as more credible (Wyer et al., 1985).

Situational factors also play a role in the cognitive processing of rape-related information. Alcohol consumption by both parties decreases the likelihood of labelling unwanted intercourse as rape (Norris and Cubbins, 1992). Sexual encounters between strangers are more readily defined as rape than sexual encounters between friends (Tetreault and Barnett, 1987). However, attributions of rape also vary according to the type of acquaintanceship. Women, for example, are more likely to define forced intercourse on a 'pick-up date' as rape than forced intercourse in a more traditional dating situation (for example, man asks the woman for a date and pays for the evening's expenses) (Jenkins and Dambrot, 1987).

Trivialization

Feminists have discussed society's indifference to sexual violence and have suggested that the reluctance to address this issue critically is based on assumptions about the nature of male–female relationships and sexual encounters. Along these lines they have identified a particularly insidious rape myth that equates rape with sex. Starting with this erroneous supposition, the reasoning continues: Women generally want sex, and if they do not, they could at least still enjoy it. Consequently, if rape is really only sex, what, then, are women complaining about?

Attribution research implicitly confirms the existence of the 'rape = sex' myth and the consequent trivialization of sexual violence. More specifically, experimental investigations have demonstrated that victim characteristics mediate perceptions of the psychological effects of sexual violence. Rape is presumed to be less damaging to sexually experienced women and to 'unrespectable' victims (Luginbuhl and Mullin, 1981). The effects of sexual assault are also trivialized if women do not respond in the anticipated fashion. For example, the consequences of sexual assault are presumed to be less serious if victims appear emotionally stable and remain calm (Krulewitz, 1982).

Situational features are also seen to mitigate the significance and consequences of forced sex. Not only is acquaintance rape perceived as less serious and traumatizing than stranger rape, but varying degrees of seriousness are attributed to different types of date rapes (Bridges, 1991). For example, forced sex among dating partners is considered more justifiable if the woman asked the man to go out and if the man paid for all the expenses (Muehlenhard et al.,1985). Overall these attributions tend to trivialize the impact of sexual violence on the bulk of sexual assault victims.

Denigration

In addition to trivializing the consequences of sexual assault, it is common for victims to be denigrated, even to be seen as deserving of sexual violence. In this vein a number of attribution studies have considered emotional and evaluative responses to victims of sexual assault. As would be expected, people respond more favourably to victims who appear to possess positive qualities and victims with whom they can readily identify.

Physical attractiveness appears to have powerful effects on perceptions of sexual assault victims. Unattractive victims evoke more negative feelings; attractive victims, by contrast, are liked more and elicit more sympathetic reponses even though they are perceived as more seductive (Deitz et al., 1984; Jacobson and Popovich, 1983). Respectable victims (most typically defined in terms of occupations) are liked more than unrespectable victims and are likewise seen as better persons (Luginbuhl and Mullin, 1981; Smith et al., 1976). They are also judged as more similar to observers (Mazelan, 1980).

Both pre- and post-rape behaviours affect evaluations of victims. In the first instance, cautious victims are perceived more positively than careless ones (Wilcox and Jackson, 1985). In the second, emotionally expressive victims are liked more than emotionally controlled victims (Calhoun et al., 1981); they also elicit stronger feelings of identification (Krulewitz, 1981). Situational aspects of sexual assault may also influence perceptions of victims. For example, studies show that women who are raped by strangers are liked less than those assaulted by acquaintances (Tetreault and Barnett, 1987).

Blame, Fault and Responsibility

The Victim Perhaps one of the most significant areas of experimental research on perceptions of rape victims is the area of blame and responsibility. In this context victim characteristics such as physical attractiveness and pre-assault behaviours have received special attention. On the first count research demonstrates that unattractive victims are generally perceived as more at fault than attractive victims (Seligman et al., 1977; Thornton and Ryckman, 1983; Tieger, 1981). This may be in line with a general contention that beautiful is good, a typical finding in social psychological research. Beyond that, some researchers have inferred that an unattractive victim is liable to be perceived as acting in some way to precipitate her rape, and, therefore, is more at fault.

As commonly held rape myths perpetuate the notion that victims are generally responsible for their assaults, provocativeness has been considered an important element in the attribution process. Although provocativeness can be perceived in many ways and is often differentially interpreted by men and women, victims' mode of dress and seductive behaviours have been highlighted in experimental investigations. As would be expected, provocative appearances evoke greater responsibility attributions to women and elicit stronger expectations of rape (Kanekar and Kolsawalla, 1980; Kanekar et al., 1981) – despite the reality that the victim's mode of dress is unrelated to the likelihood of sexual assault. In addition, normal social behaviours are often perceived as provocative. For example, visiting a bar before a rape (even if the rape is perpetrated by a stranger) increases the perceived blameworthiness of a victim (Best and Demmin, 1982). Similarly, date rape is considered more justifiable if the victim initiated the date than vice versa.

On the whole, women are expected to play traditional gender roles and to restrict their behaviours accordingly. There is little sympathy for women who are judged to be daring, careless or imprudent. Careless behaviours such as failure to lock one's car result in greater attributions of responsibility (Damrosch, 1985a). More daring behaviours such as hitch-hiking result in greater attributions of blame, fault and responsibility, all of which serve to limit and restrict women's behaviour.

The unjust character assassination of female victims of sexual violence has received particular attention in the feminist literature. Feminists point out that rape is forced sexual intercourse and that women's characters and previous sexual behaviours are irrelevant to the commission and punishment of the crime. However, this does not coincide with popular visions of sexual violence. Victim respectability is a major factor in influencing interpretations of sexually violent encounters. Studies have considered both dispositions and behaviours which relate to this issue, and, as would be predicted, less respectable women are attributed more blame and responsibility.

In terms of sexual experience, sexually active women are assigned more responsibility in sexual assault than inactive women (Cann et al., 1979; L'Armand and Pepitone, 1982). People are also more likely to see intoxication as contributing to the woman's responsibility in sexual assault. A particularly interesting study on this theme was undertaken by Deborah Richardson and Jennifer Campbell (1982), who examined attributions for acquaintance rape. The researchers relied upon written vignettes to describe an incident where the victim had given a party, was tidying her apartment after the event, and was visited by her neighbour, who had attended the gathering and had returned to offer assistance with the clean-up. The rape occurred after the man re-entered the apartment and had rendered some assistance. While the core features of the rape scenario remained the same, the researchers varied the intoxication state of the victim and the assailant. The findings revealed that when the woman was intoxicated, she was assigned greater responsibility for the rape; however, when the man was intoxicated, he was assigned less responsibility for the assault!

In the main it appears that women are expected to be prudent, cautious and respectable. If they are sexually assaulted, they are also expected to stage vigorous resistance. Studies show that women who resist attempted rape are perceived as less responsible and less to blame for their assault than those who do not resist (Shotland and Goodstein, 1983; Wyer et al., 1985). In addition, women are seen as less responsible in the case of an attempted, compared to a completed, rape (Kanekar and Vaz, 1983). If rape is accomplished, women are expected to be devastated by the event and to have little emotional control. Emotionally expressive, compared to calm, victims are seen as less responsible for sexual assault (Calhoun et al., 1981; Krulewitz, 1982).

Attributions of victim blame are also affected to some extent by characteristics of the assailants as well as features of the crime itself. For example, assailant premeditation enhances positive evaluations of victims. In terms of situational factors, more fault is attributed to victims of date rape than of stranger rape and to victims of rape than of robbery. In addition, greater responsibility is assigned to survivors of completed compared to attempted rape (Kanekar et al., 1985, 1991).

The Offender Far less research has been undertaken on attributions of blame, fault and responsibility of the offender; however, studies do indicate that victim characteristics influence perceptions of the rapist. Rapists are apportioned less blame when victims behave provocatively (Best and Demmin, 1982; Yarmey, 1985) or unconventionally (Acock and Ireland, 1983). Similarly, they are blamed less if victims are sexually experienced (L'Armand and Pepitone, 1982). Studies of victim attractiveness, however, have failed to demonstrate an influence on blame attributions for the offender.

The impacts of offender characteristics and behaviours and situational features of sexual assault have been even less frequently considered, although there is evidence that alleged rapists' attractiveness diminishes the certainty of guilt (Deitz and Byrnes, 1981). Offenders are attributed more responsibility for a completed versus an attempted rape (Krulewitz and Nash, 1979) and are blamed in relation to amount of force exerted in the commission of a sexual offence (Krulewitz and Payne, 1978). There is also evidence that greater responsibility is assigned to an offender if the premeditation and intention to rape was present and if he is motivated by internal (dispositional) as opposed to external (situational) factors (Wiener and Rinehart, 1986).

Individual Differences and Attributions
Experimental studies of attribution have sometimes incorporated demographic variables and individual difference measures into the research to assess their impact on rape attributions. It must be borne in mind that although researchers tend to employ these measures as if they are independent variables, the experimenter does not retain the experimental control over these factors which is necessary to draw conclusions about causal relationships. For example, a researcher cannot control, manipulate or randomly assign subjects to age groups or racial categories. However, sex differences or differences in personality dimensions may legitimately be observed in conjunction with other experimental manipulations.

Personality and Attitudes   While there is some evidence that men with hyper-masculine (macho) personalities and individuals with rigid or dogmatic traits tend to assign more responsibility to victims in the commission of sexual assault (Beaver et al., 1992; Thornton et al., 1982), personality, for the most part, has received scant attention in relation to the attribution literature. In line with the overarching theoretical framework, however, the locus of control construct has merited some scrutiny. In this domain psychologists have distinguished the relatively stable tendency or disposition to rely on 'internal' or 'external' explanations for behavioural events. In the simplest terms an internal orientation reflects the belief that individuals can and do exert direct control over life events. An external orientation, by contrast, is associated with the perception that events are shaped by outside forces such as fate or chance. While these orientations relate to cognitive strategies and causal attributions, personality theorists believe that the strategies are employed with some consistency and vary across individuals. When locus of control is measured as a personality trait, it is found that internals assign more causality, fault and blame to victims of sexual assault than do externals (Paulsen, 1979; Thornton et al., 1981).

On the whole, attitudes have received more attention in relation to attributions. In fact, it has been argued that the readiness to endorse rape myths is one of the most powerful factors affecting both the social and legal evaluations of victims. When experimental research has been combined with attitude scales as measurements of individual differences, a strong association emerges between these dispositions and attributions. On the most fundamental level acceptance of rape myths is linked to attribution of responsibility to victims of sexual assault (Krahé, 1988). Those who readily endorse rape myths are also less likely to define ambiguous situations as rape and are more likely to see ambiguous behaviours as indicative of women's desire for intercourse (Jenkins and Dambrot, 1987).

Studies by Sheila Deitz and colleagues (1984) with the Rape Empathy Scale have similarly revealed that individuals who have empathetic dispositions toward victims of sexual assault are more likely to attribute responsibility for rape to the assailant, less likely to attribute responsibility to the victim, and more likely to judge the assault as serious. They also have more favourable and positive perceptions of victims.

Charlene Muehlehard, who is well known for her research on women who say 'no' but mean 'yes', specifically investigated the belief that 'leading men on' justifies rape and the relationship of that belief to various rape attributions. She divided 206 university women into three groups – low, medium or high – on the basis of the strength of their 'leading men on' beliefs. As expected, women who strongly held the justification belief were less likely to define forced intercourse between dating couples as rape, more likely to see rape encounters as justified, perceived victims as more responsible for the sexual episodes and evaluated them more negatively. Interestingly enough and in contrast, Muehlenhard also found that those who did not see rape as justified by 'leading men on' were less likely to have been involved in unwanted sexual intercourse themselves. She went on to suggest that the 'justifiers' may be at greater risk of sexual coercion (Muehlenhard and MacNaughton, 1988).

The influence of attitudes on rape attributions is not specifically limited to rape myths or rape empathy. Cognitive processing of rape-related information is also linked more broadly to gender stereotypes and attitudes toward women. As would be expected, individuals with more traditional stereotypes rely on more stringent criteria for defining rape (Willis, 1992). In contrast, those with liberal attitudes toward women are less likely to blame or find fault with victims (Thornton et al., 1982). They are also more likely to cite societal causes for sexual violence (Krulewitz and Payne, 1978). Men with traditional attitudes are more likely to see a wider range of behaviours as justifying rape than are men with liberal dispositions. Traditionalists are also less likely to see victims as traumatized by sexual abuse (Howells et al., 1984).

Sex Differences Women generally have more favourable percep-tions of rape victims, and their attributions about sexual violence reflect this perspective. In line with the attribution framework described above, sex differences may be considered in relation to defining sexual violence and to issues of victim credibility, denig-ration, trivialization and blame. On the most fundamental level, women are more likely to define an ambiguous sexual encounter as rape than are men and are more likely to believe a victim of sexual assault (Jenkins and Dambrot, 1987; Tieger, 1981). Women also view rape as a more serious offence and see it as more psychologi-cally damaging and socially stigmatizing (Feldman-Summers and Lindner, 1976; L'Armand and Pepitone, 1982; Levett and Kuhn, 1991). As would be expected, women are less likely to derogate victims (Deitz and Byrnes, 1981) and, in general, they attribute less blame, fault and responsibility to victims and more to assailants than do men (Fulero and DeLara, 1976; Howells et al., 1984; Rumsey and Rumsey, 1977). However, empirical findings are not as straightforward as might be predicted. Some research has failed to demonstrate sex differences in attributional patterns, and other studies have revealed that women attribute *more* responsibility to victims, at least under certain circumstances (for example, Krulew-itz and Payne, 1978; Luginbuhl and Mullin, 1981).

There is some evidence that the distinction between behavioural, characterological and situational 'blame' is a useful one in predict-ing male and female attributions. Men appear to apportion more blame and responsibility to victims on the basis of their characters than do women. For example, their attributions are often more affected by victims' sexual history and appearance, and they are also more likely to perceive women as having an unconscious desire to be raped (L'Armand and Pepitone, 1982; Selby et al., 1977). In this sense men may respond to victims' dispositional characteristics more so than do women. In many cases they are also more likely to acknowledge a behavioural basis for the blame – particularly if the behaviours are provocative ones. More specifically, men are more likely to perceive a victim as contributing to the incident because of her appearance and seductive activities. Women, however, are more likely to rely on situational and chance explanations for sexual violence and, compared to men, are more likely to perceive the victim as merely 'being in the wrong place at the wrong time' (Luginbuhl and Mullin, 1981; Selby et al., 1977).

The conceptual distinctions of blame, fault and responsibility should also be borne in mind in interpreting sex differences in attributional patterns. Although the three concepts are similar and interrelated, they cannot be used synonymously (Krulewitz and

Nash, 1979; Pallak and Davies, 1982).[1] The most fundamental distinction among the terms is based on moral and causal dimensions of attributions (Harvey and Rule, 1978). Along these lines the concept of responsibility is directly linked to causality – although this may or may not imply intention or foresight. Blame and fault, by contrast, are pejorative terms and function primarily as moral evaluations. The moral 'responsibility' attached to blame and fault evaluations necessarily implies causal responsibility, while causal responsibility may or may not imply moral 'responsibility'. More succinctly, causal responsibility is a necessary, but not sufficient, precondition for blame and fault attributions.

A more careful scrutiny of the literature reveals that when sex differences in attributions are apparent, men routinely ascribe more *fault* to victims. From the masculine perspective, women are held as morally responsible for the assault. This is congruent with the tendency to attribute blame on the basis of the victim's character and seductive behaviours, and suggests that men readily respond to the victim's dispositional characteristics. Although a similar pattern generally emerges for *responsibility* attributions, women sometimes attribute more responsibility to victims (Kanekar et al., 1985; Kanekar and Vaz, 1983; Krulewitz and Nash, 1979). In these conditions the responsibility attributions appear to have a behavioural basis but are linked to activities that might be regarded as careless or lacking prudence. It is of note that such behaviours – which may enable sexual violence to occur – are generally situation-specific and controllable.

A study by Judith Krulewitz and Elaine Payne (1978) in the United States illustrates this point. University students were presented with a rape scenario in which the victim was described as walking across campus alone after a night class. On approaching her car she was accosted and raped by a stranger who had followed her for a short distance. In response to this scenario female subjects ascribed more responsibility to the victim than did males. It is interesting to note, however, that they also perceived her as more respectable.

A similar line of investigation has been pursued by Suresh Kanekar and his colleagues in India. Kanekar likewise differentiates fault and responsibility, but defines the latter in terms of perceived likelihood of sexual violence. As both intention and foresight are typically considered in conjunction with the attribution of responsibility, this approach implies that the victim may be causally responsible for sexual violence merely through lack of foresight. In a series of studies with Indian university students Kanekar found that women perceived greater likelihood of the victim's sexual assault than did men, that is, they viewed the victim as more responsible for the assault; however, they simultaneously attributed less fault to the victim.

More sophisticated studies which have contrasted types of 'blame' or have differentiated responsibility and fault can be summarized as follows: men apparently rely more on victim dispositions as a basis for attributions of blame and responsibility, and women apparently rely more on situational determinants. Attributions based on behavioural factors, however, produce a mixed pattern of sex differences with men appearing more victim-blaming when seductive behaviours are apparent and women perceiving the victim as more responsible when careless behaviours are involved. These patterns will be elaborated later in relation to motivational elements of causal attributions.

Cultural Differences

The bulk of research on rape victimology and attributions described in this chapter has been carried out in the United States. Limited work in the United Kingdom has also been cited. For example, Barbara Krahé (1988) and Kevin Howells and associates (1984) have undertaken research which links attitudes and attributions and reports findings which are consistent with American studies. In a similar vein Suresh Kanekar and associates (1980, 1981, 1983) have pursued experimental research on rape attributions in India and have investigated the impact of factors such as victim respectability, provocativeness and attractiveness. While these studies suggest that there are many similarities in rape attributions across cultures, explicit cross-cultural comparisons have not been made, and the research tells us very little about genuine cultural differences.

Starting from a cross-cultural perspective and employing experimental methods, Kathleen L'Armand and colleagues (1982) investigated rape attributions in India and the United States. Their research followed a typical attribution paradigm. Students were presented with a simulated newspaper article which described the rape of a 20-year-old woman and the subsequent arrest of the assailant. The news item reported a guilty verdict from a recent trial and provided additional information that the man's defence had been based on the victim's consent. The story also indicated the woman's denial of consent, the corroboration of medical evidence, and the story of two police officers who heard screams, investigated the incident and made an arrest. While these features were present in all rape accounts, two factors were varied in the story. First, the victim's past sexual history was not mentioned, described as limited (consensual sexual relations with one boyfriend) or described as extensive (casual intercourse with a number of men and a reputation for promiscuity). Secondly, in half of the simulated news reports the victim and the assailant were described as strangers and in half they were described as acquaintances.

The results of the study demonstrated a number of similarities between American and Indian respondents. For example, there were no significant differences in the perceived seriousness of the crime, the estimated damage to the victim or the amount of blame attributed to the assailant. There were also tendencies in both groups to trivialize the impact of rape for victims who were sexually experienced. Furthermore, women in both cultures attributed more blame to the offender than did men.

There were also some interesting cross-cultural differences. Indian subjects, compared to Americans, blamed the victim more for the sexual assault. However, this was due to their perceptions of sexually experienced women. Indians blamed the 'innocent' victim less and the sexually experienced victim more than did Americans. The researchers also pointed out that the presence versus the absence of previous sexual experience affected attributions of victim blame for Indians while Americans were more likely to be influenced by the extent of sexual experience in making their attributions.

In addition to the conventional use of rating scales in attribution studies, the researchers requested respondents to generate reasons for their judgements and then subjected these spontaneous attributions to content analysis. Results indicated that both groups perceived victim sexual experience as a mitigating circumstance, while the Indians, but not the Americans, also commented on the 'uncontrollable nature of lust'. Indians and Americans were also differentiated by their interpretations of victim suffering. Americans explained the damage to the victim in terms of psychological distress, while the Indians viewed it in terms of social repercussions, more specifically the impact of rape on future marriageability. While the work by L'Armand and colleagues represents a single piece of cross-cultural research, it does serve to remind us that there are cultural differences in the perceptions of rape victims and causal attributions.

Evaluating Theory and Method

Evaluating Theory
Experimental research on causal attributions has shown that individuals rely on specific cognitive strategies to understand and

explain sexual violence. As feminists would predict, rape myths underlie these cognitive processes. For the most part, rape, including its causes and effects, is interpreted in line with stereotyped views of sexual assault. Individuals are more likely to define a situation as rape with increasing male force and female resistance. They are also more likely to interpret a sexual encounter between strangers as rape than one between acquaintances. This holds despite the reality of sexual violence – that rape occurs more often between people who know each other and that compliance is generally achieved through verbal coercion.

As feminists have suggested, there is also a common notion that rape can be equated with sex and that male lust is often unleashed by an attractive or provocative woman. People are generally more willing to believe that an attractive woman has been raped, compared to an unattractive woman, and they are more likely to see the unattractive woman as being at fault. The effects of rape are also trivialized if the victim is sexually experienced or if forced intercourse occurs between people who know each other. Again, this disadavantages the typical victim of sexual violence.

In general, social psychological research has demonstrated that people rely on different patterns of attributions when explaining their own behaviour as compared to explaining the behaviour of others. In the context of rape attributions there is some evidence that this might be motivated by the 'just world' rationalization. Original work in victimology emphasized that when a person is behaviourally blameless, and compensation cannot be offered, there is a tendency toward victim denigration. The phenomenon has been interpreted as supporting and maintaining the belief that people get what they deserve and deserve what they get. Despite the popularity and intuitive appeal of the 'just world' theory, the original proposition has not been explicitly investigated by attribution studies of sexual assault. Support of the 'just world' hypothesis can nevertheless be inferred from some rape research. For example, when victims are described as being raped by strangers (and with no implication of inappropriate behaviour) they are liked less than when described as being raped by acquaintances.

What has been explicitly investigated in experimental studies of rape attributions is the converse of the original 'just world' phenomenon; that is, the attributional consequences of blameless characters. More specifically, when victims' characters or dispositions are beyond reproach, what attributions will be made about their behaviours? Cathleen Jones and Elliot Aronson (1973) hypothesized and found that when a victim is of high moral character, she is held as more at fault in her victimization.

Obviously, individuals rely on both behavioural and characterological causes for explaining sexual assault, but defining and predicting the relationship between these two dimensions have not been adequately achieved by the 'just world' hypothesis. In addition, a number of studies have cast doubts on the comprehensiveness of the theory. Contrary to 'just world' predictions, a separate line of empirical investigations has shown that: (1) victim responsibility is inversely correlated with perceptions of likeability and intelligence (Miller et al., 1976); (2) victims of high moral character are both liked more and attributed less responsibility in their sexual victimization (Smith et al., 1976); and (3) as respectability decreases, perceived responsibility for rape increases (Feldman-Summers and Lindner, 1976).

One of the most challenging studies to the 'just world' hypothesis was presented by Jurgis Karuza and Thomas Carey (1984). They considered the impact of victim behaviour (careful/careless) and character (high/low respectability) on behavioural and characterological blame attributions and victim derogation. Contrary to the 'just world' hypothesis, they found that bad character was associated with victim derogation, but that victim derogation was not affected by pre-rape behaviours. The researchers also queried the proposed motivational underpinnings of the 'just world' hypothesis and the influence of blame attributions on perceptions of adaptive environmental control. Their findings revealed an adaptive value of behavioural blame for preserving a belief in a meaningful and controllable world, but not so for characterological blame.

Despite these findings, the 'just world' hypothesis has remained popular in the victimology literature. One argument has been that the effects of 'just world' motivations become apparent when the situation is ambiguous and when responsibility cannot be assigned to another agent. Another position is that there are individual differences in the tendency to cling to a 'just world' philosophy. Zack Rubin and Letitia Peplau (1975), for example, found that individuals who scored highly on a 'Just World' measurement were more likely to evoke victim derogation in experimental situations. In addition, some tangential support for the theory has been gained by earlier research – at least in the case of male subjects. James Luginbuhl and Courtney Mullin (1981), for example, found that when victims were respectable, blame attributions increased for males, but decreased for females. It is possible, then, that the 'just world' theory explains some patterns of rape attributions, particularly if it is linked to personality or sex differences.

On the whole, defensive attribution styles have received greater support in the victimology literature. As preconditions for the defensive styles to emerge, a sense of identity with the victim and perceived likelihood of a similar fate are required. As such, it would be expected that women would be more prone to exhibit these defensive styles; certainly it has been demonstrated that women identify with victims to a greater extent than do men.

Attribution research has suggested that men rely on dispositional attributions in explaining sexual violence whereas women are more prone to utilize situational factors in their explanations. This is consistent with the literature on self-serving biases which documents the tendency for individuals to assume internal and stable causes for their positive behaviours and external and unstable causes for their negative behaviours. This pattern holds constant when explaining the behaviours of members of an ingroup (say, people of the same sex or race) but the opposite pattern typically emerges when explaining outgroup behaviour.

Certainly women have more sympathetic responses to victims. They are more likely to find victims credible and to define an ambiguous situation as rape than are men. They are less likely to derogate victims and, in general, attribute them less blame, fault and responsibility. Of course, perceived similarity with victims may be influenced by a number of features and is not limited to victim sex. Age, race, occupation and general background might affect perceived similarity. When these characteristics are considered, research tells us that less fault and responsibility are assigned to similar, compared to dissimilar, victims (Fulero and DeLara, 1976).

These defensive styles serve obvious ego-enhancing functions. In general, people with whom we identify are perceived more favourably and are attributed less blame and fault. This reassures us that they, like us, are good people who do not deserve misfortune. However, defensive styles, like 'just world' rationalizing, may also relate to instrumental goals, that is, the need to perceive the environment as controllable. As noted above, in some instances, women, who more readily identify with victims of sexual violence and who perceive a greater likelihood of victimization than men, sometimes assign more responsibility to rape survivors. When this occurs, the responsibility attributions appear to be linked to situations in which the victim behaved carelessly. In these cases such behaviours can be modified – both by the victim and by the observer, who shares a sense of identity and common fate. The attribution of rape responsibility to situational, unstable, but controllable causes can assist in gaining a sense of environmental control. Although defensive attribution styles have not typically been interpreted in this framework, it is easy to see how these attributions reaffirm the adaptive value of behavioural blame.

Evaluating Methods

Experimentation in social psychology has conventionally been regarded as one of our most powerful investigative tools. The research method is rigorous, robust and has the capacity to test hypothesized cause and effect relationships. In terms of experimental studies on rape attributions, psychologists can confidently conclude that characteristics of the victim, such as her reputation, sexual history and her pre-rape behaviours, characteristics of the offender, such as status and premeditation, and situational features of the assault, such as the use of alcohol and relationship between the victim and the perpetrator, affect definitions, perceptions and attributions about rape. While these studies have generated a massive amount of data, psychologists would also be quick to point out a number of shortcomings of the research.

A fundamental issue relates to the generalizability, or external validity, of the research samples. The majority of investigations have been undertaken in the United States, and the samples have been almost completely confined to university students. The extent to which the same patterns of attributions are apparent in other groups, such as people of different ages, educational and religious backgrounds, and cultural origins, is not clear, although survey research tells us that attitudes toward rape are certainly affected by these demographic factors.

The question of external validity extends even further and additionally relates to the issue of mundane realism. More specifically, what is the relationship between the research experience and everyday experience? To what extent do paper and pencil tests predict real life behaviours? While the evidence suggests that there is a considerable overlap between attitudes and attributions, it is difficult to predict confidently how an individual will make attributions in response to a genuine rape case. There is also the issue of the discrepancy between psychological dispositions and processes, such as attitudes and attributions, and behaviour, which has been mentioned in the previous chapter.

Psychologists have been socialized in the world of science, and they rely on explicit criteria to assess the robustness of scientific method in their evaluation of experimental studies of rape attributions. Feminists, however, have different criteria for making methodological evaluations. From a feminist perspective experimental studies could be criticized on a number of grounds; however, one point is in accordance with the standard psychological critique – a concern for the external validity of the research. Feminists would argue that the methods employed in experimental studies of attribution remove the research subjects from the real world and expose them to artificial and meaningless manipulations. The artificiality of the research might also be noted in terms of the use of quantitative rating scales, instead of more spontaneous and unconstrained attributions which are rarely considered. The relevance of this 'artificial' research endeavour would be carefully scrutinized. As with survey research, feminists would also point out that the researcher stands in a vertical power relationship with the subjects, exerting control over the content, theoretical framework and methods to be employed in the research. This top-down approach hinders the two-way flow of information and power-sharing in the research enterprise.

Despite these criticisms of the experimental method, feminists would be quick to note the application of the attribution studies. The research is consistent with feminist theorizing and provides basic information about perceptions of rape and the cognitive strategies that individuals rely upon in interpreting sexual violence. Such information is a necessary prerequisite for moving on to attitude change.

In Conclusion

Social psychology has rendered empirical support for feminist claims that rape myths influence the perceptions of and responses to victims of sexual assault. Attribution theory and research, which informs us about how people make sense of the world, demonstrates that causal explanations and assignment of blame and responsibility for sexual assault are in accordance with common misconceptions about the nature of sexual violence. For example, individuals more readily define a situation as rape when forced intercourse occurs between strangers and trivialize its consequences when it occurs between acquaintances – even though the bulk of actual rape cases occur between people who know each other. Individuals are also more likely to recognize a sexual encounter as rape with increasing use of male force – even though most forced intercourse is achieved by verbal coercion.

Attributions are not only influenced by specific misconceptions of sexual violence, but also relate more generally to widely held, conservative, patriarchal attitudes toward women in society. The tendency to blame women for sexual assault and to see them as responsible for their own victimization is apparent – just as many powerless groups in society are blamed for their own misfortunes. What women wear, how they behave, and with whom they choose to associate come under careful scrutiny. Women are implicitly expected to restrict their behaviours and to conform to societal expectations about 'good' girls. This relates not only to sexual behaviours specifically, but also to limitations pertaining to curfews, being out alone, drinking alcohol and leading what many would regard as a normal social life. Victims of sexual assault who have transgressed conservative social restrictions are seen as more deserving of their sexual abuse and elicit less sympathy.

By employing experimental tools psychologists have been able to investigate effectively feminist claims of the influence of rape myths in patriarchal societies on the perceptions of victims of sexual violence. Going beyond anecdotal accounts of sexual abuse, this line of research has provided sound empirical evidence of factors which affect perceived causes and consequences of sexual assault. In this context feminism has provided a spark, and social psychology has fuelled the fire via attribution theory and experimental method. Despite its limitations, the research has implications for understanding rape perceptions and attributions in the real world, and provides a theoretical framework for field research, which is examined in the following chapter.

Note

1 Krulewitz and Nash (1979) reported correlations between victim blame and fault (.64), responsibility and blame (.59) and responsibility and fault (.54).

4

Social and Institutional Responses to Rape: Field Research

Twenty-year-old Lila lived at home with her parents and sister in Singapore.[1] For a period of about two months she had received calls from Jas, who had gotten her telephone number from a mutual friend. They had many pleasant conversations, and he often invited her out. After some time Lila finally agreed to see Jas. They arranged to meet in a fast food restaurant at 4 p.m.

When Lila arrived at the restaurant, Jas was waiting for her and offered her a soft drink. Soon after she felt giddy and went to the women's room to wash her face. When she returned to the table, she felt drowsy and passed out. Lila regained consciousness in a brothel. Jas had removed most of her gold jewellery and threatened to rape her if she did not also give him her chain. She offered him the chain, which he accepted, but Jas then removed her clothes, kissed her and subsequently forced her to perform oral sex. Lila panicked. She was sexually inexperienced and complied with Jas's demands because she was afraid.

About 8:30 p.m. Lila was allowed to go home. She initially tried to trace Jas but he had given her a false name. However, he telephoned her within the next week and demanded more money. Lila agreed to meet Jas at a department store, supposedly to give him more cash; however, she enlisted the help of friends who caught Jas and forced him to the police station, where a report was lodged.

How did the criminal justice system deal with this case?

The police took statements from Lila and Jas and sent Lila for a medical examination. Medical evidence confirmed that Lila was still a virgin, but the delay in seeking medical intervention made it impossible to establish the presence of drugs in her body. Lila's allegations could be corroborated, however, by her mother and sister, who were told of the incident soon after its occurrence, and there was the additional possibility of further witnesses from the restaurant and brothel. Both the police and the public prosecutor felt that the evidence was strong enough to go to trial.

Jas was convicted of robbery and molestation (described colourfully under Singapore law as 'outraging modesty'). He was sentenced to a four-year jail term and 12 strokes of a cane. However, the case was appealed in the High Court. The defence attorney argued that (1) the victim knew the offender, (2) she had taken about one week to make the report, and (3) she continued to be in contact with the defendant after the incident. The judge agreed that the penalty was unduly harsh and reduced the sentence to two years and seven strokes of the cane.

Why should these factors function as mitigating circumstances? In most cases of sexual assault the victim knows the perpetrator. In most cases there is also a delay in reporting. While these factors represent the most common features of sexual abuse, they are none the less relied upon in the legal system to diminish the seriousness of the crime.

Both social psychologists and feminists would maintain that this line of argument reflects stereotyped misconceptions of sexual violence and prejudice against victims. As rape is seen as 'just sex', in many cases acquaintanceship with the offender and delay in reporting are taken to imply that there was some ambivalence about the sexual encounter or even that consent was given. Despite substantial evidence to the contrary, it is still hard for most people to accept that men actually rape women they know!

Research in the field gives an excellent opportunity to explore feminist claims of insensitive and unjust treatment of victims of sexual violence by legal, medical and social service agencies and to consider the application of social psychological theories on attitudes and attributions to real world settings. Anecdotal evidence of callous disregard can be substantiated by the more systematic analysis of institutional responses to sexual violence, and social psychological theory can be refined, concretized and tested in specific field situations. For example, do attitudes toward rape predict psychotherapeutic intervention styles? Are police less likely to clear cases when the victim shows no physical signs of resistance? Do victim characteristics, such as moral conduct, affect trial outcome? Do sexual offenders receive shorter sentences in cases of acquaintance rape?

Multi-method field research has provided the context for investigation of these phenomena in real world settings, and both psychological theory on attitudes and attributions and feminist theories of conflict and sexual access provide conceptual foundations for the interpretation of the research. In terms of an overarching framework for linking basic and applied theory and research the actual responses to victims of sexual violence can be conceptualized as the outcomes or consequences of underlying attitudinal dispositions toward rape and rape victims.

Theoretical Issues Underpinning Field Research

*Social Psychological Theory and Research on Attitudes
and Behaviour*

Social psychological research on attitudes toward and perceptions of rape victims has demonstrated that prejudicial and biased misconceptions of sexual violence abound. There appears to be substantial resistance to relinquishing the popular stereotype of rape as a sex crime – a vicious assault perpetrated on a provocative young woman who has been overwhelmed by a sexually deprived deviant in a fit of uncontrollable lust. In contrast, the more common forms of sexual abuse, such as date rape, are often discounted. For example, basic research in social psychology has revealed that allegations of acquaintance rape are frequently viewed with inherent scepticism and that forced sex between people who know each other is deemed less believable and less serious. The rape of sexually experienced women is often trivialized, and the issue of victim precipitation rarely goes unnoticed. Victim behaviour, moral conduct and evidence of resistance are subject to particular scrutiny. While a variety of social psychological theories on attitudes, attributions, prejudice and intergroup relations may be used to account for these phenomena, fundamental questions still remain: What effects are these prejudicial attitudes likely to produce in the field? What are their consequences? Is there more than anecdotal evidence of unfair treatment of victims of sexual violence by social institutions and by the community?

Extending theory to application, psychologists would predict that the more similar the case characteristics are to stereotypes about rape, the more sympathetic the actual treatment of sexual assault victims. More specifically, stranger rape, rape involving force or weapons, evidence of resistance, emotional upset and good moral character of the victim would evoke more supportive and favourable responses. In the field setting these supportive responses may be assessed in a number of ways, including the examination of the clearing of sexual assault cases by the police, trial outcomes, sentencing of sex offenders, and psychotherapeutic interventions offered to victims of sexual assault.

The field-based predictions which link rape stereotypes with reactions to victims of sexual violence are founded on implicit assumptions about the connection between attitudes and behaviour. Psychologists have described attitudes in terms of response dispositions and have emphasized their mediational functions; nevertheless, the attitude–behaviour link has proved to be one of the most contentious issues in social psychology. In fact, reviews of studies have cautiously concluded that, in general, there is only a modest relationship between attitudes and behaviour and the strength of that relationship may be reduced or enhanced by extraneous factors (McGuire, 1985).[2]

Although the emphasis here has been placed on the power of attitudes in predicting behaviours, it should be noted that the causal direction of the attitude–behaviour link has also prompted controversy. The more popular and intuitively appealing position is that attitudes produce actions. This is based on an information-processing approach and is consistent with the traditional conceptualization of attitudes (McGuire, 1972). However, it has also been postulated that behavioural change leads to attitude change. This theme is apparent in dissonance and self-perception theories (Bem, 1972; Festinger, 1957) and will be taken up again in Chapter 6.

Of course, it might be argued that in practical terms it is behaviour or attitudinal outcome which is most important and that it is unnecessary, even superfluous, to study underlying attitudes as mediational constructs. Attitudes have, nevertheless, made a significant contribution to theory development and have retained a revered position in social psychology (McGuire, 1985). In addition, feminists have proclaimed attitudes a major stumbling block to social reform, and in popular psychology laypeople have frequently emphasized the effects of attitudes on interpersonal interactions. Given the salient position attitudes have assumed in social, feminist and popular psychology, many are reluctant to abandon them in field research.

Feminist Theory
Although feminist perspectives on field research have been interdisciplinary, they have none the less mirrored the assumptions of social psychologists about the relationship between attitudes and behaviour. Drawing on sociology, medicine and law, the feminist-based literature has made three important points about the significance of attitudes toward sexual violence. First, like psychologists, feminist-oriented researchers maintain that there is a direct link between attitudes and behaviour. In the legal context, for example, it has been argued that 'the likelihood of convictions in rape cases will be affected by the extent to which characteristics of cases approximate the stereotypes of rape held by criminal justice personnel' (LaFree, 1980a, p. 833). Similarly, it has been contended that professionals' attitudes toward sexual violence directly affect the treatment of rape victims by medical and social service providers (Holmstrom and Burgess, 1978). Secondly, feminists maintain that the attitude–behaviour link is implied at varying levels of abstraction

and may be examined from both micro- and macro-perspectives. For example, it has been argued that not only do individuals' responses to victims of sexual assault reflect their acceptance or rejection of rape myths, but also institutional reactions to sexual violence provide evidence about broader societal attitudes toward rape (Brownmiller, 1975; Hilberman, 1977). Parenthetically, while social psychologists have generally framed attitudes in terms of individual dispositions, they have also considered them in terms of broader patterns of culture (Allport, 1935). Thirdly, again consistent with social psychological theory, feminists maintain that attitudes affect behaviours, and behaviours influence attitudes. As LeGrand stated: 'Although societal attitudes are no doubt responsible for the present construction of rape laws, it is also true that this construction serves to reinforce those attitudes' (1973, p. 919).

Feminists would further agree with psychologists in predicting that more sympathetic responses to rape victims would be found when sexual violence occurs between strangers, when there is evidence of violence and victim resistance, when the victim is of impeccable moral character, and when she has not placed herself at obvious physical risk. However, the basis of these expectations is largely situated in feminist modifications of sociological theories of conflict.

The fundamental premise of conflict theory is that political power is the basic determinant of social rewards and constraints. This is enshrined in social custom and laws which function to grant and maintain privileges for empowered groups and to restrict these benefits for others. In the broadest sense, the patriarchy has been concerned with preserving male power and authority and protecting male interest; this has resulted in social constraints on women. In the context of sexual offences, feminists have argued that rape is a violent crime perpetrated on women by men and that it serves to oppress women and confine them to narrowly prescribed gender roles. In an institutional context, feminists further maintain that both rape legislation and reactions to sexual violence punish women for deviating from these narrowly prescribed roles. For example, processing of rape cases in the criminal justice system is more reflective of attitudes to male–female behaviour than of legal evidentiary requirements.

On a more specific level, feminist scholarship makes reference to the constraints of female sexuality and its management in terms of property rights. Men retain a dominant position in society and sanctioned sexual access. As a commodity, female sexuality is regulated in a manner which protects male interests. For example, only recently have some countries adopted marital rape laws, and in many societies the idea of a husband raping his wife is still quite incomprehensible. While society may regulate various aspects of female sexuality and reproduction, laws are designed for the maximum protection of valuable property; in the case of rape this refers to the harsh punishment of men who violate conforming, chaste or virtuous women. In contrast, protection is not extended to damaged goods – women who choose unconventional lifestyles or who are sexually promiscuous. While the thrust of the feminist argument relates to these dimensions of sexual politics, it should also be noted that conflict theory has additionally been used to explain the impact of race on the institutional processing of rape cases. In these instances it has been argued that social stratification and the power retained by white men allow them greater sexual access and result in less punitive retaliation for them than for black men – particularly in cases of interracial sexual violence.

Multi-methods in Field Research

Field research is a general label applied to a variety of research methods which are concentrated on the direct or indirect observation of naturally occurring events (Dane, 1990). Field research may be descriptive or quasi-experimental; however, its distinguishing characteristic is that it occurs in a natural environment – the 'real world' – without the creation, manipulation or discontinuation of events for investigative purposes. Naturalistic observations, which involve the selection, recording, coding and interpretation of behaviours, are at the core of field research. Direct behavioural observations may be additionally supplemented by intrusive research methods such as surveys or interviews, and field data may also be derived from secondary sources such as archives. This illustrates a multi-method approach to research in field settings.

The array of methods available to field researchers parallels, to a large extent, the techniques employed by feminist ethnographers. For example, both naturalistic observations and archival studies are commonly used. However, the way in which these approaches are implemented and the research designs with which they are linked tend to vary. As previously mentioned, feminists generally take a very active and integrated role in participant observational research, often joining with their 'subjects' in producing social and political change. In contrast, social psychologists and sociologists are less likely to adopt a participatory, interventionist or change-oriented approach in their observational studies. On a second count, feminists are more inclined to rely on qualitative data and latent content analysis in their archival research while psychologists generally prefer quantitative statistics and manifest content analysis. Most notably, however, social psychologists often combine their naturalistic observations with quasi-experimental designs whereas feminists generally opt for more basic descriptive studies.

Along these lines, a substantial portion of the field research presented in this chapter constitutes natural or quasi-experiments and parallels work described in Chapter 3 on attribution theory and experimental psychology. Field researchers, for example, might also consider the influence of victim, defendant and crime characteristics on trial outcomes. In contrast to true experimental investigations, however, the field researcher is unable to control or manipulate victim, offender or situational factors or to manage random assignment of jurors to various conditions. Rather trial outcomes, such as verdict and sentencing, may be examined as naturally occurring consequences of antecedent case characteristics. Obviously, there is an implied causal link between the case characteristics and trial outcome; however, as quasi-experimental research is not as rigorous as true experiments and admits the possibility of alternative explanations and the influence of extraneous variables, it is more appropriate to refer to the case characteristics as indicators (rather than causes) of trial outcomes.

Quasi-experimental research may result from first-hand observations, such as direct monitoring of criminal cases, or the research data may be derived from public records known as archives. In the first instance, direct observations can be a powerful research tool. In order to study the police processing of rape cases, for example, the researcher may act as an independent observer, riding with patrol officers to crime scenes, scrutinizing their incident reports and recording the reactions of investigating officers. These observations may be supplemented by more intrusive measures such as interviews, as was the case in Vicki Rose and Susan Randall's (1982) research on the police management of sexual offences. Alternatively, court records, trial transcripts and police reports may be relied upon in archival field research on sexual assault, as illustrated by Gary LaFree's (1980a, 1980b) work on reactions to rape in the criminal justice system.

Some of the research presented here is more accurately described as field-based in that it is somewhat more intrusive and relies on self-report of behaviours rather than direct behavioural observations. For example, Carol Bohmer (1974) interviewed judges about their courtroom responses to rape cases. Similarly, a survey approach may be used to gain information on self-reported behaviours, as was undertaken by Ellen Dye and Susan Roth (1990) in their study of psychotherapeutic interventions for victims of sexual violence.

Field Research and Attitudinal Outcomes

Psychotherapy for Victims of Sexual Violence: Responses from Mental Health Professionals

On the whole, survey research has demonstrated that therapists have relatively supportive attitudes toward victims of sexual violence (Resick and Jackson, 1981; Ward, 1988a) – despite the influence of psychological and medical literature which, even in the post-Freudian era, has undermined the significance of sexual abuse with its emphasis on women's rape fantasies, incestuous impulses and masochistic tendencies (for example, Coons and Milstein, 1984). Far less work, however, has been undertaken on the outcomes of therapeutic interventions or on linking the attitudes and behaviours of mental health professionals in the treatment of victims of sexual assault. A major exception to this trend is a study by Dye and Roth (1990), who examined psychotherapists' knowledge of sexual assault, attitudes toward victims of sexual violence and treatment approaches to sexual abuse.

Dye and Roth surveyed 257 psychologists, psychiatrists and social workers about their practices with sexual assault victims. While the researchers found that psychotherapists were reasonably knowledgeable about sexual abuse, there was evidence of sexist practices in their therapeutic interventions. Exploring the link between attitudes and behaviour, Dye and Roth reported that rape myth acceptance was associated with the endorsement of victim blame. However, the most salient finding was that therapists whose attitudes reflected stereotypic misconceptions about sexual violence were also more likely to use psychological interventions which were directed at victim blame. Based on their clinical experience, 64 per cent of the therapists said they would work with a victim on more appropriate and less seductive behaviours with men, and 56 per cent said they would discuss ways in which she unconsciously desired or enjoyed the sexual assault. Dye and Roth sadly concluded that a sexual abuse victim is just as likely to be treated with blaming than non-blaming therapies and that there is little way to anticipate and distinguish professional responses as therapeutic orientation was not predicted by demographic factors.

The Investigation and Prosecution of Sexual Offences:
Responses from Police, Judges and Juries
Although there is cross-national variation in the institutional management of sexual offences, a brief overview is merited to give some
indication of the complexity of the criminal justice system processing of sexual assault cases and to provide the necessary background
information for interpreting subsequent empirical findings. As the
bulk of the empirical data on police investigation and trial outcome
is based on studies from the United States, the American system of
investigation and prosecution is used as a reference point for the
following description.

Sexual offences initially come to the attention of the authorities
when the police receive a complaint, and an incident report is filed.
These reports may be brief but would include a description of the
offence, personal particulars of the victim, details of the suspect and
information about other leads such as witnesses etc. These reports
are often taken by junior officers and are then sent to a case
investigator who will pursue the investigation, including taking a
more detailed statement from the victim. At this stage the investigator may conclude that no offence has been committed, that is, the
complaint is unfounded. S/he may also decide that an actual offence
has been committed but that the suspect cannot be apprehended. In
those instances the case will be suspended. If there is no prosecution
due to insufficient evidence the case will be termed 'exceptionally
cleared'. In none of these instances would the case progress to
court. Alternatively, the case may be cleared by arrest (Galton,
1975–6). As may be inferred from the above description, the
preliminary disposition of the case may be determined by a variety
of factors, including somewhat arbitrary decisions made by investigators based on extra-legal criteria.

Cases pass out of the hands of the police investigators and on to
prosecuting attorneys who evaluate the strength of the case and the
probability of conviction. This is based on evidentiary requirements
but is also affected by extra-legal considerations. At this stage the
accused may plead guilty to the original charge or may claim trial.
However, it is not uncommon to plea bargain sexual assault cases so
that the accused pleads guilty to a lesser offence. If this is the
situation, the case again does not reach trial.

If the accused claims trial, there are essentially three defences
available. First, it may be argued that sexual intercourse did not
occur; therefore, no rape was committed. Secondly, it may be
agreed that sexual intercourse took place, but that it was not with
the accused. In this instance, the defence attorney would argue a
case of mistaken identity, and the defendant would require an alibi.

Thirdly, it may be admitted that sexual intercourse occurred between the victim and the accused but that it was consensual. This is the defence which is most relevant to feminist and social psychological theorizing on rape because it highlights the victim's character and behaviour. Additionally, the defendant may admit to guilt but plead mitigating circumstances, for example intoxication etc. In these cases attempts are often made to discredit the victim and make her share responsibility for the sexual assault.

The conclusion of a trial will require a verdict. In most cases this responsibility is placed in the hands of a jury; however, in some countries, such as Singapore, trial is by judge alone. If a conviction results, the judge is entitled to determine the sentence and to consider any requests for leniency. These determinations are also likely to be influenced by extra-legal factors, especially perceptions of the victim.

Police Intervention   Eric Galton's (1975–6) work has been frequently cited as providing some of the earliest empirical evidence of police mistreatment of victims of sexual violence. In the course of his field research in a large metropolitan police department in Texas, Galton interviewed police and complainants and relied upon structured questionnaires for the additional assessment of police management of sexual assault cases. As a starting point Galton noted that the police investigators involved in the research project did not perceive rape as a special crime, nor did they agree that it required female investigators or a specialized police unit. The officers were also sceptical about actual rape reporting and estimated that 26 per cent of their cases (in contrast to documented estimates of 1–2 per cent) involved fabrication (Katz and Mazur, 1979). Rape was perceived primarily as a sexual crime, and there was a strong tendency to trivialize sexual violence. While female investigators were more sceptical of victim veracity, male officers were likely to view rape merely as unwanted sex. Galton reported, for example, that a common response was 'She only got raped.' Notwithstanding these findings, the main thrust of Galton's research made reference to the link between attitudes and behaviours. In this context he argued that 'subjective attitudes concerning rape complainants undoubtedly extend into and affect their technical analysis of the elements of a rape offence' (1975–6, p. 20).

Along these lines Galton considered key characteristics of the cases under investigation. A fundamental issue involved the notion of consent. While rape laws specify non-consensual sexual intercourse achieved by force or threat, the presence of a weapon in itself was not taken to be indicative of force. Rather, the police were more concerned with how a weapon was used. Ninety per cent of the investigators believed that a woman should resist if she is only threatened (although this increases her chances of being brutally beaten). Overall the police demanded far more resistance than was required by the law. Lack of screaming was taken to imply consent in many cases, and investigators also expected to see bruises and lacerations to document resistance.

Twenty per cent of reported rape cases in Galton's research were classified as unfounded; that is, the police concluded that no offence took place. This is not surprising given that investigators estimated that one in four cases is based on fabrication. A particularly distressing conclusion of Galton's study, however, was not only that police hold victims to more stringent criteria of proof than is required by the law, but also that changes in rape legislation will not affect police field actions as investigators independently determine what must be present in viable rape cases.

A more recent and comprehensive study was undertaken by Rose and Randall (1982), who participated in observational research involving 610 reports of sexual assault during their field work in a metropolitan police department in Texas. They combined interview and observational techniques to monitor all rape and sexual assault cases received during a six-month period. The researchers concentrated on investigators' responses to sexual assault cases after receiving the initial offence incident reports (OIR) from patrol officers. These reports include general information regarding the time, place and date of the offence, classification of the offence and the modus operandi, information about the complainant (such as injuries sustained), suspect and witness information, a description of weapons (if any), and a brief narration of the offence with reference to victim–perpetrator relationship, coercion, resistance and victim reaction.

The researchers concluded that police officers based their investigative decisions on the evaluation of four factors: (1) victim credibility: promptness in reporting and receiving a medical exam, emotional state, cooperation with officers, and corroboration by physical evidence and witnesses; (2) victim consent: the proximity and intimacy of victim–offender relationship, circumstances surrounding initial contact, evidence of force and resistance; (3) seriousness of the offence: extent of injuries and use of weapons; and (4) victim characteristics such as age, occupation, race, marital and socio-economic status. The criteria used for the assessment of sexual assault clearly disadvantage the typical rape victim. For example, most victims know the offender, delay the reporting and do not sustain signs of force or violence. In addition, extraneous victim characteristics such as age or race are irrelevant to the commission of a crime. While the concern for corroborative evidence is clearly appropriate, it appears that investigators relied substantially on extra-legal factors in determining their responses to charges of sexual offences. Rose and Randall concluded that it is not enough that the allegation of sexual assault can be believed but also that the victim is 'worthy of being believed' (1982, p. 28). This is evidenced by behaviour which corroborates the genuineness of her character. In this instance it is helpful if she is compliant (with the police, but not the rapist), cooperative and appropriately upset.

The researchers emphasized that the criteria relied upon by police investigators are more stringent than those embodied in the legal code. For example, although they expected prompt reporting of sexual offences, the law requires only that the victim tell a third party within six months of the offence. The issue of consent is also problematic. Consent was routinely questioned if women knew the assailant, if they had previously had sex, if they had put themselves at risk by accepting rides from strangers or walking alone, if they worked in nightlife occupations or if they were teenagers or young women. And although the law does not require use of a weapon for the commission of rape, police investigators put considerable weight on this factor in determining case legitimacy.

The police may represent the victim's initial contact with the legal system; however, the courts are also responsible for the management of sexual assault. The next section considers research on trial outcomes.

The Criminal Justice System   One of the earliest studies on judge and jury responses to rape was undertaken by Ross Barber (1974) in Queensland, Australia. He examined trial verdict by juries and the severity of sentencing by judges in relation to victim, defendant and situational crime characteristics for all rape cases over a 10-year period. Barber argued that jury reactions reflect general societal attitudes toward rape and went on to report that the most salient determinant of trial outcome was the *victim's moral character*. Twenty-two per cent of convictions versus 74 per cent of the acquittals occurred when victim's moral character was described as 'dubious'. Virginity also affected trial outcome, with convictions more probable in cases when unmarried females had no previous experience of intercourse.

In terms of judges' responses to convicted sex offenders, Barber classified victim, defendant and case characteristics as either aggravating or mitigating factors in terms of their impact on length of sentence. Judges, like juries, were strongly influenced by their impressions of the victim. In this context poor moral character functioned as a mitigating influence while virginity acted as an aggravating factor. For the offender both alcohol abuse and prior criminal record were aggravating factors and served to increase the length of sentence. Finally, certain features of the crime also influenced the severity of sentencing. Extensive injury done to the victim functioned as an aggravating circumstance although in gang rape cases sentencing was less severe than in cases involving a single assailant. It is interesting to note, however, that the amount of force exerted in a sexual assault had no significant effect on sentencing recommendations.

Some of the most comprehensive work on outcomes of rape investigations and trials has been undertaken by Gary LaFree and colleagues. Relying heavily on archival resources, he initially studied 124 forcible rapes reported over a three-year period via recorded evidence from the prosecution files, defendants' criminal histories from police records, and the final case disposition from the court documents. LaFree (1980a) examined characteristics of the victim, the defendant and the crime with particular concentration on victim and defendant moral conduct and character. He hypothesized that without corroborative evidence decisions involving allegations of sexual assault may depend less on whether a rape has actually occurred and more on whether the victim and accused are viewed as the 'kinds of people that are likely to have been involved in a sexual offence' (1980a, p. 834).

In considering trial outcomes, LaFree reported that non-conforming behaviour on the part of the victim had the greatest impact on trial outcome. Women who allegedly engaged in sexual misconduct, women who were acquainted with the offender, and women who did not report the incident promptly were less likely to have their complaints come to trial and less likely to achieve subsequent convictions in court. Cases of women who were assaulted in their homes were also less likely to result in conviction. Again, the more typical forms of sexual violence, particularly rape between people who know each other, tend to go unpunished. Although victim characteristics appeared to be the most powerful predictors of trial outcomes, offender and case characteristics also exerted some influence. Assaults by defendants with more serious criminal records and rape involving more than one assailant were more likely to end in conviction. Finally, victim and defendant race influenced the conviction and sentencing. Cases involving black women were less likely to end in conviction. However, in the less common case of interracial sexual violence, black men accused of raping white women were more likely to have their cases filed as felonies, to be given longer sentences, and to be incarcerated in the state penitentiary (LaFree, 1980b).

In addition to trial outcomes, LaFree and colleagues (1985) investigated jurors' perceptions of rape and their decision-making processes in rape trials. This project entailed post-trial interviews with 331 jurors who served in the trials of 38 forcible sexual assault cases in Indianapolis. The trials under study involved attempted and completed rape and sodomy of victims aged 12 years and above. In quasi-experimental field-based research the investigators considered characteristics of the complainant, defendant, the crime and the jurors. In the first instance the victim's race and marital status were considered in addition to conformity to traditional gender roles as indexed by drug and alcohol use and sexual experience. Defendant characteristics such as race, criminal record and lifestyle were examined in conjunction with situational crime factors such as availability of eye-witnesses, use of weapon and injuries sustained by the victim. Finally, juror characteristics including sex, race, age, occupation and education were tapped with supplementary questionnaires used to assess their attitudes toward women's roles, social and sexual freedom and crime control. The impact of these factors was examined on jurors' reports of their verdicts after the trial but prior to deliberation.

For the purpose of data analysis the forcible sexual assault cases were divided into two groups. The first group included cases which were based on either a no sex or victim consent defence; the second group was composed of cases in which mitigating circumstances were pleaded. The most striking finding in cases of no sex or consensual intercourse defences was that even when there was explicit evidence that the victim had been forced to submit to intercourse, such as physical injury or the use of weapons, these factors did not affect verdict. Rather, jurors were primarily influenced by the moral character of the victims. Jurors were less likely to believe in the *defendant's* guilt if the *victim* engaged in sex outside marriage, if she drank or used drugs, and if she had been acquainted with the assailant.

Defendant characteristics also exerted influence on the judgements, and jurors were more likely to render a guilty verdict if the defendant had few social ties, a negative courtroom appearance or a criminal record. Attitudes toward women's roles and attitudes toward social and sexual freedom did not directly impact on trial verdict; however, these factors interacted with victim characteristics. More specifically, jurors who had conservative attitudes in these domains were more likely to render innocent verdicts when victims did not assume traditional gender roles. Attitudes toward crime control influenced trial outcomes, with more guilty verdicts rendered by those who were generally disposed to take a tough stance on crime; however, juror demographics did not affect pre-deliberation verdicts.

Findings for diminished responsibility pleas were influenced by somewhat different factors. Use of weapons and eye-witnesses increased the likelihood of a guilty verdict; however, victim relationship with offender also affected outcome. If rapists fitted a conventional stereotype, for example, if they had prior sexual offences, guilty verdicts were more likely. Outcomes were not affected by juror demographics or attitudes toward women, but more guilty verdicts arose from jurors who held 'tough on crime' attitudes.

On the whole LaFree's work has been more rigorous than previous investigations; however, it should be noted that his results concur with the findings of others. When the victim is acquainted with the rapist, the latter is less likely to be charged or convicted (Williams, 1978). Furthermore, if convicted, he is likely to receive a shorter sentence (Hibey, 1973). Convictions are also less probable in cases which involve complainants with bad reputations, unconventional living arrangements and/or a pattern of chronic alcohol abuse (Clark and Lewis, 1977; Kalven and Zeisel, 1966; Williams, 1976). It has also been noted that the criminal justice system is less likely to react to cases involving hitch-hiking (Brodyaga et al., 1975, cited in Myers and LaFree, 1982). There is considerable evidence, then, that extra-legal factors affect the outcomes of sexual assault cases in the courts. Indeed, Harry Kalven and Hans Zeisel (1966) reported that 60 per cent of the simple rape cases that were acquitted by juries on extra-legal criteria would have been found guilty by judges on points of law!

In addition to work on the effects of complainant, defendant and crime characteristics on trial outcomes of sexual assault cases, LaFree also compared the management of rape cases to other crimes in the criminal justice system. Myers and LaFree (1982) studied 945 defendants of sexual, property and other violent crimes in Indiana. They found that sexual assault crimes were more likely than property crimes to go to trial and less likely than either property or other violent crimes to result in a guilty verdict or prison sentence. There were fundamental differences between sexual assault victims and complainants of other crimes in that sexual assault victims were more likely to be younger, unemployed, single, known to the defendant, and more likely to report physical injury. Sexual assault cases also more frequently involved eye-witness identification, expert testimony and additional charges and less frequently involved evidentiary statements from witnesses or defendants. On the whole their findings concur with earlier work of others such as LeGrand (1973) who reported a higher acquittal rate for rape than for any other felony in California.

Myers and LaFree argued that there are differences between sexual assault and other crimes, but when relevant case characteristics such as strength of evidence are controlled, these features are not translated into discriminatory reactions in the criminal justice system. This represents one point of view on the complex issue; however, their argument seems to miss a more fundamental point. The nature of sexual offences and the framing of these offences under the law may make it proportionately more difficult to produce evidentiary requirements in a typical rape case. For example, sexual assault generally occurs as a private act between two people who know each other and, in the majority of cases, does not result in marked physical injuries to the victim which could corroborate resistance. Comparative crimes are more likely to involve witnesses. Unlike theft, rape does not admit the possibility of the culprit being caught in the possession of stolen goods. In short, the alternatives for substantiating allegations of sexual assault are typically more limited and less accessible. In contrast to the Myers and LaFree position, then, it may be argued that discrimination does exist in the treatment of complainants of various crimes but that the biases in the criminal justice system are merely found at a different level of analysis. In his analysis of forcible rape in the criminal justice system Gerald Robin (1977) has come to a similar conclusion, citing institutionalized sexism as responsible for the focus on corroboration, consent and character which has established a standard of proof in rape cases which is considered more stringent than 'beyond a reasonable doubt'.

Carol Bohmer (1974) took quite a different approach in her investigation of judicial attitudes toward sexual assault. In her field-based research she interviewed 38 Philadelphia judges about their attitudes and behaviours in the courtroom. She was particularly interested in judges' reactions as the judge is perceived as a source of legal authority and is responsible for maintaining control of the courtroom. The judge additionally has the discretion to decide the amount of evidence that can be admitted about the victim's reputation, which, in turn, exerts a direct effect on trial outcome (Borgida and White, 1978).

Bohmer found that judges tended to divide rape cases into three categories, based primarily on their evaluations of the credibility of the allegations. The first category was what the judges regarded as 'genuine rape'. These largely fit the stereotype of sexual assault with a sex-starved stranger leaping out of the bushes to attack a helpless victim. In these cases judges tended to be sympathetic to victims and to react punitively toward rapists. They displayed quite different attitudes to cases which, although defined as rape under the law, were perceived as consensual. In these instances, judges often believed that the victim was 'asking for it' and used terms such as 'friendly rape' or 'assault with failure to please' to describe the incidents (Bohmer, 1974, p. 305). The third category was seen as either alleged rapes clearly involving consensual sex or alleged rapes which did not entail actual intercourse. In these cases the judges did not hesitate to attribute a motive to the victim – female vindictiveness and a desire to punish a specific man.

In assessing cases judges put the most weight on circumstantial evidence; that is, facts that can be inferred from circumstances. However, they tended to make grossly inaccurate judgements about which circumstances are actually relevant to veracity – these included speed of reporting (which is almost always delayed and often done by someone other than the victim), amount of co-operation with legal authorities (which is often hindered by insensitive treatment), and indecision about testifying (a realistic response in light of the reactions of the criminal justice system) (Weis and Borges, 1973). In addition, motives for filing rape complaints received special scrutiny and often influenced the judge to doubt victim veracity. Concluding her research, Bohmer noted that the judicial attitudes are far less impartial than generally supposed, and she further maintained that her investigation supported the allegation of courtroom victimization of at least some rape survivors.

Finally, our own research in Singapore has included monitoring of press reports of appeals for convictions for sexual assault. First, it should be noted that convictions for rape in Singapore are sparse. Between 1978 and 1984 555 rapes were reported; during the same period 60 convictions were obtained in High Court. In addition, Singapore differs from the United States, United Kingdom and most Western countries in that there is no trial by jury; rather, both the verdict and the sentencing are rendered by the judge.

Our archival research indicates that defence attorneys often play on popular misconceptions about sexual assault in order to overturn convictions or to reduce sentencing. This includes emphasis on victim–offender relationship, victim's lifestyle and previous sexual experiences. In turn, the judges tend to favour the defendant when the victim's character or behaviour is dubious. For example, the Chief Justice stated that the evidence which convicted a 29-year-old man of raping a woman that he had formerly dated was 'inherently incredible'. He pointed out that 'An allegation of rape is one of the

easiest to make and one of the most difficult to refute' in overturn-
ing the guilty verdict. Among others, the Chief Justice cited the
following reasons for the judgement: (1) the victim and the accused
had known each other for some time and had clearly been more
than friends; (2) the woman was sufficiently composed at the time
of the assault to ask the accused not to ejaculate inside her; (3) the
victim had not wanted to make a police report, but had been
persuaded to do so by friends; and (4) there was no corroborating
medical evidence (as the woman was sexually experienced) or
physical evidence of resistance. The Chief Justice erroneously
concluded that 'all of these hardly fitted into any of the conventional
accounts of rape which have been committed' (*Straits Times*,
January 12, 1991, p. 23) and further maintained that the woman was
clearly in no fear of death or hurt during the sexual assault.

Community Responses to Sexual Violence
Pervading social values and attitudes toward rape victims are
reflected and embodied in social institutions and official responses
to rape; these shared values and attitudes also influence the way
individual members of a community respond to sexual violence. In
one sense, then, all responses to rape are community responses;
however, analysis of these responses may occur on different levels
and with different emphases. From one perspective the development of rape crisis services, changes in rape legislation, or the
implementation of rape prevention programmes may be considered
and interpreted as community responses to rape victims in general.
From another perspective the assessment of community responses
to specific rape victims may be examined. Along these lines Lynn
Chancer (1987) has provided a poignant analysis of the New
Bedford gang rape and the community responses to the victim in the
aftermath.

Chancer's research is field-based and derives from archival
sources. She relies heavily on media coverage, particularly newspaper reporting of the incident, to track the history of the community responses to the victim, Cheryl Araujo. Her analysis of the
events after the sexual assault derives both from feminist theorizing
and from social psychology. In particular, she emphasizes the
impact of the victim's characteristics, especially her moral conduct,
on the community's unsympathetic responses.

Background   On March 6, 1983, at about 9 p.m., after putting her
two children to bed Cheryl Araujo went into Big Dan's bar in New
Bedford, Massachusetts, to get some cigarettes and to have a drink.
After midnight she was found running, half naked and screaming on

the roadside. Cheryl maintained that she had been gang raped on a pool table in the middle of a bar while a group of male customers watched and cheered. After assistance from the passerby, the police were called.

The following description of the rape was compiled by Chancer based on trial information reported in the *New York Times* and the *New Bedford Standard Times*. The 21-year-old victim was having a drink at the bar while several men were playing pool in the middle of the room. There was some verbal exchange between the victim and one of the men, following which she was carried, screaming and crying, across the room by him and a second man. Once at the pool table two other men joined in by pulling off her pants while a third pair of men held her down. At least one man raped her on the pool table, and two forced her to perform oral sex. Another two men prevented the bartender from calling the police and shouted 'do it, do it'. The rape lasted for over two hours with 9 or 10 men present at Big Dan's.

Community Responses   The community response to the incident was initially one of shock and horror. Emotions ran high with expressions of outrage, indignation and sadness. One week after the rape between 2500 and 4000 people marched in a candle-lit protest in New Bedford. However, the initial support for the victim diminished, and the Portuguese community, of which both Cheryl and the accused were members, shifted their allegiance to the sexual offenders.

The gang rape and following trial grabbed the attention of the nation, and the media provided extensive coverage of the court-room activities, including 15 hours of testimony by the victim. The New Bedford rape became the first criminal trial to be broadcast nationally, and over the next four weeks the newspapers printed detailed accounts of witness testimony. The accounts of the trial, the verdict and the sentencing of the defendants were supplemented by descriptions of the community responses to the rapists and the victim.

Victim-blaming began in the courtroom with one of the defence attorneys, Judith Lindahl, stating that Cheryl had been willing and that she had encouraged the men's advances (*New Bedford Standard Times*, cited in Chancer, 1987). Nevertheless, four of the six defendants were convicted of rape. After the first verdict was announced for Daniel Silva and Jose Vieira on March 17, 1984, a waiting crowd shouted and cursed. As the offenders were led from the courtroom the crowd cheered, and someone yelled 'Why wasn't she home with her kids?'; another shouted 'Why don't they bring that girl out in handcuffs?' (*New Bedford Standard Times*, cited in Chancer, 1987, p. 249).

It was five days before the remaining verdicts were determined, and during the interim several jurors received threats against their lives and were given police protection. Cheryl's sister and nephew left town permanently, and on a local radio station a caller referred to Cheryl as 'dead meat' (*New Bedford Standard Times*, cited in Chancer, 1987). When Victor Raposo and John Cordeiro were convicted of rape and Jose and Virgilio Medeiros were acquitted, Virgilio ran from the courtroom into a cheering crowd proclaiming that a rape had never occurred at Big Dan's.

On March 22, 1984, between 6000 and 8000 people participated in a candle-lit demonstration protesting that the defendants were convicted on flimsy evidence. On March 23, between 10,000 and 15,0000 people assembled outside the courthouse in a rally led by Jose and Virgilio Medeiros. Catherine Gabe, a journalist, interviewed women marchers and found unsympathetic blaming attitudes toward the victim of a brutal gang rape.

> 'They did nothing to her. Her rights are to be home with her kids and to be a good mother.'
> 'She should get punished, too. If they raped her, she was the aggravator.'
> 'I'm also a woman, but you don't see me getting raped. If you throw a dog a bone, he's going to take it – if you walk around naked, men are just going to go for you.' (*New Bedford Standard Times*, cited in Chancer, 1987, p. 251)

The Portuguese community were clearly in support of the rapists rather than the victim. And on the the morning of March 26, 1984, when Daniel Silva, Jose Vieira, Victor Raposo and John Cordeiro were sent to prison, the judge who sentenced them had received petitions signed by 16,000 people requesting leniency. Cheryl Araujo, like her sister and nephew, moved to Miami. Less than two years after that, she died tragically in a car accident in Florida.

While Chancer's analysis of the New Bedford rape case highlights the impact of media-fuelled ethnic discrimination on the Portuguese community's unsympathetic reactions to sexual violence, she is also quick to point out that characteristics of the victim contributed to the intensity of victim blaming. Cheryl Araujo was not a virtuous maiden; she did not lead an exemplary life. She was a Portuguese woman who dared to leave her children at home, who dared to enter a bar, and who was raped by men known to her. All of these factors contributed to the perception of victim precipitation. In the conservative Portuguese community the victim was considered a whore and deserving of her assault. Chancer further argues that the antagonism toward the victim and support of the rapists symbolizes the same kind of social control that Brownmiller (1975) referred to when she described male oppression of women through sexual violence. In this case, community reactions inflicted the second wound.

Evaluating Theory and Method

Evaluating Theory

The theoretical implications of research findings arising from field studies may be evaluated on a number of counts. On the most fundamental level the distinction between 'pure' and 'applied' psychological research becomes useful. Although the boundary between the two is sometimes blurred, basic theorizing on rape attitudes and perceptions may be seen to culminate in field research. After all, both social psychological and feminist theories are ultimately aimed at the explanation of real world phenomena. In this context, field research provides the most appropriate testing ground for theories about antecedents and consequences of rape-related attitudes and attributions.

The results of field studies are consistent with feminist theorizing on conflict and sexual access and mirror the findings of basic psychological experimental and survey research. For example, a portion of the studies on attributions and rape victimology has been conducted as simulated jury trials and has concentrated on trial outcome, particularly verdict and recommended sentencing. In these instances, as in the field, perceptions of victim characteristics tend to be more powerful predictors of trial outcomes than defendant traits (Sealy and Wain, 1980). Simulation studies have demonstrated that guilty verdicts are less likely to be rendered in rape cases when there is no evidence of victim resistance (Deitz et al., 1984; Johnson and Jackson, 1988) or assailant force (Burt and Albin, 1981). In addition, if the victim's behaviour is considered contributory, that is, she acted in an imprudent manner which may have facilitated the commission of a sexual offence, this decreases the likelihood of conviction and length of sentence (Pugh, 1983). Victims' moral character and conduct are crucial indicators of trial outcome and sentencing. Sexually active victims are less likely to have their cases result in conviction (Pugh, 1983). In fact, Eugene Borgida and Phyllis White (1978) reported that any testimony on prior sexual history reduces the probability of a guilty verdict. Along similar lines, longer imprisonment is recommended for offenders who assaulted virgin, compared to non-virgin, victims (Kanekar and Vaz, 1983).

Research demonstrates a fundamental consistency between the

field- and lab-based studies. However, field-based studies, which evidence actual, rather than hypothetical, prejudice against victims of sexual violence, are often taken to substantiate the link between attitudes and behaviours. This is in line with the contentions of legal analysts who frequently argue that on many occasions the evidence presented at a rape case does not reliably predict a verdict as trial outcome is based more on jurors' attitudes about rape (Feild, 1978b, 1979; Hibey, 1973; LeGrand, 1973; Mathiasen, 1974).

From a methodological point of view the proposed link between attitudes and behaviour is difficult to assess empirically as attitudes and behaviours are rarely measured concurrently in the same field study. The link is inferred: as attitudes and attributions are believed to be predictive of behaviour in basic research, behaviours are taken to be indicative of attitudes in the applied domains. However, it is worth noting that there is some evidence of an attitude–behaviour link which is found in basic survey and experimental research. More specifically, a number of studies have examined rape myth acceptance, rape empathy, general attitudes toward rape and victim perceptions in conjunction with responses to rape cases, including the likelihood of criminal conviction and the proposed length of sentencing, and have substantiated a relationship between attitudes and self-reported behaviours.

Mock jurors whose attitudes reflect empathy for victims of sexual violence see the victim in a less precipitatory role, are more certain of the defendant's guilt, and recommend longer sentences (Deitz et al., 1981, 1982, 1984; Spanos et al., 1991–2; Weir and Wrightsman, 1990). Similarly, rape myth acceptance and attributions of victim fault reduce the probability of labelling a sexual encounter as rape and convicting an accused (Burt and Albin, 1981; Fischer, 1991). Attitudes toward rape also affect proposed sentencing. Jurors recommend more lenient sentences when they believe that women should be responsible for preventing rape, that rapists are normal, that rapists should not be punished harshly, and that rape victims precipitate their own rape (Feild, 1978b).

Field studies provide invaluable information about the treatment of rape victims. First, consistent with feminist allegations, research reveals that sexually assaulted women are plainly disadvantaged in the criminal justice system. Their cases are often handled in a way which demands greater evidence requirements than is circumscribed by the law. For example, women are expected to show signs of vigorous resistance. In addition, extra-legal considerations about victims' moral behaviour affect police processing and trial outcomes. If there is an acquaintanceship between the victim and the offender, this also reduces the probability of successful prosecution.

The factors which affect police and prosecutorial management of rape cases imply that rape myths underlie the institutional process- ing of these cases. As feminists have argued, and as basic psycho- logical research has corroborated, there is more sympathy for cases which conform to the classic stereotype of rape and for victims who conform to restrictive gender roles and norms.

The emphasis in this chapter has been placed on the treatment of rape victims by the police and the courts due to the prevalence of field studies in this area; however, the biased management of rape cases is by no means limited to this domain. Research has also demonstrated that mental health professionals engage in victim- blaming 'therapies'. It is likely, although undocumented by field studies, that the same type of responses would be found in the medical profession. As reported in Chapter 2, doctors and nurses cling to stereotyped perceptions of rape and hold relatively un- favourable attitudes toward victims of sexual violence (Best, 1983; Cochrane, 1987; Ward, 1988a). Attribution studies with nurses have further indicated that they are influenced by the amount of emotional upset in determining the extent of therapy required and that they are affected by the victim's character in assigning responsi- bility for rape (Alexander, 1980; Damrosch, 1985b).

On a theoretical basis, then, field studies imply that the unjust and biased treatment of victims by police, lawyers, judges and counsellors is the consequence of stereotyped misconceptions about sexual violence and prejudicial attitudes toward victims of sexual assault. The nature of this prejudice is consistent with the feminist framing of rape as an expression of male dominance and social control of women and the perception of women as male property. Taken together, basic and field research provide powerful and persuasive support for both feminist and psychological theorizing.

Evaluating Method

The evaluation of field studies must be undertaken from a slightly different perspective than the methodological analyses in the preceding chapters. What should be obvious at the outset is that field research is defined by its location in the real world, that is, in natural settings. Methodologically, this type of research combines a variety of research designs and techniques. Field investigations may rely on quasi-experimental methods or may be descriptive studies; they also incorporate survey research with the use of both question- naires and interviews, naturalistic observations of behaviour, and data derived from archival sources. The appraisal of the merits of field studies, then, should be based on the overall package of design and technique. This may include consideration of the strengths and weaknesses of survey and questionnaire research and quasi-experimental studies. As these methods have been previously discussed, and as the bulk of field studies involve naturalistic observations and archival research, a further comment on observational and archival techniques will be made. This is particularly appropriate as observational and archival methods tend to be applied somewhat differently by psychologists than by feminists.

Systematic observation necessarily involves the selection, recording, coding and interpretation of naturally occurring behaviours. In some types of field research it may be possible to observe subjects without their knowledge, which, while raising ethical issues, ensures more natural behavioural responses. In the studies described here researchers have operated, for the most part, as known observers, for example Rose and Randall's (1982) study of police investigation of sexual offences. The awareness of these research observations is likely to reduce the spontaneity of subjects' activities and influence the treatment of rape victims. Consequently, behavioural responses may be subjected to the same type of distortion and social desirability influences described in Chapter 2 with reference to questionnaire research.

It is particularly important in field observations that the researchers have a clear idea of which behaviours will be monitored and how the data will be collected and coded. Some behaviours are easier to observe and categorize than others. For example, it may be relatively easy to observe an investigator's classification of an alleged sexual assault case. In contrast, it may be more difficult to evaluate his or her general positive or negative behaviour towards a rape victim. Nevertheless, the final assessment of any naturalistic observational study rests on the reliability and validity of data collection and coding, including the adequate sampling of representative behaviours.

In contrast to observational investigations, archival research derives from public records. It is important to recognize that in archival studies the research data under scrutiny are used for purposes other than for which they were originally collected and that someone other than the researcher has been responsible for data compilation. In this sense key measurement decisions have already been made and may limit the testability of relevant hypotheses. For example, police and court records are likely to provide clear information about case disposition or trial outcome; however, information on selected victim or defendant variables may be missing. Along these lines Rose and Randall (1982) noted that police offence incident reports often omit important details of the crime.

Like archival and observational studies, survey research, interviewing and quasi-experimental approaches have their strengths and weaknesses. A major point in favour of field studies, however, is that they incorporate a range of these techniques, balancing the positive and negative features of the various approaches. Multimethod studies in psychology have been heralded as a particularly robust approach to the explanation of human behaviour (Campbell and Fiske, 1959). In addition to this advantage, field studies are especially powerful because they have excellent external validity; that is, the findings are based on real world phenomena.

It should be noted that field studies on the treatment of rape victims not only rely on multi-methods but are also multidisciplinary. This is in line with feminist approaches to social issues which are more concerned with the investigation of a social problem than with disciplinary boundaries. In addition, a large portion of field research mirrors the feminist preference for non-intrusive techniques situated in a natural environment. It also reflects, in some instances, the participative interaction of the researcher with the 'subjects'. While there are other feminist recommendations which have not been adopted in the field research described here such as power-sharing between the researcher and the researched, this line of social psychological and interdisciplinary investigations comes closest to methods advocated by feminist scholars.

The strength of field research is obvious. It has good validity and does not suffer from the criticisms directed at artificial laboratory-based studies. Field research provides much-needed concrete information about the actual treatment of victims of sexual assault in various systems, particularly their treatment by the police, courts and mental health professionals. Despite some limitations of the multi-method approach, the combination of naturalistic observations, interviewing, surveys, archival data and quasi-experimental studies, increases research reliability and validity.

In Conclusion

Field-based research has provided powerful evidence of the prejudicial treatment of victims of sexual violence by the police, legal system, mental health professionals and the wider community. The research lends a strong empirical base to allegations which had previously been regarded as partisan and anecdotal (LaFree, 1980b). Interdisciplinary research, including studies by social psychologists, has documented what feminists have known all along – that victims of sexual violence are perceived as precipitating their own victimization, that sexual assault is often trivialized, that women are expected to conform to traditional and restricted gender roles, and that both rape itself and the institutional reactions to sexual violence function as a means of exerting social control over women.

In terms of an overarching conceptual framework, the treatment of victims of sexual violence in the legal system, the social services and in the community is seen as the consequence of underlying misconceptions about rape and prejudicial attitudes toward women. The societal and institutional reactions to rape victims both reflect negative attitudes and values and reinforce them. As such, attitudes and behaviours are sustained in a symbiotic relationship – developing in a circular fashion and continuing to disdavantage victims of sexual violence. Changing these attitudes is a major challenge and will be considered in the second part of this book.

While this chapter has emphasized the interaction of the victim with various social institutions from the institutional perspective, it is also important that the interaction be examined from the victim's perspective. The next chapter explores the consequences of rape myths for the victim's psychological recovery from sexual assault by examining her appraisal of and reactions to both sexual violence itself and the subsequent responses from others.

Notes

1 The names of the victim and the perpetrator have been changed to protect their identities. The case study was taken from our research on sexual violence in Singapore.

2 These include the type of research setting (Hanson, 1980), the intensity of the attitude (Sample and Warlund, 1973), the familiarity of the action domains (Fazio and Zanna, 1981), felt responsibility for one's actions (Schwartz, 1973), the attitudes of significant others (Acock and DeFleur, 1975), expectations about how one should behave (Fishbein and Ajzen, 1975), a sense of moral obligation (Gorsuch and Ortberg, 1983), and the public scrutiny of behaviours (Raden, 1977).

5

Returning to the Victim: Theory and Research on Psychological Reactions to Sexual Violence

> Everybody in the system blames us. Right? From the court, hospitals, boyfriends, family. You know it is really hard for a woman who has been raped to not blame herself. It comes at you from all the other sides, and very often the rapist himself will say it.
>
> (A rape victim meeting sexual offenders in therapy, in Bruyere et al., 1982)

In the end we return to the beginning . . .

The examination of attitudes toward and perceptions of victims of sexual violence began with broad descriptions based on personal anecdotes and poignant observations. The experiences of rape victims, the reactions of significant others, the treatment of survivors of sexual assault by social, legal and medical services, social customs, laws and 'expert' opinion which carry implicit values about the role of women and the regulation of their sexuality were presented. From personal anecdotes and passing observations of social trends, a more solid base of empirical research was described.

This commenced with ethnographic and archival studies and continued with the quantitative assessment of biased and prejudicial attitudes toward rape victims. The antecedents and predictors of these attitudes and attributions were discussed, and the influence of diverse dispositional and situational factors on perceptions of rape and rape victims was highlighted. The study of antecedents of rape attitudes then shifted to emphasis on the consequences of rape myths. Macro-analysis featured field studies of institutional responses to victims of sexual violence, including clearance of police cases, trial outcomes and therapeutic interventions. Throughout these presentations both theoretical and methodological issues were critically assessed, but in the end we return again to the victim and consider the impact of negative, prejudicial misconceptions of sexual violence on her psychological well-being and recovery from sexual assault.

Clinical case studies of victims of sexual assault and broad-based survey research have provided the context for investigation of psychological reactions to sexual violence while psychological theories on stress, coping and self-perceptions have offered the conceptual foundations for interpretation of the findings. On the one extreme, clinical case studies have been employed for in-depth information-gathering pertaining to single individuals. On the other extreme, large-scale community surveys have been conducted to enable investigators to access a wide range of sexual assault victims, including those who have never reported to the police or social service agencies.

The analyses of victim responses have drawn on cognitive-based theories in both clinical and social psychology. From the broadest perspective theories of stress and coping have provided an overarching conceptual framework for the examination of victim responses; within this framework specific factors are assumed to mediate victim reactions to sexual violence. Of particular concern in this context are: (1) victims' cognitive responses and self-perceptions and (2) the availability of social support. Both of these factors affect psychological recovery from sexual violence, both are modified by social influences, and both are linked to perceptions of and expectations about sexual violence.

Clinical Case Studies

Case studies are a form of descriptive research which is distinguished by data gathering in a structured setting and emphasis on a single individual. In most instances the researcher attempts to construct a detailed description of the personality and behavioural characteristics of an individual. The most common method for obtaining this information is the interview, although in some cases this is supplemented by questionnaire administration and even naturalistic observations. In traditional psychological research the interview is usually conducted via a set of structured questions directed by a researcher who attempts to remain somewhat detached from the interactive process so as to avoid biasing the participants' responses. In contrast, feminists tend to adopt a somewhat different style by becoming more involved in interactive interviewing and empowering strategies.

As case studies are descriptive in nature, conclusions cannot be drawn about cause and effect relationships. The researcher may merely describe psychological phenomena such as the presence of social support or the absence of self-blame. Nevertheless, reliability and validity are still important considerations. Selective observations and recording of case study data can affect research results, and the case study method is often criticized for biases in data interpretation.

Case studies also suffer limitations with respect to generalizability. Findings from the study of a single rape victim, regardless of the quality and quantity of case information, cannot be applied to rape victims in general. For this reason some researchers have collected a series of in-depth case studies to look for common patterns of psychological and social responses to sexual assault. Survey methods, described previously in conjunction with attitude research, have also been used to examine psychological reactions to sexual abuse.

An Overview of Stress, Coping and the Consequences of Sexual Assault

Sexual assault may be viewed as a traumatic life event which produces overwhelming stress and demands the extensive use of personal adjustive resources to restore a stable level of pre-crisis functioning. In the clinical literature, maladaptive symptoms arising from rape and other forms of sexual abuse are generally classified as post-traumatic stress disorders (PTSD); this acknowledges that the psychological, emotional and behavioural disruptions are transient and that they are due to severe stressors which would typically overwhelm even the most stable and competent individual. Post-traumatic stress disorders are particularly devastating if the distressing life event is unexpected and unfamiliar as in the case of sexual violence, other forms of criminal victimization, and serious accidents.

As a crisis-evoking life event, sexual assault may be understood and analysed within the conceptual framework provided by a clinical model of stress and coping. The model, illustrated in Figure 5.1, is adapted from Coleman's (1979) and Lazarus's (1976) work on psychological adjustment (Ward, 1988b).

While sexual assault routinely precipitates psychological trauma, individuals respond in different ways to crisis. A variety of factors influence the severity of the stress experienced, the choice of psychological coping mechanisms and the prevalence of maladaptive responses. In addition to the cognitive appraisal of and subjective distress during sexual assault, specific features of the sexual violence may be important in predicting reactions and coping capacities (Girelli et al., 1986; Koss and Burkhart, 1989). For example, there is some evidence of differential responses to stranger and acquaintance rape. It is also the case that victims of multiple offences have more difficulties with psychological, social and sexual readjustment after sexual assault (Ellis et al., 1982). The amount of force exerted in the commission of a sexual offence affects the severity of psychological symptoms of sexual abuse (McCahill et al., 1979), and although maladaptive psychological responses to sexual violence are intense and long-lasting, they do tend to diminish over time (Atkeson et al., 1982; Kilpatrick et al., 1979; Resick et al., 1981).[1]

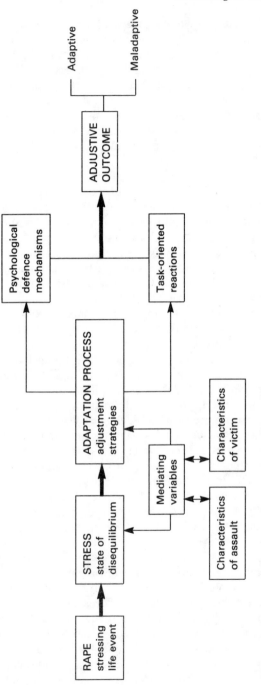

Figure 5.1 *Stress and coping framework (Ward, 1988b, p. 167)*

Victim characteristics are also significant in understanding responses to sexual violence. Pre-existing factors such as previous victimization (Cohen and Roth, 1987; Frank et al., 1980), physical illness (Atkeson et al., 1982), chronic life stressors (Burgess and Holmstrom, 1978), psychological problems and substance abuse (Ruch and Chandler, 1983) aggravate stress reactions. Attitudes may also play a role in the recovery process; there is some evidence that victims who have tolerant attitudes toward interpersonal violence suffer more severe psychological symptoms in response to sexual assault (Mynatt and Allgeier, 1990).

A considerable body of psychological research has been amassed in recent years which documents substantial, often long-term, negative consequences of sexual assault. The Rape Trauma Syndrome proposed by Ann Burgess and Lynda Holmstrom (1974b) occurs in two phases – an acute stage and a long-term reorganization stage. During these periods maladaptive symptoms may include: somatic complaints such as muscular tension, gastro-intestinal irritability and genito-urinary disorders (Burgess and Holmstrom, 1974b); sleep and appetite disturbances (Ellis, 1983); psycho-emotional responses such as powerful feelings of fear, anxiety and depression (Atkeson et al., 1982; Frank et al., 1979; Kilpatrick et al., 1979, 1981); behavioural problems such as role disruption, poor social adjustment, sexual dysfunction and substance abuse (Burgess and Holmstrom, 1979a; Feldman-Summers et al., 1979; Miller et al., 1982; Orlando and Koss, 1983); negative effects on self-concept and lowered self-esteem (Burgess and Holmstrom, 1979b; Libow and Doty, 1979); and interpersonal difficulties (Ellis et al., 1981).

The psychological symptoms arising in connection with sexual abuse may emerge as a direct effect of sexual violence or may be linked to accompanying life changes or stress situations. In this context it is useful to refer to the distinction between primary and secondary victimization proposed by Shelley Taylor and colleagues (1983). The former refers to the psychological, behavioural and emotional consequences of the sexual assault itself; the latter relates to responses engendered by the negative reactions of hostility, derogation and rejection that can follow sexual abuse. In the case of secondary victimization, experiences with the police, courts, medical authorities, social service agencies and friends and families may affect victims' psychological recovery. These experiences influence victims' cognitive appraisals of the sexual violence; they may expand or limit perceived sources of social support and exert influence on victims' self-perceptions and attributions. The following sections examine the dynamics of self-concept and social support in the stress and coping process. Viewing these phenomena from a social psychological perspective, the chapter attempts to merge current theory and research with previous studies on antecedents and consequences of rape myths.

The Social Definition of Self

Social psychological theories of self have emphasized that self-concept is acquired through social interaction. More specifically, the primary way in which we come to know about ourselves is through the reflection of ourselves provided by others. This was originally articulated by Charles Cooley, who first coined the term 'looking glass self'. Cooley's (1922) theorizing was later extended by George Herbert Mead (1934), who adopted a dynamic view of self and emphasized the interaction between our own behaviour and others' responses to it. In his theory of symbolic interactionism he proposed that the self develops as a social process in which we view ourselves reflexively as an object from the perspective of others. In this reflexive viewing Mead reiterated the importance of attitudes and expectations, a point later taken up by contemporary sociologists.

The influence of others' expectations on our behaviour and self-concept was also highlighted by Robert Merton (1948) in his research on the self-fulfilling prophecy. Merton noted that events, experiences and behaviours can be created by the mere expectation that they will occur. Although his original research was undertaken in the classroom and related to teacher expectations and student performance, there have since been over 300 studies on the self-fulfilling prophecy, which has been corroborated in both the field and the lab (Rosenthal and Rubin, 1978). This theme has been carried on in contemporary research on social cognition; for example, studies have demonstrated that when observers respond to others on the basis of prior expectations, they elicit behavioural confirmation of the expectations and influence individuals' self-perceptions (Fazio et al., 1981; Snyder and Swann, 1978).

In the broadest sense symbolic interactionists have argued that society shapes self and self shapes society. This is consistent with the feminist position that women are socialized into a victim role which leads them to accept responsibility for the victimizing events which befall them (Brownmiller, 1975). Again, on a general level if society responds to rape victims with the clear message that they are deserving of sexual coercion, that they are demeaned and devalued by their abuse and that they should accept blame for sexual violence, this is likely to result in their internalization of these negative appraisals and to have detrimental effects on their behaviours and self-concepts. In fact, some have argued that self-blame merely reflects victims' internalization of the negative perceptions held by society at large (Goffman, 1963).

It is important to recognize the vicious circle involved in moulding self-concepts of rape victims, particularly the dynamics of blame attributions and perceptions. Social attitudes frequently reflect victim blame, victims often internalize these attitudes and then, in turn, others respond negatively to victims who admit to self-blame for sexual assault (Coates et al., 1979). Even counsellors hold victims more responsible for sexual assault if they engage in self-blaming attributions; they also perceive their emotional health to be at greater risk (Thornton et al., 1988).

Perceptions of Rape, Perceptions of Self: Cognitive and Behavioural Responses to Sexual Violence

Although rape victims are required to confront a variety of pressing demands in the recovery from sexual assault, a fundamental response is centred on the cognitive understanding of sexual violence. Victims have a basic need to find meaning in their sexual abuse, to understand or to explain an essentially incomprehensible event (Frankl, 1963; Koss and Burkhart, 1989). Cognitive appraisals are tremendously important in this undertaking (Lazarus and Folkman, 1984), and the elaboration and interpretation of sexual coercion have marked consequences for victims' psychological well-being. These cognitive and perceptual processes also significantly influence victims' self-concepts.

Both social psychological and clinical literatures emphasize that victims' cognitive interpretations are inherently influenced by pervading misconceptions of sexual violence. As such, rape myths exert direct and indirect influences on self-concept and mental health. In one instance, victims may already hold negative and prejudicial attitudes toward sexual violence which affect their interpretation of rape, undermine their self-esteem, and have detrimental consequences for their psychological recovery. In another instance, stereotyped misconceptions of coercive sex can influence others' responses to victims, which, in turn, colour victims' perceptions of themselves, and influence their subsequent emotional and behavioural reactions to rape.

Making Meaning
There is considerable evidence that cognitive elaboration of sexual violence in itself facilitates recovery. Understanding the incompre-

hensible appears to be a fundamental need for victims of sexual abuse. Roxane Silver and associates (1983) reported that victims of incest persist in attempting to make meaning of the events some 20 years after the episodes. Research by John Harvey and colleagues also indicated that account-making, defined as 'story-like constructions of events that include explanations, descriptions, predictions about relevant future events and affective reactions' (Harvey et al., 1991, p. 516), is associated with post-rape recovery. Burgess and Holmstrom (1979c) likewise reported that individuals' conscious efforts at explanation aid in stress reduction and facilitate post-rape readjustment.

While making meaning is of considerable importance, the actual strategies used and explanations relied upon can also have psychological and behavioural consequences. Stereotypes of rape, reflecting dominant societal values and attitudes, can affect a victim's psychological recovery, decision to deal with the authorities and, most significantly, her perceptions of self-blame.

Social Stereotypes and Victim Responses
Research has repeatedly demonstrated that the most widely held stereotype of rape includes the following components: (1) a crime of sexual passion (2) which occurs between strangers, (3) generally in unsafe public places, (4) involves the use of physical force and (5) entails evidence of victim resistance. These rape myths are widespread and common, and, although endorsed more strongly by males than by females, are still held with some degree of confidence by both sexes. The internalization of misconceptions about sexual violence can have subsequently devastating effects on a woman if she is later forced to confront her own sexual victimization. In short, rape myths are likely to influence the interpretation of coercive episodes and psychological responses to sexual violence. Not only are victims' definitions of rape affected by these stereotypes, but it is also likely that behaviours, such as willingness to seek help in response to sexual abuse, will be influenced by pre-existing perceptions of sexual victimization and concurrent responses from others (Dukes and Mattley, 1977).

These contentions have been borne out in a study by Mary Koss and her colleagues (1987) which demonstrated that only 27 per cent of women who experienced a sexually coercive incident which met the legal criteria of rape perceived themselves as victims. As expected, forced intercourse with a stranger is more likely to be perceived as rape by the victim herself (Koss, 1985). Women also seem to cope somewhat better with sexual violence which reflects the popular stereotype of rape – physical coercion by strangers. For example, subsequent adaptive reactions to sexual assault, including enrolment in self-defence courses and adoption of more security conscious measures, are more likely to occur when the victim has a more distant relationship with the perpetrator (Wyatt et al., 1990). There is also evidence that women who had been sexually coerced by physical, rather than psychological, force have fewer post-rape adjustment problems (Mynatt and Allgeier, 1990).

Rape stereotypes similarly affect choices to interact with the criminal justice system and social service agencies. Stranger rape is more likely to be reported to the police and to receive support from rape crisis centres (Koss, 1985). In fact, the likelihood of victims reporting rape and seeking assistance from social services decreases as pre-rape intimacy with the perpetrator increases (Koss et al., 1988). Victims are also more likely to report rape in instances when they have corroborative evidence of physical force. Shirley Feldman-Summers and Jeanette Norris (1984), for example, found that 74 per cent of those who reported sexual assault to the authorities had cuts and bruises compared to 44 per cent of those who did not report.

In short, rapes which correspond more closely to the stereotype of sexual violence are more likely to be interpreted as such, to be reported to the police and social service agencies, and, in some instances, to result in fewer adjustment problems. The link between societal expectations about sexual violence and victim responses, including psychological reactions to sexual assault, is also implicit in the dynamics of blame attributions. Self-perceptions and attributions, which have received substantial attention in the social psychological and clinical literature, are considered in the next section.

Internalizing Stereotypes: Self-blame in Victims of Sexual Assault

The Nature of Self-blame   Judith Libow and David Doty (1979) commented on the prevalence of self-blame and its relationship to self-derogation in an early paper which included case studies of rape victims; however, the most cited theorizing on self-blame comes from Ronnie Janoff-Bulman (1979). Distinguishing behavioural and characterological forms of self-blame in victims of sexual assault, Janoff-Bulman maintained that blame may be attributed to a victim's disposition or behaviour. For example, victims may perceive themselves as worthless persons or as victim types and attribute blame accordingly; alternatively, they may ascribe blame to careless behaviours, such as failure to lock windows or accepting a lift with a casual acquaintance. Janoff-Bulman reasoned that characterological blame, causal perceptions based on relatively stable, global personal dispositions, would inhibit recovery from sexual violence. In contrast, behavioural self-blame, linked to specific transitory situations, may facilitate recovery by allowing an individual to regain a sense of control and to reduce feelings of vulnerability. This, of course, is predicated on the assumption that victims believe that they can alter rape-prone behaviours.

Janoff-Bulman began her research by requesting counsellors at rape crisis centres to estimate the extent to which victims of sexual violence engaged in self-blame. Counsellors indicated that approximately 70 per cent of those seeking therapeutic intervention attributed blame to their behaviours while about 20 per cent ascribed blame to their characters. Estimates of blame prevalence, however, have varied enormously in subsequent studies, depending upon research methodology and the blame alternatives provided. Sharon McCombie (1975) reported that 18 per cent of victims interviewed immediately after rape stated explicitly and spontaneously that they were disturbed by their role in the episode. This contrasts markedly with Gail Wyatt and colleagues' (1990) community-based research which reported that 61 per cent of sexual assault victims attributed victimization to something about themselves. Sommerfeldt and associates' (1989) study which relied upon the content analysis of written descriptions of sexual assault found that 46 per cent of the victims evidenced some form of self-blame; in contrast, 40 per cent blamed the aggressor. In a multi-method investigation Buf Meyer and Shelley Taylor (1986) found that 56 per cent of victims attributed blame to the rapist, 20 per cent to themselves, 15 per cent to chance and 11 per cent to society when asked who/what they blamed most for the rape; however, nearly half of the victims mentioned some form of self-blame in response to an open-ended question about blame.

Daryl Bem (1972) has argued that the processes by which people make attributions about themselves are essentially similar to attributional processes relied upon by others. Not only do victims internalize society's tendency to blame them for their sexual assault, but the factors which affect self-blame attributions largely reflect popular misconceptions about sexual violence. Smith and Ousley's (1982) study indicated that victims who were using drugs or alcohol at the time of the assault indulged in self-blame to a greater extent than those whose cases did not involve the use of intoxicating substances (see Richardson and Campbell, 1982). It is also interesting to note that these victims additionally saw themselves as suffering greater blame attributions from friends and family members. Similarly, Bonnie Katz (1991) reported that women who were raped by strangers engaged in less self-blame and perceived themselves in a more positive light than those raped by acquaintances. Wyatt and colleagues (1990) likewise found that self-blame increased with proximity to the offender. Victims tended to perceive the man as more responsible in stranger rape, although there was no difference in their perceptions of the clarity with which they communicated their own non-consent (Koss et al., 1988). On the whole, attributions of self-blame do reflect common stereotypes of rape. For example, women are more likely to see themselves as responsible for sexual victimization when they were less assertive, had been coerced by someone they knew well, who had used psychological rather than physical force, and when there was little evidence of physical injury (Mynatt and Allgeier, 1990).

Outcomes of Self-blame   The consequences of self-blame for post-rape adjustment remain subject to dispute (Abbey, 1987). Originally it was argued by both feminists and crisis counsellors that self-blame was detrimental to psychological recovery. There is also a clinical literature which suggests that negative self-perceptions, including blame, are part of a depressive syndrome (Seligman, 1975). Despite these arguments, Janoff-Bulman (1982) further pursued her distinction of behavioural and characterological blame and mustered empirical support for her contention that behavioural self-blame could produce psychological benefits for victims. She distinguished the effects of blame in actors and observers by requiring half of her subjects to imagine themselves as the victim of a sexual assault described in a vignette and half merely to read the description and comment on it as an outside observer. Subjects were then queried about their perceptions of blame. Janoff-Bulman reported that (1) behavioural blame was more likely to be engaged in by 'victims' than by observers, (2) behavioural self-blame was associated with high levels of self-esteem in 'victims' and perceptions of future avoidability of sexual violence, (3) characterological self-blame was linked to low levels of self-esteem in 'victims', and (4) both behavioural and characterological blame of the 'victim' were associated with high levels of self-esteem in the observer. Although the results are consistent with her theorizing on self-blame and adjustment, the findings are limited in that the 'victim' status had been experimentally manipulated in responses to hypothetical scenarios – real rape victims were not employed in this research.

More substantial findings have been presented by Catalina Mandoki and Barry Burkhart (1991). In a study of over 150 female undergraduates who had experienced forced intercourse the researchers found that blame attributions were the most important variable in the prediction of post-rape adjustment. Characterological blame was associated with both initial and later levels of distress; however, blame attributed to victim behaviour or more generally to society did not bear a strong relationship to psychological adjustment.

Evidence appears consistent concerning the negative impact of characterological self-blame; however, Meyer and Taylor's (1986) study found that both behavioural and characterological self-blame were associated with poor adjustment in rape victims. More specifically, behavioural blame, that is, acknowledgement of poor judgement, was associated with depression and sexual dissatisfaction while characterological blame, that is, seeing oneself as the victim type, was linked to depression and fear. In contrast, societal blame was unrelated to adjustment. The results, which were based on factor analytic studies, supported Janoff-Bulman's distinction of blame models; however, both forms of self-blame were associated with aversive outcomes.

The functions and consequences of self-blame are intertwined with issues of mastery and control and with the dynamics of self-derogation. Characterological blame is self-defeating; it reflects negative, global dispositional attributions which evidence poor self-concept and lowered self-esteem. The consequences of behavioural blame are less clear, but it has been postulated that victims may regain a sense of control and diminish feelings of vulnerability by attributing sexual violence to changeable, situation-specific behaviours. Certainly there is an extensive clinical literature on mastery and control which has documented that perceptions of personal control are associated with enhanced mental health. In rape victimology studies it has also been demonstrated that women who are led to believe that sexual violence is uncontrollable experience more fear and anxiety than those who are made to believe that they can avoid sexual victimization (Heath and Davidson, 1988).

Self-blame does not occur in a socio-cultural vacuum. It is prompted both by general ideologies and by specific responses from others. The powerful impact of others' tendencies to attribute blame to victims of sexual assault was demonstrated in a recent study by Gail Wyatt and colleagues (1990). Simply put, the researchers found that self-blame increased in proportion to unsupportive responses from others. Self-blame was predicted by involvement with the authorities and was associated with aversive psychological outcomes such as fear, anxiety, depression, sleeplessness, relationship problems, sexual dysfunction and negative attitudes toward men. Again, the circular relationship between attitudes and behaviours of others and victim self-perceptions is demonstrated.

Social Support

A variety of factors affect stress and coping in victims of crisis, and both situational and dispositional factors are important in predicting adjustive outcomes. In the domain of interpersonal influences on victims' stress reactions, basic perceptions and expectations of significant others are of obvious importance; however, their broader capacity to render social support is also critical to the recovery process. Social support has been defined as 'social interactions or relationships that provide individuals with actual assistance or that embed individuals within a social system that is believed to provide love, caring or a sense of attachment to a valued social group or dyad' (Hobfoll, 1988, p. 159). There is an extensive literature which has documented the relationship between social support and enhanced psychological well-being (Leavy, 1983). For example, social support has been reported to reduce stress and facilitate coping with life changes in general (Williams et al., 1981) and serves an adaptive function in relation to specific events such as pregnancy (Nuckolls et al., 1972), job loss (Pearlin et al., 1981), economic, parental and homemaking problems (Kessler and Essex, 1982), and widowhood (Bankoff, 1986).

Theory and research on social support has been traditionally situated in the stress and coping literature. In this context it has been argued that the use of social networks is a major factor in the moderation of the relationship between stress and adjustment. The functional benefits of social support include the provision of feedback, validation of crisis reactions, and assistance in regaining a sense of mastery. Social support may also serve to influence individuals' perceptions of a stressful event, their selection of coping responses and their resultant self-esteem. In this sense social support entails a feedback loop with support-providers offering advice and assistance which often convey both implicit and explicit values. The assistance may be accepted or rejected by the person in crisis; it may be perceived as helpful or unhelpful, but the underlying assumptions upon which support is based are often recognized by individuals in crisis and, whether positive or negative, are tacitly accepted and subsequently internalized. In this way, social support also exerts an influence on self-concept.

People rely on a variety of sources for social support when they are confronted with crisis situations. However, studies reveal that individuals turn most frequently to friends and families and that professional services are more commonly used as a later resource (Litman, 1974). Although the effectiveness of a social support source may be dependent upon the crisis situation (Hobfoll, 1988), intimate ties, especially with spouses, significantly contribute to stress reduction (Kessler and Essex, 1982). Husbands and wives are often the most salient and powerful source of social support (Reibstein, 1981). However, it is also important to note that intimate relationships have their costs as well as benefits. Rook (1985) has discussed this in some detail, remarking that close relations are more likely to include negative reactions than more distant ones, and that intimates are more sensitive to rejection, criticism and unwillingness to help. Intimate relations are also especially potent in reinforcing a person's self-image (Swann and Predmore, 1985).

Unsupportive responses from intimate others are particularly difficult for crisis-stricken individuals to manage; nevertheless, there are many reasons why potentially supportive people are unwilling or unable to give assistance. First, individuals may be unfamiliar with the crisis situation and lack the competency to be supportive. Secondly, they may hold negative perceptions of the crisis situation and be concerned about social stigma. There is some evidence that the more severe the problem, the more likely this is to occur (Dunkel-Schetter and Wortman, 1982). Thirdly, and along similar lines, support-providers may be influenced by misconceptions about the crisis situation. It has been argued that in instances where expectations differ significantly from what actually constitutes crisis, providers are more likely to react inappropriately and are unable to offer substantial support (Silver and Wortman, 1980). In these situations victims of crisis are particularly vulnerable; studies have shown that it is the *negative*, rather than the *positive*, responses from significant others which are the best predictors of psychological maladjustment in distressed individuals (for example, Brown and Andrews, 1986).

What, then, is the relationship between rape myths and social support? First, stereotyped misconceptions of sexual assault can limit an individual's capacity to render the much needed social support to victims in crisis. If this is the case, the psychological recovery of rape victims may be directly impaired by the absence of supportive responses from significant others. Secondly, these myths can be implicitly or explicitly filtered back to victims through the inappropriate or unsupportive reactions of friends and family members. As mentioned previously, this may affect the cognitive appraisal of sexual violence and have detrimental consequences for victims' self-esteem and mental health.

Social Support for Victims of Sexual Assault

Social Support from Significant Others
It is often the perception of social support, rather than the size of support networks or the quantity of interactions, which predicts psychological recovery from crisis situations (Hobfoll, 1988). Subjective perceptions of social support are particularly relevant to the cognitive appraisal of sexual violence and have obvious consequences for victims' self-images. Research has shown that rape victims tend to view reassuring behaviours, staying in close contact, talking, understanding their emotions, providing an open atmosphere to express thoughts or feelings without a view of criticism, encouragement to resume normal activities, and provision of information as supportive responses. Less directed or less constructive activities such as talking about the assault, doing things for the victim and feeling sorry for the victim, encouraging the victim to keep the assault a secret, overprotection, patronization and distraction are regarded as less helpful (Popiel and Susskind, 1985; Silver and Wortman, 1980; Silverman, 1978). In the main victims look to their support persons to be sympathetic and understanding.

Supportive responses demand non-judgemental and accepting attitudes toward the victims (see Ward and Inserto, 1990); they do not convey victim blame or denigration. Supportive responses are likely to engender psychological benefits for victims. The presence of an understanding other diminishes the impact of rape (Norris and Feldman-Summers, 1981). Positive responses from others reduce detrimental effects on close relationships and predict successful coping by rape victims (Harvey et al., 1991). In contrast, lack of social support is associated with reduced coping capacity (Silver and Wortman, 1980), a slower recovery from sexual abuse (Burgess and Holmstrom, 1979b), and elevated levels of depression (Atkeson et al., 1982).

Despite these obvious benefits, the provision of social support is often difficult for significant others due both to their own rape-related trauma and to their pre-existing conceptions about sexual violence. Personal acquaintanceship with a victim of sexual violence does not appear to affect rape myths and attitudes (Burt, 1980; Feild, 1978a), and there is no reason to expect that close friends or family members are necessarily equipped to deliver the supportive services required by victims of sexual violence. Silverman (1978), for example, has noted that family members are also often traumatized by sexual assault and are unable to render social support – the trauma that they experience influences the manner in which they interact with the victim, which, in turn, may facilitate or inhibit her psychological recovery from sexual abuse.

Victims with more positive family backgrounds have fewer long-term symptoms (Sales et al., 1984); however, fathers and brothers, affected by pervading patriarchal values, often engage in victim-blaming and revenge-seeking, neither of which is perceived as helpful by victims. Evidence suggests that friends and family members are strongly influenced by stereotyped expectations of rape and its seriousness; victims of completed assault receive more social support than victims of attempted assault (Popiel and Susskind, 1985). Family and friends are also more supportive of victims of brutal rapes (Frank et al., 1979).

Particular attention has been paid to the role of husbands and boyfriends in victims' post-rape recovery. While a variety of reactions have been observed in husbands and boyfriends, they are not necessarily supportive (Popiel and Susskind, 1985). In fact there is some evidence to suggest that spouses provide less effective support than either parents or friends and that married women experience greater behavioural, emotional and cognitive trauma (Ruch and Chandler, 1983).

Along these lines it has been argued that partners who are insensitive to victims' needs reinforce their distrust of men (Shainess, 1976). Although husbands' responses exert direct effects on sexual satisfaction (Skinner et al., 1982), the effects are not limited to that domain. In fact, sexual violence puts a general and severe strain on intimate relationships. Crenshaw (1978) estimated that between 50 and 80 per cent of raped women lose husbands or boyfriends after sexual assault, and McMillan (1976) reported that approximately 50 per cent of married women divorce after rape. It is important to note that the negative impact of rape on intimate relations is not limited to heterosexual couples. The same pattern of trauma and coping difficulties has also been noted in lesbian couples (Burgess and Holmstrom, 1979a).

Looking at empirical research on stress, coping and social support it is easy to see the symbiotic relationship between attitudes and perceptions of significant others and victim responses to sexual assault. Victims worry that their partners might believe that the rape is their fault, that they are different after the assault, that they would not be believed, and that there would be suspicion of sexual enjoyment during rape. Partners, in turn, are often more pre-occupied with the damage they have experienced, rather than the victim's trauma. In a number of cases they speak of being betrayed, repulsed or ashamed. In these instances they clearly perceive rape as sex, that is, intercourse with another man. Some husbands and boyfriends feel ashamed and blame their partners for the incident. These responses, in turn, precipitate negative psychological consequences in victims. As one victim articulated, 'It's like being unfaithful, but I couldn't help it. I am afraid my husband will have the feeling I let him down' (cited in Burgess and Holmstrom, 1973, p. 1744).

Social Support and Institutional Responses

Social support can also come to victims via the social institutions with which they must interact. The successful handling of rape cases by the police or the criminal justice system in terms of case clearance and successful prosecution of the offence in the courts can validate victims' experiences, contribute to their perceptions of a just world and enhance their sense of mastery and control. Yet both survey and field research have shown that victims of sexual violence rarely receive satisfaction from these authorities. Professionals frequently espouse victim-blaming attitudes and manage sexual assault cases from that perspective. It becomes important, then, to examine victims' responses to their interactions with the authorities. This includes both their overall satisfaction with the systems and their perceptions and interpretations of responses from the agencies.

Clark Ashworth and Shirley Feldman-Summers (1978) examined perceptions of the criminal justice system held by sexual and physical assault victims as well as a comparative group of non-victimized citizens. They measured perceived effectiveness at one and two weeks, six months and one year after the assault. The research demonstrated that rape victims' perceptions of the effectiveness of the criminal justice system declined over time. In addition, the system was seen as less effective by sexual assault victims than by physical assault victims or by the non-victimized sample. This is not surprising given that the researchers noted only one in 26 rape victims saw the offender convicted and imprisoned within the duration of the study.

Not only are interactions with various agencies important in terms of general satisfaction, but institutional responses can also affect victims' self-concepts and psychological well-being. Victim interface with the police and legal establishment exerts a direct influence on mental health. It has been argued, for example, that good police–victim relations lead to better victim adjustment (Brown, 1970). In addition, research has shown that self-derogation is more prominent in rape victims whose assailants were not apprehended by the police (Libow and Doty, 1979).

A more comprehensive longitudinal study of victim interface with the criminal justice system was undertaken by Esther Sales and colleagues (1984), who conducted multiple interviews with 127 victims of rape. At the time of the initial interview those who had successfully brought charges against an assailant experienced a reduction in psychological symptoms. The researchers considered this to be evidence of tentative legitimization of their victim status. However, further progess toward an actual trial exacerbated psychological distress. Those whose cases were tried showed heightened psychological symptoms, obviously affected by the trauma of interacting with the criminal justice system, compared to those who did not pursue their cases through legal means.

Both the outcome of the institutional intervention and the manner in which the victim interfaces with the system can affect psychological responses to sexual assault. In Debra Popiel and Edwin Susskind's (1985) study the police were seen as supportive and helpful; in fact, there was no difference in the perceived support rendered by husbands, boyfriends and the police. Physicians, by contrast, were perceived as the least helpful and supportive, differing from friends, relatives and other professionals such as attorneys and nurses. More significantly, victims' perceptions of negative reactions by doctors were related to both the level of stress and the psychological symptoms experienced – documenting again the powerful process of secondary victimization. These results are consistent with studies which report that unsupportive responses from others are the most reliable predictors of post-rape recovery. Sales and associates, for example, noted that victims' perceptions of police and doctors were positive and unrelated to post-rape readjustment; however, the criminal justice system evoked more varied responses, and victim interface with the system was linked to psychological distress.

Putting It All Together

There are two premises which bind together the literature on rape attitudes, attributions, institutional management of sexual violence and victim reactions. First, rape myths are widespread; they have been documented over time and across cultures. Secondly, these myths, or misunderstandings, about the socio-cultural phenomenon of rape have far-reaching consequences for both individuals and societies.

What are the myths and misunderstandings? Rape is rare. It happens to 'other people' and generally involves sex-starved, deviant men and/or provocative, deserving women. Rape usually occurs between strangers, and physical force and coercion distinguish it from consensual sexual intercourse. These inaccurate stereotypes persist despite evidence which shows that rape occurs most frequently between people who know each other, often quite intimately, that coercion is more commonly achieved by threat or psychological tactics, and that victims only occasionally show signs of physical resistance. Most people also fail to recognize that rape is a form of sexual coercion which falls along a continuum of male violence and control of women; it is more often perceived as an exception to, rather than an extension of, conventional male and female interpersonal behaviours. In this context unsympathetic attitudes abound, and tendencies to blame and denigrate victims, to trivialize their experiences, and to doubt their credibility are common.

These inaccurate and prejudicial stereotypes are linked to attitudes about male and female roles, the nature and control of female sexuality, and the acceptance of interpersonal violence. They are also associated with perceptions of rape victims, the cognitive processing of rape-related information, and the attributions of blame, fault and responsibility. For example, victims are seen as more to blame if they are acquainted with the rapist, if they are dressed in a provocative fashion and if they have had previous sexual relations.

While attitudes and attributions lie in the cognitive domain, social psychological theories suggest that these cognitive structures and processes are also linked to behaviours. From this perspective the treatment of victims by social institutions can be viewed as a consequence of pervading rape myths and attitudes. Indeed, field studies have shown that institutional responses, such as clearance of police cases, convictions in court, sentencing outcomes and even psychotherapeutic interventions, reflect the common misconceptions of rape. For example, convictions and length of sentencing are affected more by victims' moral character than by features of the crime. Successful prosecution is also more likely in the case of stranger rape and when there is corroborative evidence of physical force.

The consequences of rape myths can be observed not only in macro-level analysis of institutional responses to sexual assault, but can also be considered on the micro-level in connection with individuals' responses to victims of sexual violence. In this context, as well, it appears that rape myths and attitudes colour the behaviour of significant others, in particular their ability to render social support. Research has shown, for example, that husbands and boyfriends are often incapable of being supportive because they view rape as a sexual crime of infidelity and question what their partner may have done to precipitate sexual assault.

In the end rape myths have serious consequences for victims of sexual abuse. Victims' acceptance of pervading stereotypes of sexual violence and their encounters with others who are similarly influenced by myths and misconceptions perpetuate a vicious circle of self-blame and -denigration. As social psychological theories of self have indicated, we come to form our self-concepts based on others' reactions to us. If friends, families, husbands, boyfriends, courts, hospitals and police blame victims of sexual assault, they are also likely to blame themselves. And as clinical theory and research has confirmed, this, in turn, has detrimental effects on psychological recovery from sexual violence.

In the end, self-defeating cognitions and behaviours in victims of sexual abuse not only adversely affect their psychological well-being but also serve to sustain prejudicial and destructive rape myths. In Part II we will consider breaking the vicious circle. Changing attitudes toward sexual violence and changing social systems will be discussed in the next chapters.

Note

1 The relationship between the amount of force used in the commission of a sexual offence and the severity of victims' psychological symptoms is reported to be curvilinear (McCahill et al., 1979).

PART II
A CIRCLE IN THE BREAKING

Part I – 'A Circle in the Making' – reviewed basic research in feminist studies and social psychology which identified and elaborated common rape myths and misconceptions. A substantial body of empirical literature, based on ethnographic, archival, survey and experimental methods, clearly demonstrated the widespread acceptance of stereotyped, prejudicial attitudes toward victims of sexual violence. It has been suggested that these attitudes, which tend to trivialize rape and denigrate and blame victims, are an inevitable product of patriarchal, male-dominated societies. It has also been proposed that rape myths underpin both individual and institutional responses to victims of sexual assault. As field research has indicated, rape myths affect the treatment of victims of sexual violence and influence institutional processing of sexual offences by medical, legal and social service professionals. In addition, evidence has suggested that these negative attitudes and perceptions are ultimately internalized by rape victims themselves and have detrimental psychological and social consequences for their recovery from sexual assault.

The emphasis placed on the widespread existence and negative consequences of rape myths in society suggests that the situation for rape victims is bleak. The formation of negative attitudes is strongly influenced by and appears to be an unavoidable outcome of pervasive social forces, ubiquitous patriarchal influences which serve to limit and oppress women. The causes and consequences of rape myths are inextricably intertwined, and the cycle of misunderstanding seems self-perpetuating. On the macro-level, rape myths exert influences on and are reflected in social institutions and political legislation. Institutional standards and responses, in turn, implicitly encourage the social acceptance of unsympathetic, victim-blaming attitudes. On the micro-level, negative attitudes underpin behavioural responses to individual victims which, in turn, further illustrate and reinforce rape myths. The circular relationship between attitudes and behaviours, observed on both the individual and institutional level, presents a challenge to feminists and applied social psychologists. Taking this challenge aboard, Part II – 'A Circle in the Breaking' – concentrates on changing attitudes and changing social systems.

The two chapters which follow are concerned with applied research on attitude change. Although the approaches taken by social psychologists and feminists are very different, both have successfully demonstrated that substantial modifications in attitudes can be achieved. In the first instance, social psychological research has concentrated on changing *individuals'* attitudes toward sexual assault. The mainstream body of social psychological literature on attitude formation and change, which has highlighted the links between attitudes and behaviours and the role of cognitive dissonance in effecting attitude shifts, has provided the theoretical basis for these investigations. Psychological research on persuasibility has examined various factors which influence the likelihood of changing attitudes toward rape victims. These include, but are not limited to, the source of persuasive communication, programme content and format, and active versus passive participation in attitude change programmes.

Methodologically, social psychological research on attitude change has relied heavily on experimental designs which involve exposure to various intervention programmes and pre- and post-testing of precisely defined and measured attitudes. In many instances the results of rape-related attitude change programmes are compared with the outcomes of other interventions to determine their relative effectiveness. In some cases, attitudes are also compared between those who have and those who have not been exposed to educational interventions. In both instances studies have provided compelling evidence that attitudes toward rape victims can be altered via intervention programmes; however, the most potent factors in precipitating more positive attitudes toward rape victims remain to be successfully identified.

In contrast to social psychological studies of attitude change, feminist approaches offer alternative theoretical and methodological perspectives. A fundamental distinction is that feminists largely concentrate on changing *social systems*. While acknowledging the empowering consequences of attitude change for individuals, emphasis is placed on systemic changes; consequently, the feminist approach is more all-encompassing and situated in a wider socio-political context.

In addition, feminist research is guided by praxis – the interplay of theory and practice in the achievement of social change. The theoretical basis of the research is rooted in the feminist vision of the patriarchy and the acknowledgement that rape myths are embodied and reflected in social and political institutions. From this perspective, changing attitudes and changing institutional responses to sexual violence go hand in hand. An apparent consequence of this type of feminist action-oriented research, however, is that attitude change is, for the most part, implicitly, rather than explicitly, investigated. In the main, feminists have neither precisely defined nor quantitatively measured attitudes toward victims of sexual violence. While undoubtedly concerned with rape myths and attitudes, these are seen as part and parcel of the more tangible mistreatment of women in society. Again, eliminating the social and institutional mistreatment of rape victims via action-oriented research is believed to improve simultaneously attitudes toward victims of sexual violence.

The more specific methods used by feminists in their work on socio-political change can also be contrasted with standard social psychological research tools. Feminists have relied upon a variety of descriptive, ethnographic techniques, including interviews, surveys and participant observations, in their action-oriented research. Although experimental methods have been largely neglected, feminists have blended data collection and information dissemination to accomplish social and institutional change. Consciousness-raising and other forms of political activities have also been commonly used in conjunction with more traditional research methods.

On the whole, then, Chapter 6 on social psychological studies of attitude change and Chapter 7 on feminist action-oriented research provide encouraging evidence that the widespread acceptance of rape myths is neither inevitable nor immutable. The patriarchal circle which misrepresents, constrains and oppresses women can be broken. Complementary approaches from social psychology and feminism, spanning individual and systemic levels of analysis, offer hope for the future.

6

Changing Attitudes

Suppose you are on the staff of a large university where there has recently been an allegation of rape of a student by a professor. The allegation has divided the student population. There are those who believe that the victim was exploited and sexually assaulted by her mentor and others who argue that the sexual contact was one of mutual consent, that the student was provocative and flirtatious, and that even if there was an element of coercion, she essentially 'got what she deserved'. While you are unable to draw conclusions about this case, you are generally concerned about the prevalence of rape myths and stereotypes which have surfaced in response to this incident. You are also concerned about the increase in reported sexual assaults on campuses and believe that there is a need for greater rape awareness. More specifically, you would like to see an improvement in knowledge about sexual violence and attitudes toward victims of sexual assault. You decide to design a programme to enhance rape awareness in university students and to encourage empathy towards victims of sexual coercion. How would you do this? What would you include in the programme, and how would you assess any resultant change?

Lynn Borden and colleagues (1988) considered this issue, proposed and implemented a rape prevention programme for university students, and evaluated the outcome of the programme. The training package was developed within the university and presented to undergraduates by the coordinator of a varsity programme on sexual violence. Rape-related information was emphasized, and lectures included an explanation of the legal definition of rape, biographical descriptions of rapists, and discussion of the rape trauma syndrome, rape prevention strategies and post-rape assistance.

Students participated in the rape awareness programme in undergraduate classes. They completed questionnaires about their attitudes toward rape and empathy for victims before the educational programme and then again four weeks after the intervention. Unfortunately, the researchers found that the intervention programme did not impact on rape-related attitudes – neither general attitudes nor empathy toward victims improved. *Why*?

There are many factors that could have diminished the effectiveness of the educational programme. Perhaps the students already had very positive attitudes toward rape victims, and the content of the educational programme was not discrepant enough to induce a subsequent attitude shift. Alternatively, the participants may have held negative perceptions of rape victims but were unmotivated to change their attitudes as they regarded the issues as of peripheral importance. Perhaps the format of the workshop demanded little student involvement, which consequently decreased the likelihood of attitude shift. Or the fact that the programme was undertaken in a classroom setting may have detracted from the overall impact of the persuasive communication. The message itself may have been rather dry and factual, and the probability of attitude change might have been increased if persuasive techniques were based on emotional rather than rational appeal. Or perhaps the students did not view the presenter as an authority on rape victimology. Any of these factors could have reduced the probability of attitude change. Certainly, social psychological studies have indicated that a wide variety of factors influence attitudes, including the characteristics of the communication source, the target and the persuasive message. Theories on attitude formation and change have provided the conceptual framework for the analysis of these factors, and experimental method has provided the technique for examining attitude change.

Theories of Attitude Change

As attitudes have proved to be one of the central areas of research in social psychology, it is no surprise that a great deal of theorizing has been directed toward attitude formation and change. More than seven decades of research on the topic has generated a wide variety of theories; however, the most popular contemporary approaches reflect the pervasive influence of cognitive psychology and emphasize individuals' perceptions and evaluations of persuasive communications. Consistency theories have been particularly prominent and have highlighted the significance of self-awareness in the analysis of attitudes and behaviours. The core of consistency theories is based on the assumption that we are motivated to maintain consistency across our attitudes and coherence between our attitudes and behaviours.

Along these lines the best known and most well-researched theoretical framework for the study of attitude change derives from Leon Festinger's (1957) work on cognitive consistency. His theoretical framework provides the discussion of both the function and consequences of attitudinal consonance and dissonance. The fundamental assumption of Festinger's theory is quite simple: Dissonance occurs when two cognitions (attitudes, opinions, beliefs) or behaviours contradict each other. Dissonance is unpleasant; it is an uncomfortable state of psychological tension which individuals are motivated to avoid or to reduce. However, the strength of the motivation to decrease dissonance, and consequently the likelihood of attitude change, depends upon both the number and importance of discrepant attitudes, opinions and behaviours. If an individual holds cognitions which are generally consistent and coherent or if discrepant attitudes and behaviours are perceived as peripheral and unimportant, there will be little motivation for dissonance reduction and attitude change.

There are a number of methods that individuals employ to reduce cognitive dissonance. The first line of defence may involve diminishing the number or importance of the discrepant thoughts or attitudes. For example, an individual may undermine the significance of the discrepant attitudes or behaviours. If one finds that an admired and much loved friend has been sexually assaulted, but generally believes that rape victims get what they deserve, one might argue that this incident is an exception to the rule, that rape rarely happens to nice people, that it is unlikely to impinge further on one's own experience and, therefore, is not worthy of much thought one way or another. While this strategy may reduce dissonance in the short term and in relation to a specific case, a more long-term solution involves altering cognitions so that inconsistencies no longer occur – in short, changing attitudes. Attitude change expends substantial psychological energy, but may prove more beneficial if the dissonance arises frequently or if it pertains to attitudes and behaviours that are regarded as central and important. Further down the line changes in cognitions may lead to behavioural shifts; however, Festinger also emphasizes that changes in behaviour may likewise precipitate cognitive shifts.

Programmes which are specifically designed to produce attitude change rely heavily on the induction of cognitive dissonance. Their effectiveness largely depends upon generating a substantial number of significant and discrepant cognitions, inducing dissonance and promoting attitude change as a method of dissonance reduction. While this represents a general approach to attitude change, research has shown that some types of interventions are more effective than others in generating a state of psychological discomfort and producing subsequent shifts in attitudes. In this context the effects of message, target and source on attitude change have been considered.

Extensive research on the variables affecting attitude change has been undertaken in contemporary social psychology, and a comprehensive review is beyond the scope of this book. However, in general terms the persuasiveness of a message may be affected by the 'what, how and who' of a communication. The message content itself is central to the appraisal of persuasiveness. On the most basic level clarity is obviously important, and it is imperative that the message be designed for specific audiences in terms of their comprehension abilities and familiarity with the topic. For example, different messages would be expected to be delivered to adolescents and to adults. Positive messages are more effective for longer-term attitude change than negative, fear-arousing communications, and strong messages are more persuasive than weak ones. While the specificity of an argument may influence attitudinal responses, attitude change generalizes, at least to some extent, and shifts have often been observed in related attitudes (for example, McGuire, 1981).

The content and presentation of persuasive messages influence, and in some cases interact with, recipient responses. If an individual perceives an issue as having personal relevance, she or he is more likely to consider the persuasive message carefully. Attitude change is less likely if the arguments are implicit and subjects must draw their own conclusions about the communication (Hovland and Mandell, 1952). There is some controversy, however, surrounding the value of constructing arguments which run counter to an individual's initial position. Although consistency theorists such as Festinger (1957) have inferred that counter-attitudinal advocacy should result in attitude change, active participation in attitude change programmes has produced mixed results. In many instances, passive reading of prepared persuasive messages evokes greater attitude change than the construction of one's own argument (McGuire, 1961).

There is some evidence that forewarning produces anticipatory attitude change, particularly if it is known that attitudes will be measured after exposure to persuasive communications (Saltzstein and Sandberg, 1979). The persuasiveness of the message is also affected by the amount of discrepancy between the communication and the individual's original attitudes. In general, arguments which are more discrepant with an individual's original attitudinal position are more effective in inducing dissonance and precipitating attitude change; however, when the discrepancies hit extremes, credibility becomes suspect, and a boomerang effect may result (McGuire, 1985).

The impact of various media on attitude change has also received attention in social psychological studies; however, research findings on this topic tend to be ambiguous. Printed material is superior for inducing attitude change when issues are difficult to grasp and the arguments are complex (Chaiken and Eagly, 1976). Television and video are more effective in prompting attitude change than audio channels; however, physically present source persons may be more adept at precipitating change as they are liked more than electronically mediated sources (Keating and Latane, 1976).

The source of the persuasive communication can also have a powerful effect on attitude change. In particular, source credibility, often influenced by evaluations of expertise or trustworthiness, is important in predicting the likelihood of attitude change. For example, you are more likely to be influenced by an Oxford expert on rape victimology than a secondary school student who presents statistics on date rape. Perceived trustworthiness, often evaluated in terms of the source's personal loss and gain, can also affect attitude change. Those people who appear to present arguments which are obviously not to their own benefit are often seen as more trust-worthy and effective in producing alterations in attitudes. In this context, it may be the case that a man who presents an anti-rape speech could effect greater attitude change than a woman. Source attractiveness, often influenced by familiarity and likeability, also exerts a positive effect on communication persuasiveness, as, indeed, does source power (McGuire, 1985).

Altogether, then, social psychological theory suggests that arousal of cognitive dissonance can precipitate attitude change. In cases where attitudes and behaviours are discrepant, attitude shifts provide one avenue for achieving the much desired cognitive consistency. Predicting the eventual likelihood of attitude change, however, is dependent upon not only features of persuasive messages which may arouse dissonance, but also characteristics of the target audience. While there has been substantial research on attitude change in general, social psychologists have made only brief experimental sojourns into the specific area of changing attitudes toward rape victims.

Research Methods

Social psychological research on attitude change has typically relied upon experimental studies which assess the impact of various intervention strategies on rape myths. In the most common designs research participants are assigned either to an experimental condition, that is, they are exposed to an attitude change programme, or to a control condition in which they experience no interventions. Attitudes may then be compared between groups who do and do not receive exposure to educational programmes or between groups who participate in different types of educational interventions. In many instances the researchers will also examine the potential effects of attitude testing per se, by considering whether the completion of a questionnaire in itself sensitizes individuals to attitude change. If this is incorporated into the experimental design, a portion of the research participants will be tested before and after the educational programme while another portion will be tested only after the intervention. By assuming an experimental approach the researcher is then able to examine the impact of various features of educational packages on attitude change.

Although the research on changing attitudes toward rape victims has arisen very much from an applied context, it is inspired by both survey research on attitudes and experimental studies of rape perceptions and attributions (see Chapters 2 and 3). Standard measurements for the assessment of rape-related attitudes are typically employed, such as Burt's (1980) Rape Myth Acceptance Scale or Deitz et al.'s (1982) Rape Empathy Scale; however, in some cases the perceptions of victims and perpetrators are tapped by simple rating scales. In either case, the investigators are concerned with changes in attitudes or perceptions as a result of specially designed intervention programmes.[1]

Empirical Research

Despite the long-standing tradition of social psychological research on attitude change, surprisingly little has been undertaken in the domain of rape attitudes. One of the earliest studies emerged in relation to the evaluation of a Rape Prevention Education Project designed for teenage and adult men. The training programme, conducted by male volunteers, consisted of three parts: (1) the presentation of didactic information on rape myths and realities, (2) experiential empathy exercises and (3) group discussions. Although the rape prevention programme had been implemented with various populations, in one instance, pre- and post-workshop attitudes toward rape were assessed in a sample of university men. Findings revealed a significant improvement in attitudes after participation in the rape prevention programme (Lee, 1987).

A more ambitious project was recently undertaken by Mary Fonow and colleagues (1992). Employing a sophisticated experimental design the researchers considered the impact of two rape education programmes on rape myths and victim blame. In the initial phase 582 undergraduate sociology students were randomly divided into three groups. The first group of students received no educational intervention while the remainder were exposed either to a participative rape education workshop or to a video of the workshop. Half of the students in each of the three conditions were pre-tested on their rape myths and rape attributions. All students were post-tested three weeks after the intervention programmes.

The rape education workshop was undertaken with small discussion groups and commenced with the description of a rape scenario. The female facilitator then invited participants to identify the rape myths embedded in the depiction. These included the myths that women precipitate rape by their appearance or behaviour, that rape occurs between strangers, outdoors, at night, and that it generally involves the use of a weapon. In addition to the active participation by the workshop attenders, the programme provided rape statistics including information on reports and convictions. The facilitator also offered a reconceptualization of rape emphasizing its violent nature, the humiliation of women, power and control issues, and the effects of sexual violence on all women and men. These themes were subjected to further discussion before the conclusion of the programme. In the second intervention a video of the 25-minute workshop was shown under the same circumstances and presented to small groups of students.

Although the results indicated that students were largely rejecting of rape myths at the time of the initial testing, the intervention treatments were still effective in inducing attitude change. Rape myths (Burt, 1980) and victim-blaming attitudes (Resick and Jackson, 1981) were reduced by both educational programmes, and the workshop and the video sessions were equally effective in producing attitude change. Despite the finding that female students initially held fewer myths than male students, both men and women learned equally from the interventions. The researchers also noted that the pre-test itself acted as a sensitizing factor; all students who were pre-tested concluded the study holding fewer rape myths than those who were not pre-tested, regardless of the intervention. The effect was not powerful, but discernible nevertheless.

A similar study, but with specific emphasis on date rape, was undertaken by Patrick Harrison and colleagues (1991) at San Diego State University. Their educational intervention programmes entailed either viewing a video or participating in a group discussion in conjunction with video viewing. The video itself included a series of media clips which relied upon sexual themes in advertising. This was followed by selected interludes of the interaction between a couple which featured mixed messages that are often conveyed in a dating context. For those groups who participated in a post-video discussion, structured guidelines were adopted by a facilitator to analyse issues related to date rape. The facilitators also presented facts about date rape and prompted additional discussion. As in the previously described study, some students received no educational intervention, and a portion were given both pre- and post-tests, while others completed only post-intervention measures of knowledge about rape and victim-blaming attitudes.

The study revealed that both interventions improved rape knowledge and attitudes; however, in this case changes were found only for men. There was no difference in the effects of the two training packages. And, as in the study by Mary Fonow and colleagues, pretesting acted as a primer, increasing rape knowledge and decreasing victim-blaming attitudes, regardless of the presence, absence or type of the educational programme. While resistance to attitude shift was unanticipated in females, the researchers suggested that the already supportive attitudes in women, which were significantly more positive than those of men, left little room for change.

Programmes for changing rape-related attitudes have also been designed by researchers at Eastern Illinois University. Genie Lenihan and associates (1992) compiled an educational package which combined lectures by male and female facilitators with video presentations. Factual information included rape statistics and legal definitions, the effects of sexual assault, prevention strategies, help resources, characteristics and attitudes of offenders, and cultural myths and stereotypes. The programme also incorporated the sharing of information about a personal rape experience by one of the facilitators. In an attempt to reduce rape myth acceptance audience questions and participation were also encouraged.

Approximately half of the 821 students in this study were exposed to the attitude change programme, and half received no intervention. In each of these groups about half of the participants completed Burt's (1980) Rape Myth Acceptance Scale before the implementation of the educational programme. All students were subsequently post-tested one month after the intervention.

The study reported differential effects for men and women. As in the other studies, women were less accepting of rape myths; however, in this case the intervention programme was only effective in shifting attitudes in female students. While all women lowered their rape myth acceptance, the magnitude of the change was greater in those women who were exposed to the educational programme. The pre-test acted as a primer for attitude change in this study, but again the effect was confined to women. No significant differences were found among the male groups.

While these studies represent the most common experimental approach to the implementation and evaluation of programmes for the improvement of attitudes toward victims of sexual violence, two variations in design have been observed in recent research. First, some investigations have incorporated assessments of rape *perceptions* in addition to the standard *attitude* measures; secondly, a portion of research on changing rape-related attitudes has been linked to studies of violence and pornography.

Along these lines Margaret Intons-Peterson and colleagues (1989) compared men's perceptions of rape victims and rape myth acceptance after exposure to educational films. Participants were either presented with a film about rape, which was designed to debunk rape myths and to describe the trauma of sexual violence, or they viewed a film about social and sexual interactions between men and women, which highlighted societal expectations about male sexuality and emphasized the emotional benefits of sexual intimacy and honesty. After viewing the educational briefing films participants additionally observed a video of a mock rape trial. Their perceptions of rape victims and their myth acceptance were assessed and compared to those of participants who had not received educational interventions. The assessment and comparison were repeated again after a two-week interval.

The researchers found that groups who had viewed films on both rape and male–female interactions were less accepting of rape myths than those who received no educational briefings. In addition, these participants further reduced their rape myth acceptance in the subsequent testing. With regard to perceptions of characters in the mock rape trial, the briefed groups perceived the victim as less responsible and as more seriously injured. They also perceived the victim as demonstrating more substantial resistance and as deserving greater sympathy. Finally, they were more likely to perceive the perpetrator as guilty of rape. However, the researchers found no differences between the participants who had been exposed to the rape film or to the film on male–female interactions.

Daniel Linz and colleagues (1990) also examined changing attitudes toward and perceptions of rape victims; however, they situated their study in the broader context of pornography and violence. In this instance the researchers created an educational programme which concentrated on three social issues: (1) male–female sexual encounters, (2) rape myths and stereotypes and (3) the effects of violence in the media. After exposure to a compilation of educational films on these topics participants engaged in one of the three following activities: (1) they composed anti-rape essays, had a video made in which they presented their arguments and then viewed the video playback; (2) they composed anti-rape essays which were read and taped, but then exchanged amongst participants; or (3) they composed neutral essays with reading and video playback. As contrasts to these programmes and interventions two additional groups of students participated in the study. One group viewed a neutral film about general television topics and produced neutral essays with reading and playback while the second group merely completed the attitude measures without receiving any educational materials.

Two weeks after the educational programmes all participants viewed violent pornographic films, which they evaluated. They additionally viewed a film of a mock rape trial and completed questionnaires pertaining to rape-related attitudes. These included rape myth acceptance and tolerance of interpersonal violence, as well as perceptions of victim and perpetrator responsibility in the mock rape trial (Burt, 1980). Male participants also completed a questionnaire about their sexually coercive behaviours. In the analysis of findings the researchers reported that the interventions decreased the tendency to perceive the victim as responsible for rape, reduced self-reported sexually coercive behaviours in men and moderately reduced the acceptance of rape myths. They did not, however, find significantly different effects for the two intervention programmes.

The explicitly feminist conceptualization of rape as an issue of dominance and control has also been incorporated into studies of attitude change. As feminists have argued that rape is a reflection of the generally oppressive treatment of women, James Johnson and Inger Russ (1989) considered the impact of educational interventions which were focused on the role and status of women in society rather than specifically concentrated on sexual violence. In this research students were exposed to videotaped speeches. While the speeches spanned a number of topics, one elaborated the historical mistreatment of women in society. No speech, however, dealt specifically with rape or other forms of sexual violence. After exposure to a series of speeches, participants read several passages, one of which depicted an episode of sexual violence. In each instance they were queried about the passages; in the rape episode they were explicitly asked about their perceptions of the victim and the perpetrator. The post-session analysis indicated that participants whose video exposure included the speech on the status of women attributed less responsibility to victims of sexual assault. In addition, males who heard this speech reported a diminished likelihood of committing rape.

While experimental studies in social psychology have, in the main, demonstrated that attitudes toward rape victims can be changed, there are inconsistencies and limitations in the research literature. On one extreme there are some studies which have failed to document attitudinal shifts (for example, Bailey, 1985; Borden et al., 1988). On the other extreme, minimal interventions, such as a single-paragraph debriefing, have been shown to affect attitudes toward rape causality and perceptions of victim responsibility (Malamuth and Check, 1984). In between, there are studies which demonstrate attitude change in certain limited domains (for example, Gottesman, 1977) and with specific subject groups (for example, Brakensiek, 1983). A more significant problem, however, is that the relative effectiveness of various persuasive techniques has not been established.

Attitude change has been accomplished with an array of educational materials which, while generally incorporating specific information about rape, have also included varying amounts of additional information about male–female relations, interpersonal violence and pornography. Attitude change has been equally effected by programmes which demand active and passive participation. More specifically, there has been no reported difference in attitude change from those who participate in active discussion and those who passively view educational materials. And in those more active conditions which require participants to construct anti-rape arguments, there is no significant difference in attitude shift between those who do and do not receive media feedback. Similarly, attitude change has been precipitated by both video and written presentations with no distinction in consequent outcomes from the two techniques (Nelson and Torgler, 1990). Given this line of research, and the effects of priming on attitude change, it is impossible to gauge just what it is about intervention programmes which precipitates attitude shifts.

To consider this question in more detail Sally Baker (1987) examined the influence of message (what), source (by whom) and target (to whom) characteristics on attitude change. More specifically, Baker evaluated the influence of argument strength, source credibility, motivation and sex on attitude change in 204 New Zealand secondary school students. In this research pupils were presented with either strong or weak arguments for inducing supportive attitudes toward survivors of sexual assault. The source of the arguments was attributed to either a Harvard expert on rape victimology or to a secondary school student who had collated a variety of arguments. Approximately half of the students were then motivated to respond to the arguments by being told that they would be required to present and justify their own positions in class; the other half were merely informed that they might deal with rape as a topic in a future class session.

Students' attitudes were examined via Ward's (1988a) Attitudes toward Rape Victims Scale; they were tested prior to the presentation of educational materials and then again four weeks later. As in other studies, Baker found that girls had more supportive attitudes toward rape victims than boys. Consistent with the priming effect, she also found that all students improved in their attitudes over time, but that students who were motivated to appraise the arguments showed greater improvement in rape-related attitudes than those who were not motivated. The strength of the persuasive arguments and the credibility of the source, however, did not affect attitude change.

In Conclusion

While a variety of studies have shown that rape-related attitudes can be improved by educational interventions, the findings have not been synthesized and directed toward the establishment of reliable and effective intervention programmes. Research has demonstrated that a variety of educational packages are capable of improving attitudes toward victims of sexual assault and increasing general knowledge about sexual violence. Despite the reported success of intervention programmes in social psychological studies, a systematic investigation of the factors affecting attitude change has not been achieved, and the empirical findings are difficult to synthesize. Fundamentally, we know that rape-related attitudes may be altered, but there is little precise information about what specifically prompts an attitude shift.

Along these lines, the most effective content for persuasive messages has yet to be identified. While the bulk of the intervention programmes has relied upon rational rather than emotional appeal, there has been considerable variation in the actual content of educational information. Presentations which have concentrated on male–female relations in general, sexual coercion specifically or women's status in society have all proved effective in inducing attitude change but have not been distinguished in terms of their overall impact on rape-related attitudes. Similar criticisms apply to the research domain which has considered the effects of presentation media on attitude change. Attitude shifts have been effectively evoked by written material, direct observation and video viewing; however, there have been no reported differences in resultant attitude change via these channels.

In terms of audience characteristics there are conflicting results about sex differences in persuasibility. In some studies men and women benefit equally from educational interventions, in others attitude change has been achieved only in female participants, and in still others the positive impacts have been limited to males. It is likely that amount of discrepancy from initial attitudinal position, general knowledge and level of motivation underlie these findings. For example, women are known to have more sympathetic attitudes toward rape victims in general. In this case it may be that educational programmes are not sufficiently discrepant from their general attitudes toward sexual violence to induce attitude change. In past research (see Chapter 2) it has also been noted that women are more knowledgeable about sexual violence. Traditional social psychological studies on persuasibility have shown that attitude change is easier to induce in those individuals who are less knowledgeable about the topic under discussion (Eagly, 1978), suggesting that male attitudes may be easier to alter. However, as women are more typically the victims of rape, they may be more motivated to respond favourably to educational packages on sexual violence. We do know that motivation plays an important part in attitude change and that individuals who are motivated to consider carefully the content of a persuasive message are more likely to change their rape-related attitudes.

Characteristics of intervention programmes and characteristics of the target audience are undoubtedly important in understanding the process of attitude change. Similarly, the interaction of the two is likely to affect resultant attitudes. Unfortunately, we know little about this interaction in the context of rape-related research. An obvious starting point is the consideration of the level of audience participation in educational interventions. However, active and passive programmes have proved equally effective in inducing attitude change. For example, viewing a video of a rape workshop is no less potent than direct workshop participation in improving attitudes toward victims of sexual violence.

Despite the inconclusiveness of the research findings on the factors affecting attitude change, some features which are apparently shared by successful intervention programmes may be identified. Harrison and colleagues (1991) have argued that the success of their programmes has been reliant upon knowing the existing attitudes and beliefs of the target audience and structuring messages designed specifically for that group. In general, persuasive messages in educational interventions have included clear information and strong arguments about sexual violence. It is also likely that educational interventions have relied upon credible source persons. Although the effect of argument source has not been systematically investigated in connection with attitudes toward rape victims, those programmes which rely upon workshop facilitators have tended to employ trained counsellors. It is likely that these source persons are perceived as experienced and as at least moderately authoritative on the topic.

Given the scarcity of studies on altering attitudes toward rape victims and the inconsistencies in the research findings, it is impossible to identify confidently the most effective components of intervention programmes. One possibility that must be seriously considered is that the apparent change in rape-related attitudes is a research artefact. In many cases the purpose of the investigation and intervention techniques would be obvious to participating students. In such circumstances there is a great likelihood that the apparent shift in attitudes is due largely to social desirability influences. Students may be motivated to present a liberal and enlightened picture of themselves. They may also be motivated to assist the investigators in achieving their research objectives. The influence of social desirability forces is particularly plausible given that a number of studies have reported attitude shifts in comparative (control) groups who have not been exposed to intervention programmes. It appears that completing an attitude questionnaire on rape sensitizes an individual to salient issues and prompts an observed attitude shift. The legitimacy of the shift, however, remains suspect, and the potential effects of social desirability cannot be discounted.

In addition to legitimacy, the resilience of attitude change may also be questioned. In this instance, the duration of the applied research projects may be subjected to criticism. Only one of the reported studies included two post-testings, and not a single investigation assessed attitude change for a period of greater than one month after the educational interventions. Consequently, the permanence of attitude change remains undetermined. This is cause for particular concern as Robert Cialdini and colleagues (1976) have commented upon the elasticity of attitude change. More specifically, they have noted that attitudes 'snap back' to their original position after an external pressure to change is withdrawn. The permanence of attitude change, then, like the legitimacy, is questionable.

In short, there is simply not enough research on the topic of changing rape-related attitudes to draw firm conclusions. The theoretical base is substantial, and the empirical results are tentatively encouraging both for applied social psychologists and for feminists. However, there are notable limitations, and more systematic research is required in this area. Along these lines it is imperative to retain connections between theoretical and applied branches of social psychology, and as more innovative approaches to attitude change have been proposed in the field (Shepard et al., 1991), such as peer training (Ellis et al., 1991; Hight and Skinner, 1991; Walter-Brooks et al., 1990) and men-to-men workshops (Berkowitz and Capraro, 1989), researchers should be on the spot to evaluate these intervention techniques.

Note

1 Discussion of psychological research on attitude change is limited to programmes or interventions designed to improve attitudes toward rape victims. In contrast, there is a vast experimental literature on the *negative* effects of exposure to pornography on attitudes toward and perceptions of rape victims. See Linz (1989) for a review of this literature.

7

Changing Systems: Feminist Action-Oriented Research

As early as 1978 Women against Rape (WAR) in London began its first research inquiries into sexual assault. At that time a small survey in the King's Cross area suggested that rape was far more common than believed and that more information was needed to assess the extent of sexual assault, institutional responses to sexual violence and preventive measures for women's protection. Despite the recognition of the need for such a project, WAR acknowledged its limited experience in research. The group, a grassroots organization composed of women from diverse backgrounds and situations, was better known for its political activities: campaigning, lobbying, directing pickets, initiating petitions, invading courtrooms, acting as women's advocates, liaising with various women's groups, promoting public education and monitoring the popular media. In short, WAR was directed toward social and political change for the benefit and protection of women and the eventual elimination of sexual violence.

In the course of the war on rape, however, the women's collective was able to attract research consultants and assistants and to secure funding from the Greater London Council in order to implement a Women's Safety Survey in the London area. The project involved more than 100 volunteers working to collect questionnaire responses from 1236 women and to conduct interviews with scores of others in relation to their experiences and perceptions of sexual assault and institutional reactions to sexual violence. Paralleling the survey and interview work, WAR continued to stage pickets and lobbies, to meet with Members of Parliament, government bodies and other organizations, and to utilize the media to mobilize public awareness. This allowed the organization to maintain high visibility and to exert more effective political pressure for the policy changes recommended on the basis of the safety survey findings.

After more than four years of hard work, *Ask Any Woman: A London Inquiry into Rape and Sexual Assault* was published (Hall, 1985). It summarized the findings of the Women's Safety Survey, including information about the prevalence and characteristics of sexual offences, experiences with police and perceptions of police intervention, and attitudes toward sexual assault and the law. The report also included recommendations for institutional management of sexual assault and rape prevention. These recommendations covered public transportation and housing requirements, environmental issues pertaining to street safety, police practices, legal definitions of sexual assault, trial procedures, conviction and sentencing issues, and victim compensation. The recommendations were accompanied by sustained pressure for social and political reform.

The major objective of the WAR research was to make London a safer place for women – preferably in terms of reducing or eliminating sexual violence, but also by way of improving institutional and legal treatment of victims of sexual assault. The project also attempted to raise public consciousness and to change misperceptions about sexual violence. As such, the research encompassed feminist grassroots activities and multi-method approaches designed for social change. However, the WAR campaign went beyond that. The study also provided an example of praxis, the dynamic interplay between theory and practice in feminist research.

But how does this relate to the issue of attitudes and attitude change? Is there a connection between feminist research, the feminist movement, changing attitudes and changing social systems? *Ask Any Woman* has been described as the first major survey on rape and sexual assault in Britain, and it has been credited with 'overturn[ing] accepted notions about rape, and about what life is really like for women and girls'.[1] However, while the WAR research undoubtedly contributed to undermining rape myths in society, the group's feminist approach is obviously very different from experimental social psychological documentation of persuasion and attitude shifts. This chapter considers feminist action-oriented research in the context of the women's movement and its connection to changing attitudes toward sexual violence.

Praxis: Feminist Theory and Methods

> The integration of activism and scholarship is essential to the emerging feminist consciousness of the last decade.
>
> (Golden, 1981, p.1)

Feminist research, whether focused on sexual violence or on other aspects of women's lives, commences with a vision of the patriarchy as defining, limiting and misrepresenting women's experiences and realities. In the context of sexual violence, rape and other forms of sexual assault are seen as inevitable outcomes of women's social, psychological and economic subordination. Underpinned by feminist insights and theorizing, feminist research on sexual violence seeks to remedy that inequitable situation. Like other feminist research, it aims to precipitate social, political and individual change, to empower women and to improve their status in society.

Feminist research on rape is typically action-oriented. It is often connected to the grassroots women's movement and frequently has explicit objectives involving social change. Change may occur in the form of general consciousness-raising. Demystification – or the very act of obtaining knowledge – creates the potential for change as in many instances it is the lack of information about women's experiences that contributes to their powerlessness (Reinharz, 1992). Or change may occur in connection with more concrete and specific objectives such as the establishment of specialized services for victims of sexual assault. In either case, rape-related attitudes do not escape the attention of feminist researchers. Indeed, some have argued that with respect to rape as a social problem, 'attitudes and assumptions constitute a focal point of feminist concerns' (Rose, 1977, p. 77).

Although feminists do not generally use the term 'attitude' with the same precision as do social psychologists, a major tenet of feminist thought is that attitudes both influence and reflect social and institutional responses to sexual violence. Feminist analyses of sexual assault and the law, institutional policies and practices in the medical, legal and social service professions, popular media descriptions of rape, and academic writings on sexual violence are based on the assumption that rape myths are inescapably intertwined with, if not largely responsible for, the widespread misunderstanding and mistreatment of rape victims. Furthermore, the feminist literature argues that attitude change, which may be achieved via consciousness-raising activities, can precipitate changes in social structures and modifications in institutional responses to survivors of sexual assault. Similarly, although it is less frequently made explicit, feminists also suggest that social, political and institutional changes can contribute to enhanced knowledge and improved attitudes towards victims of sexual abuse.

A considerable portion of feminist scholarship emphasizes macro-socio-political transformation via action-oriented research and consciousness-raising and its significance for rape myths and prejudicial attitudes toward survivors of sexual abuse. However, some scholars have argued not only that feminist research can be a vehicle for broad-based social change, but also that transformation may occur on a more personal level for both the researcher and the research participants (Bristow and Esper, 1988). Susan Brownmiller (1975), for example, described her personal transformation during her participation in rape workshops and speak-outs, her research and writing *Against Our Will*. Similarly, Ann Bristow and Jody Esper (1988) discussed how a number of women altered their perceptions of sexual assault and reformulated their definitions of rape after participating in research interviews or attending community presentations. Whether transformation occurs on the societal or individual level, however, feminist action-oriented research emphasizes praxis, the significant contribution of both theory and practice in maximizing social change. As such, feminist research has both political implications and theoretical significance. As Maria Meis has pointed out, 'In order to understand a thing, one must change it' (1991, p. 62).

Action-oriented research starts with applied objectives, the quest for social change and the acknowledgement that the study is *for* women not *on* women. With the explicit statement of feminist values and the goal of social transformation feminist scholars argue that science and politics do mix. In doing so they diverge from the traditional claim of scientific objectivity, the hallmark of conventional scientific wisdom, and replace it with acknowledgement of partial subjectivity.

Although feminist research may be distinguished by explicit value statements, it is not differentiated by the specific methods or the techniques that it employs. In fact, feminist action-oriented programmes rely on a range of methods common to the social sciences, including interviews, surveys and participant observational techniques. However, the ways in which these methods are implemented often distinguish action-oriented feminist research from mainstream social psychological investigations (Harding, 1987).

One of the most notable features of feminist research is power-sharing between the researchers and the research participants. Along these lines, feminists attempt to replace the traditional vertical relationship between the researcher and the researched with a more horizontal or egalitarian association. Interviewing techniques are particularly amenable to power-sharing and have been discussed in detail by Ann Oakley (1981). Following her recommendations, feminist scholars have tended to adopt open-ended, informal, involved, interactive and empowering methods which allow the research participant to exert considerable influence over the direction, pace and content of the interview. This differs from the more popular structured interview in social psychology which is directed by a relatively detached and allegedly objective researcher.

Power-sharing between the researcher and research participants in feminist studies is not confined to interviewing strategies. It has been extended in many instances to the actual design and implementation of studies (for example, Meis, 1983) as well as the interpretation of data and the dissemination of research findings (Acker et al., 1991). The politics of power-sharing is consistent with feminist theory; however, this approach is also popular with feminist researchers because it is conducive to personal growth and empowerment. As such, the consciousness-raising and personal transformation which emerge in feminist research unfold as facilitated change, a change from within, rather than a manipulated and controlled change induced from without, as in experimental studies of attitude shifts.

In addition to the power-sharing element, feminist action-oriented studies and social psychological research are often distinguished on the basis of preferences for field- versus lab-based studies and qualitative versus quantitative data. As feminist research is designed to foster personal consciousness-raising and socio-political change, it usually occurs in field settings. Women are studied in their natural environments, and emphasis is placed on understanding wider social and structural issues. Studying women in the real world diverges from lab-based research in experimental social psychology, which is preferred as a means of maintaining control over the research setting. In addition, feminists usually favour qualitative methods in their action-oriented projects to enhance the meaning and significance of their research findings, while applied social psychologists typically prefer quantitative techniques and sophisticated statistical analyses to ensure research reliability and validity.

Feminist Research: Grassroots Activism and Social Movements

Feminist action-oriented research has emerged with the specific objectives of empowering women and promoting social change. This description, however, does not fully communicate the extent to which a symbiotic relationship exists between feminist scholarship and the feminist movement. It is often the case that feminist research pertaining to rape arises from a collective consciousness and is undertaken in the context of the broader anti-rape movement. In this sense it is integrated with women's lives and oriented toward women's needs. Frequently feminist researchers work hand in hand with grassroots activists to produce feminist scholarship and to precipitate social change. In many instances the actual research initiative emerges from the grassroots organization, for example, WAR's study on women's safety. In other cases the major impetus comes from an individual or group of feminist scholars who work in the anti-rape campaign, for example, Cathy Roberts' (1989) research with rape victims in London. In either case, there is a close and nurturant relationship between feminist scholarship and grass-roots activities which is embodied and represented in the anti-rape movement.

An excellent discussion on the anti-rape movement and its connection to feminist theory, ideology and research has been provided by Mary Koss and Mary Harvey (1991). They have argued that feminist thought has had a major impact on shaping the structure and function of the anti-rape movement in at least four ways. First, feminist scholarship has contributed to widespread consciousness-raising in its recognition that sexual assault is an inevitable outcome of the patriarchy. Secondly, in highlighting women's perspectives on sexual violence, feminists have also drawn attention to the psychological trauma of rape and the negative consequences of institutional responses to victims of sexual abuse. Thirdly, after criticizing hierarchical structures, authoritarian decision-making practices and institutional failures to recognize and serve women's interests, feminists have implemented alternative collective strategies to meet women's needs. Finally, they have practically activated feminist organizations to look specifically at sexual violence.

In some instances feminist activism and feminist research have formally enjoyed a shared history. In 1976, for example, federal legislation in the United States made way for the creation of the National Center for the Prevention and Control of Rape to sponsor research, to initiate training and to examine the causes, conse-quences and treatment of rape. In other instances the relationship between grassroots activism and feminist research has been less formalized, but no less effective. In the main, action-oriented research on rape has been situated in the context of a social movement and has been consistent with the objectives of social change; prevention, service reform, and empowerment of women have received particular attention (Koss and Harvey, 1991).

Activism and research by Andra Medea and Kathleen Thompson exemplifies the action-oriented approach and its convergence with consciousness-raising, attitude change and service reform. Inspired by the anti-rape movement and their association with Women against Rape in Chicago, the researchers initiated a survey on sexual violence which investigated the characteristics of rape, psychological and social consequences of sexual violence, and institutional responses to sexual assault. In 1974 they published *Against Rape: A Survival Manual for Women*. The book was based primarily on the responses of women who were willing to share their experiences of victimization and to comment on the factors which had facilitated their recoveries. Relying both on these survey responses and on their own knowledge and experience with the anti-rape movement, the authors compiled information on rape avoidance and coping methods, strategies for social and institutional changes – including liaising with hospitals and courts, public campaigning and use of media publicity – and guidelines for starting rape crisis services.

The work by Andra Medea and Kathleen Thompson represented one of the first reports on rape from a feminist perspective. Although it provided considerable practical information on avoiding and coping with rape, it is particularly noteworthy that the researchers highlighted the significance of rape-related attitudes in their introduction to the book:

> Our present attitudes paralyze us, they leave us unprepared and ready to fall into man-made traps, they teach us to resign ourselves when it is unnecessary and they lead us to believe that the situation is unchangeable. As long as we accept the stereotypes that are presented to us . . . the rape situation will not change. (Medea and Thompson, 1974, p. 7)

Their ground-breaking study represented a serious attempt to alter these attitudes.

Cathy Roberts' (1989) work with the London Rape Crisis Centre also illustrates feminist research in action against a backdrop of the larger anti-rape movement. At the commencement of the project Roberts acknowledged the impact of feminist social action, the anti-rape campaign and the experiences of the women who set up and used the London Rape Crisis Centre on the development of her research. In the course of her own work with the Rape Crisis Collective and the provision of counselling and support for sexually abused women, Roberts documented the experiences of 30 women who agreed to have their stories used for research purposes. The research data were collected in an involved process of interactive information-sharing where the researcher attempted to reflect, interpret and challenge perceptions of victimization and oppression, and to understand and facilitate coping mechanisms in the recovery from sexual assault. Despite the appropriate combination of theoretical and applied objectives, Roberts was quick to recognize the limitations of the research. The analysis of change on the individual level contributed to only partial understanding of rape; broader-based political influences were also important in interpreting rape and facilitating change.

In this context Roberts acknowledged the significance of attitudes in her analysis of personal and political change. She reiterated the relationship between the personal and the political, noting the parallels between individual victims' reactions to sexual violence and public responses to the issues. In short, she argued, public attitudes and awareness of rape influenced how women felt about their own experiences. These attitudes also affected facilities for victims of sexual assault – not only the availability of services but even the counselling process itself was structured and informed by a political agenda. Roberts consequently concluded that those who controlled the public understanding of sexual violence, whether feminists or not, also directed the social and institutional responses to rape.

A similar conclusion was reached by Fanny Cheung in her description of changing attitudes and the War on Rape Campaign in Hong Kong. Cheung (1988) discussed the activities of the War on Rape Committee set up in 1977 with feminist researchers and representatives from various government and voluntary organizations in Hong Kong. The Committee concentrated on four major tasks: applied research, services for victims, training and public education, and advocacy and social action. Along these lines, the research team adopted a very practical approach to rape-related issues; they were the first to compile thorough descriptive statistics on the characteristics of sexual offences in Hong Kong and to gather comprehensive information on service provision for rape victims. In addition, they undertook survey research on attitudes toward rape, particularly those attitudes held by legal, medical and social service professionals. Research findings in these areas were later used as a basis for recommendations of the establishment of specialized services, institutional policies and procedures for dealing with rape victims, training programmes for relevant professionals, and public education for consciousness-raising and changing attitudes toward victims of sexual assault. Despite these praiseworthy undertakings, Cheung also reported that more in-depth studies on victims and offenders, though extremely important to understanding psychological and social aspects of rape, were not conducted, due to lack of access to these groups.

In terms of social action and the application of research findings, the War on Rape Committee was able to liaise with local organizations to implement specific recommendations for the development of services and changes in procedures for dealing with victims of sexual assault. These included the establishment of a Rape Victim

Aftercare Service by the Family Planning Association and the introduction of a rape crisis telephone hotline by the Samaritans. In addition, the Committee began working with the police and hospitals for improved and standardized protocols for dealing with victims of sexual assault. A manual, synthesizing medical, legal and psychological information on rape and providing guidelines for crisis intervention and counselling, was also produced for social service professionals and volunteers.

The War on Rape activists also concerned themselves with training and public education. In this domain workshops were developed for professionals and paraprofessionals working with victims of sexual abuse. Nurses, doctors, teachers and mental health workers were offered training packages. Public education was additionally provided for students and community groups with emphasis on the presentation of accurate information on the nature of sexual violence in Hong Kong and the elimination of popular rape myths which have detrimental consequences not only for victims themselves, but for women and men more generally. In some instances consciousness-raising was linked to social advocacy. Legislative and institutional changes were promoted by the War on Rape Committee. One example of socio-political change was the passage of the Crimes Amendment Bill (1978), which offered additional protection to rape victims such as the inadmissibility of evidence in court regarding the victim's sexual history, the protection of the victim's identity in the media and the provisions for *in camera* testimony.

Given the nature of feminist action-oriented studies, the comprehensive review of this research domain cannot be accomplished in the same manner as a review of social psychological studies of persuasion and attitudes shifts. The research itself is not so amenable to succinct and compact summary as each study relies on multiple methods, is situated in a specific socio-political context and demands analysis of change and development over time. Despite the numerous examples of feminist action-oriented research on rape and feminist discussions of social, political and personal transformations, few reports contextualize action-oriented studies within the larger anti-rape campaign or provide specific information about the relationship between the research and concurrent or subsequent change. Even fewer explicitly comment on the action-oriented outcomes in association with attitude change. For the purposes of illustrating and evaluating the impact of feminist action-oriented research on changing social systems, then, an in-depth analysis rather than a broad, but patchy, overview is preferred. The following section concentrates on the anti-rape movement and feminist action-oriented research in Singapore. It attempts to situate feminist research and intervention in the broader context of the women's movement and to analyse it in relationship to social and political changes pertaining to sexual assault in Singapore.

Feminist Action-oriented Research In Singapore

Although our research on sexual violence in Singapore provides only one example of feminist action-oriented research, the historical and socio-cultural background of the project renders it a particularly suitable illustration of applied feminism. The geographical concentration of a 2.8 million population in a 582 square kilometre nation-state and the relatively recent history of the local women's movement permit comprehensive monitoring of social and institutional responses to sexual violence. As such, the evolution of socio-political innovations can be easily traced, and the research project itself can be set in the context, as indeed it emerged, of broader social activism and change in Singapore.

Having suggested that feminist action-oriented research and social transformation in Singapore can be comprehensively and succinctly described, it is difficult to narrate the development of the research project and associated social change in a straightforward manner. Although a linear model may represent how the research is presented, it is not how the research was experienced (Stanley and Wise, 1991). It is also difficult to describe the unfoldings in terms of cause and effect relationships. The project in Singapore was interwoven with shared aims and personal connections with various women's organizations, voluntary agencies and government authorities. The benefits which eventually accrued for women emerged through these interconnections and convergences.

The Project
In 1981 the Singapore Council of Women's Organizations (SCWO) and the National Crime Prevention Council (NCPC) convened a public forum on 'Violence against Women' in Singapore and strongly urged that research be undertaken: (1) to assess the type and extent of abuse of women, particularly rape and battering; (2) to determine its psychological and social consequences; and (3) to formulate effective prevention strategies and treatment facilities. At that time little was known about the characteristics of sexual violence, victim reactions, or institutional management of sexual offences in Singapore. Only two published studies existed on rape, both of which were medical reports on the physical and demographic characteristics of 'alleged' victims (Ng, 1974; Sng and Ng,

1978). In addition, there was one legal commentary which urged that more stringent corroboration criteria be maintained in the prosecution of sexual offences (Koh, 1977). Despite the topic's neglect in the professional literature, police statistics indicated that rape rates, although low by most Western standards, were on the rise and that the 93 cases reported in 1981 represented a 50 per cent increase over the preceding 10 years (*Statistical Report on Crime in Singapore*, 1981). This was an object of concern for both women's groups and law enforcement authorities.

The next year, in response to the SCWO and NCPC's suggestions, a research proposal from the Department of Social Work was submitted by my Singaporean colleague, Dr Myrna Blake, and myself to the National University of Singapore for funding of a study of sexual violence. The proposal cited the initiative of the SCWO and NCPC and the necessity of understanding and supporting victims of sexual assault. The research was explicitly designed with the aim of examining the patterns and consequences of rape in Singapore and with the immediate objective of assisting victims of sexual abuse. It was also proposed that the research would serve as a basis for future recommendations for rape prevention, rape counselling and treatment and have significant implications for policy-makers and welfare officers.

The proposed project included three components: clinical, institutional and socio-cultural. The first component was centred on victims of sexual violence themselves. It examined demographic information on rape victims, characteristics of sexual offences, and psychological and social consequences of sexual assault, including trauma and readjustment processes. This portion of the project was related to direct practice, and research was conducted in conjunction with mediation and advocacy. Crisis intervention, counselling, support and referral were incorporated into the research process in an attempt to empower women and to alleviate the trauma of sexual assault.

The second component focused on the institutional management of sexual offences, including the compilation of information on rape statistics, the policies and procedures of police, hospitals and the criminal justice system, the available counselling and support facilities, and the networking strategies for the provision of services to victims of sexual offences. This part of the research involved not only data collection from victims and archival sources, but also interviewing service-providers to learn more about the institutional management of sexual assault cases. The project's third component concentrated on social beliefs and values which encourage the commission of rape and affect its consequences. Knowledge about and attitudes toward victims of sexual violence were examined with special emphasis placed on those individuals who encountered victims in their professional practices.

Although the funding for the project was obtained with relative ease, implementation proved problematic. There were no voluntary agencies which dealt specifically with survivors of sexual violence, and there was an initial reluctance of government authorities to become involved with the research and to permit access to victims of sexual offences. To a large extent these reactions were guided by negative attitudes and misperceptions. A typical response was that rape was not a problem in Singapore. A second line of defence was that it was an overly sensitive issue in Asian societies and that research interests might be more profitably directed elsewhere.[2] The third strand of resistance was the practical difficulty in setting up a research project of this type.

Of course the researchers believed, after our preliminary work in formulating the research proposal, that better services for victims were a necessity; however, policy-makers and purse-string holders understandably wanted evidence that this was indeed the case. The first few months of the research activities found us involved in the infamous Catch 22: the authorities could not respond to requests for improved services if substantial proof of need was not provided, yet the necessary access to victims to demonstrate the need was blocked, partially because 'rape wasn't a problem in Singapore'. The situation echoed Maria Meis's (1983) plight in Germany and the attempts she described of Women Help Women to establish a refuge in Cologne. It also mirrored Fanny Cheung's (1988) comments on community research and the War on Rape in Hong Kong.

Our project budget allowed for the provision of trained social workers or senior social work students to be on call for assistance with crisis intervention and counselling at hospitals or police stations. In return, the research team requested permission to conduct confidential, voluntary interviews with victims. But officials in both the Ministry of Health and the Ministry of Home Affairs initially declined permission for the research, cutting off the possibility to work directly with the public hospitals and the police. Fortunately, staff in government social services were more accommodating. The Ministry of Social Affairs (MSA) agreed for us to have access to victims of sexual abuse who were under the care of their Children and Youth Services. Our earliest work in 1983 was undertaken with children and adolescents, many of whom had been victimized much earlier. While this gave us some basic information about sexual offences in Singapore, the research team was failing to tap a broader spectrum of sexual assault victims, and although our reports were made available to MSA staff, our counselling and support services were largely redundant as the victims were receiving guidance and assistance from the Ministry's social workers.

But our early work was not without its merit. Paralleling our action-oriented research, the SCWO and NCPC continued their efforts to raise public awareness about these issues. In June 1983, a second public forum, 'Violence against Girls', was organized and presented. The forum included our contribution on understanding and counselling victims of sexual assault which was based on our preliminary observations in children's homes.

Our work with children and adolescents was soon supplemented by a liaison with the National University of Singapore's Obstetric and Gynaecology Department, who agreed to cooperate with our research and to permit access to their sexual assault patients. As the University's department received a substantial proportion of the country's police-referred sexual assault cases, we were then able to work with a broader and more representative range of victims. By 1984 we had set up an interview room in one of the local hospitals where the NUS Obstetrics and Gynaecology Department was situated. We began to work with women and girls who had attended the hospital clinic and were routinely referred to our research centre. Not all women who had been referred by the gynaecologists chose to meet with us; however, of those who did attend our sessions, all agreed to participate in the research. We employed a very loosely structured interview schedule for data collection purposes; however, we engaged our clients in a two-way flow of information, and research objectives were always secondary to the counselling and support work. In the context of the research enterprise we provided crisis intervention, counselling and a variety of practical services related either to sexual assault specifically or to everyday concerns, for example, schooling, personal relationships and employment. We also attempted to retain contact with the project participants for at least six months after the initial interview, and even longer, if requested. In the course of our study we documented the changes experienced by the participants in their recovery from sexual assault.

While the work with victims was developing we also became more involved with the study of the institutional management of sexual assault. Much of the data came from our participants' case histories, their descriptions of interactions with the police, hospitals, courts and social services. In many cases we acted as victim advocates, assisting them with lodging police reports, finding shelter and accompanying victims to court. We also interviewed a variety of professionals such as police administrators and investigators, members of the National Crime Prevention Council, lawyers, staff in the Attorney General's Chambers, gynaecologists in government and private practice, hospital administrators, and social workers and counsellors in government and voluntary organizations. In this way we maintained not only the direct experience of working with the various authorities, but were also able to gain a comprehensive overview of the interlocking systems in Singapore. Oddly enough, this had not been previously accomplished.

By 1985 the research team expanded and, in addition to the university staff, included two social workers and eight senior social work students.[3] During a two-year period we interviewed over 100 women and girls who had been victimized by a variety of sexual offences, compiled the only centralized source of information on rape victims and their treatment in Singapore, and provided extensive counselling and advocacy services. We learned more about sexual assault in Singapore and how it very much resembled sexual violence in other societies, for example in that rape victims generally know their assailants, that most offences occur indoors, that mode of dress is unrelated to sexual abuse, that psychological trauma is affected by the reactions of significant others. We learned that the agencies dealing with sexual assault rarely worked in conjunction with each other and that limited social services were provided for victims. We encountered an abundance of rape myths in legal and medical professionals. We attempted to use the media, at first very unsuccessfully, to draw attention to rape myths and misconceptions, the needs of victims, the problems with rape legislation and the limited services available. At the same time we started to network with various women's groups and social service agencies. We began to find that we were receiving referrals from schools and voluntary organizations. As the research and intervention component of the project continued to expand, we branched out and became more involved in training and community education programmes.

After two years in the field our research project became more widely recognized and accepted. Based on our research, intervention and advocacy experiences, the sexual assault team began to offer training packages for various government and voluntary organizations in 1985–6. This included social workers at the Ministry of Community Development (formerly the Ministry of Social Affairs), who dealt mainly with statutory sexual offences and incest, and medical social workers employed by the Ministry of Health in government hospitals, who had begun to receive more regular referrals from doctors. We also provided training for volunteers at the Samaritans of Singapore (SOS), a telephone crisis service. In addition we offered a programme on sexual abuse for school principals through the Ministry of Education and commenced training for the police both at police divisions and at the Police Academy. We were also asked to address the Academy of Medicine on the psychological effects of sexual assault (April 1986) and to contribute a session on sexual violence in the family to a forum on 'The Relevance of Social Policy to Domestic Violence' (May 1986).

Although the clinical component of our project concluded later that year, one of our most tangible and useful contributions to the improvement of services for sexual assault victims came in the form of *Victims of Sexual Violence: A Handbook for Helpers*, which was published in 1990 (Ward and Inserto, 1990). The book was based on our practical work with survivors of sexual assault and was intended to serve as a resource manual for local helping professionals. The volume detailed the nature and characteristics of sexual assault in Singapore, sexual offences and the law, victims' psychological and social responses to sexual assault, crisis intervention, counselling and follow-up, an overview of the police procedures, hospital management of sexual offences, the role and responsibilities of the criminal justice system, available social services, community prevention and policy recommendations.

The legacy of information provision, training and education is still continuing although our project was officially terminated in 1991 after the completion of an additional study on women's safety. Training is currently provided on a regular basis to the Police Academy and some voluntary organizations. In addition, we have become more recently involved in rape prevention, offering consciousness-raising sessions to family life educators in secondary schools. But back-tracking to the mid-1980s, our research, training and educational programmes were not unfolding in isolation. Other changes were emerging with the formation of women's groups, the expansion of social services and heightened awareness of government authorities.

In the Meantime . . .

The year 1985 became a turning point for anti-rape activism in Singapore. Impetus for social change sprang up from diverse sources – voluntary social service agencies, grassroots feminist organizations and government authorities. There were three particular advancements which had significant consequences for the awareness and management of sexual violence in the local context: (1) the formation of a special committee to study the desirability and feasibility of specialized services for sexual assault victims within the Samaritans of Singapore; (2) the establishment of AWARE, the Association of Women for Action and Research, a grassroots feminist organization which was aimed at improving the status of women in Singaporean society; and (3) the inauguration of the Ministry of Health's Working Committee on Rape, Molestation and Sexual Assault for the revision of hospital management of sexual abuse cases. As the size and compactness of Singapore contribute to the everybody-knows-everybody phenomenon, an excellent networking system allowed us to participate in some of these developments. In many instances we were able to link the aims and objectives of the research project with the needs and interests of the organizations.

Social Services Our formal and informal attempts to promote improved facilities for victims of sexual assault were met with favourable responses from the Samaritans of Singapore. Although SOS had historically specialized in suicide prevention, the organization recognized a gap in service provision relating to the area of sexual violence. It began to consider the need for specialized facilities for victims of sexual assault and invited members of our research team to submit a proposal for discussion of service development. Preliminary discussions took place between May and September 1985. Following from this, SOS's Service for the Sexually Assaulted was launched in May 1986, representing a major breakthrough in anti-rape activism in Singapore.

Modelling the Service for the Sexually Assaulted on its work with suicide prevention, SOS activated a specially trained squad of volunteers to provide crisis intervention via telephone helplines. The volunteers were also equipped to act as advocates, to liaise with the police, hospitals and the courts, and to make appropriate referrals to other agencies for additional services or follow-ups. For more long-term counselling, SOS offered face-to-face sessions with qualified social workers and counsellors. More recently it has sustained efforts to extend its colloborative work with the police and has begun to receive direct referrals from police divisions.

SOS has demonstrated its commitment to providing services for sexual assault victims by maintaining regular volunteer training programmes, in conjunction with members of our research team, and by placing senior staff in overseas rape crisis centres to learn more about counselling techniques, case management and administration. The organization has also put considerable effort into public education by producing and distributing a pamphlet on 'What You Should Know about Rape', describing rape myths and available services. The brochure, including information based on our study, has been directed towards relevant professionals such as teachers, police, doctors and lawyers. When possible, SOS has also relied upon the media to call attention to the plight of rape victims and the paucity of available services. Indeed, the organization has been a major force in disseminating our research findings to policy-makers and to the general public.

Feminist Groups and Women's Networking   While SOS was working to introduce new centralized services for sexual assault victims, AWARE was emerging as Singapore's first explicitly feminist association. Registered in 1985, the organization was devoted to consciousness-raising and the attainment of equal opportunities for women. Although AWARE concerned itself with many women's issues, including employment, health, welfare and family life, one of its first areas of activism was sexual violence. This was facilitated by the material that we had already generated on sexual assault and by the formal and informal liaisons between the founding mothers of AWARE and members of the research project team.

AWARE's early activities were concentrated on public education. The association effectively engaged the 'old girls'' network and was particularly successful in working with the Singapore Association of Women Lawyers (SAWL) and the Singapore Council of Women's Organizations. In June 1986, the three bodies presented a joint symposium on 'The Role of Legislature in Crisis Intervention' at the Association of Psychological and Educational Counsellors of Asia Conference. The following month AWARE organized a public forum on 'Violence against Women' which addressed issues of physical and sexual abuse. It continued to work hand in hand with the SCWO, an umbrella body, in the formation of a Task Force for the Prevention of Violence against Women and contributed to the 1987 'Stop Violence against Women Forum and Exhibition' sponsored again by the SCWO and NCPC.

AWARE's public forum participation was supplemented with written material on physical and sexual violence. The Task Force for the Prevention of Violence against Women continued its work, and in 1988 *Men, Women and Violence: A Handbook for Survival* was published by AWARE and SAWL. The handbook detailed the definitions of violence against women, community strategies for eliminating violence, legal protection against physical and sexual abuse, and a list of help services. In addition, AWARE took advantage of the publication and review of our handbook (Ward and Inserto, 1990) to launch a Rape Awareness Week. The media blitz in late 1990 which continued through early 1991 gave rape a high profile, widely disseminated our research findings and policy recommendations, and generated renewed interest in sexual violence in Singapore.

AWARE then expanded its activities to direct service and in 1991 opened the Women's Helpline. Although the Helpline is broadly available for crisis intervention, counselling and consultation, the organization has taken special interest in physical and sexual abuse. Volunteers are equipped to handle telephone counselling, to act as victim advocates, to liaise with the police, medical and legal authorities, and to make agency referrals. The Helpline is supplemented by face-to-face counselling sessions and a Legal Aid service.

Public awareness has traditionally been a high priority for AWARE, and in March 1991 a second public forum on 'Violence against Women' was organized. In making excellent use of feminist networking, AWARE joined with various social service associations and campaigned tirelessly for the improvement of services for sexual assault victims. In 1991 they were joined by the newly formed Society against Family Violence (SAFV) in affiliated consciousness-raising activities. In September of that year, AWARE, SOS and SAFV organized a public seminar on 'Networking for Families in Crisis: The Management of Rape and Domestic Violence'. Our research team made its presence felt by contributing a presentation on networking legal, medical and social services for victims of sexual assault. In August 1992 SAFV also mounted a public forum on 'Courtship and Family Violence', in which we added a discussion of sexual abuse in dating and marital relations.

Social activism, consciousness-raising and networking converged in 1991–2 with the formation of an AWARE, SCWO, SAWL, SAFV and SOS coalition, the Rape Study Committee, to examine policies, procedures and services provided by police, hospitals and the legal system. The Committee directed its immediate attention toward police practices, and in 1992 its members produced a working paper for the National Crime Prevention Council on streamlining procedures for the handling of sexual offences. The report included recommendations for: increased participation of counsellors and paracounsellors; specially trained women officers to process the cases; standardized investigative procedures; and improved networking with social services. The Rape Study Committee now has biannual dialogues with high-level police administrators and is currently involved with the production of a new training package for senior investigating officers. Although there have been some token gestures made towards feminist activism in Singapore, the police response to the sustained lobby and media attention appears to represent the most significant reaction to date.

All in all, feminist groups and social service agencies in Singapore have taken major strides in anti-rape activities. They have been responsible for raising public awareness and promoting specialized services for survivors of sexual assault. Members of the research project have been fortunate to assist, to some extent, with these activities and work hand in hand with the agents of social change. In many instances we have been able to provide additional ammunition for the war on rape. In turn, we have enjoyed the broad dissemination of our research findings on sexual violence in Singapore.

Government Support   While the mid-1980s saw the impact of women's groups and the influence of social service agencies on the emergence of improved facilities for victims of sexual assault, government bodies were beginning to respond to social concerns over sexual violence. The most significant response came in the form of the Ministry of Health's inauguration of the Working Committee on Rape, Molestation and Sexual Assault. The Committee, chaired by a senior government pathologist, was largely concerned with practical procedural issues such as standardizing patient interviews, clinical history-taking and medical examinations; however, it also generated recommendations to enhance physicians' sensitivity, to diminish victim trauma, and to ensure adequate social and psychological support. Its 1985 report provided guidelines for cooperation between police and hospitals in the management of sexual assault cases and advocated the acceptance of self-referrals which were previously excluded by hospital policy. In addition, it revised and standardized report forms for sexual offences and produced a sexual assault examination kit for the more thorough collection of medical evidence. The Committee also stipulated that examination of sexual assault patients should be limited to qualified specialists, and that routine referrals should be made to medical social workers for social and psychological support.

Many of the non-medical recommendations made by the Committee were previously suggested by our research team. In particular we were concerned with the acceptance of emergency cases and the consistent provision of counselling and follow-up services. Nevertheless, the Committee's work and recommendations were also an important landmark along the route to social change. Although there was little evidence to link the Committee's work directly or formally with our efforts to improve the treatment of sexual assault victims, this demonstrated official recognition of the necessity for improved services for rape victims and represented one of the earliest positive responses by the government institutions towards victims of sexual assault.

The following year the National University Hospital implemented a number of the Committee's recommendations for the treatment of sexual assault patients. These included standardized protocol for the management of sexual assault patients, examination by senior specialists and routine referrals for social and psychological services. Most significantly, however, the hospital's medical social workers initiated a 24-hour crisis intervention and counselling service for sexual assault victims. This was the first service of the kind in Singapore, and, to date, the university hospital is the only medical institution to provide this facility. The medical social work staff have retained their commitment to this service and have also organized training and educational packages for health professionals, with assistance from members of our research team, on the care and treatment of sexual assault patients.

Other Changes   In addition to changes in hospital policies and procedures and the expansion of specialized services for victims of sexual assault, the mid-1980s saw revisions in Singapore's laws pertaining to sexual offences. In accordance with the Penal Code of Singapore, the definition of rape is limited to vaginal–penile penetration and excludes marital offences. While the definition of rape has remained unchanged, in 1984 the punishment was revised, increasing the term of imprisonment up to 20 years and incorporating liability for fines and caning. In addition, amendments were made to the crime of molestation ('outraging modesty'). The offence was elaborated, and the Penal Code amendments specified the inclusion of certain conditions which warranted harsher punishment. While sentencing for molestation was previously limited to a two-year term of imprisonment with or without fines, the period of incarceration was extended for up to 10 years if voluntary hurt was caused, wrongful restraint was employed, if the offence was committed in a lift or if the victim was under 14 years of age. In these cases caning was also specified as mandatory.

There is no substantial evidence to suggest that these changes were specifically linked to increased awareness of violence against women in Singapore. Indeed, the maximum penalties for a number of crimes were increased in 1984, reflecting a generally tougher anti-crime stance. There have been no further changes in the definition of or punishments for sexual offences under the Penal Code since that time; however, many lawyers believe that the trend is currently toward harsher sentencing for convicted sex offenders.

Then and Now
Mary Koss and Mary Harvey have argued that the objective measurement of a community's beliefs and attitudes is found in the

'programs, policies and actions to which it willingly commits its limited resources' (1991, pp. 103–4). Along these lines there is considerable evidence of social change in Singapore: attitudes toward sexual violence have changed, and institutions have modified their responses to rape victims. In 1981 rape was not considered a problem. There was reluctance to talk about the issue, victims' needs went unacknowledged and services for survivors were neither specialized nor centralized. Today specialized and centralized services for rape victims are provided by two voluntary agencies. Improved, standardized management of sexual assault cases has been introduced by the police, including the provision of specially trained women police officers to assist with rape investigations. Government hospitals have also revised the procedures for dealing with victims, offering them priority treatment and standard referral to medical social workers. In addition, greater cooperation among the police, hospitals, courts and social services has been implemented, and all women who report sexual assault are now ensured access to counsellors.

Efforts have continued to sustain and further improve effective institutional management of sexual assault cases. In addition to regular training provided to police, hospitals and voluntary agencies, an ongoing dialogue between the police and women's organizations has been maintained. The criminal justice system has responded positively, evidencing an increased percentage of rape convictions – up from 11 per cent of reported cases in 1978–84 to 21 per cent in 1985–1993 (Criminal Investigation Division, 1994). Finally, rape prevention programmes have started to emerge. These have included public forums, popular publications, educational packages for the schools and media coverage to reduce violence against women.

The establishment of a rape crisis centre has not yet been achieved and has remained a controversial issue. There are those, including myself, who believe that such a centre in Singapore may be under-utilized due to the social stigma of sexual assault. As an alternative, a more generic women's resource centre has been suggested and has been established with the opening of AWARE's centre and expanding services. There is, in addition, an existing proposal for a SAFV social service clearing house for cases of all types of violence.

Praxis Revisited

The work described here has provided an illustration of feminist action-oriented research. Its theoretical underpinnings are consistent with feminist scholarship, its implementation reflective of feminist method, and its applied objectives associated with social action. Exemplifying praxis in the combination of feminist theory, method, research and practice, the project has convincingly demonstrated that both attitudes and social systems can change.

The research commenced with the objective of empowering sexually assaulted women and encouraging social and institutional changes to provide improved services for victims of sexual violence. This was accomplished through a variety of activities. Field research and intervention were undertaken with victims of sexual assault. An interactive methodology was adopted which focused on therapeutic encounters as a means of understanding and facilitating recovery from sexual abuse. The project incorporated multiple methods, including interviews, naturalistic observations and archival sources, and both qualitative and quantitative data to document the characteristics of sexual offences, victims' psychological and social responses, and their experiences with related institutions. This multi-method approach, applied at both the individual and institutional level, was also used to formulate recommendations for policy changes and improved services.

The project was based on feminist theory, which highlights the role of patriarchal values in the misunderstanding and misrepresentation of women. Viewing these values and attitudes as a major stumbling block to social change, efforts were made to demystify sexual violence, to understand women's experiences from their own perspective and in their own terms. It was important to share this information more broadly by making it widely accessible – to victims, to feminist groups and other organizations, to professionals who deal with sexual violence, and to members of the general public. In doing so the research project could contribute to the larger anti-rape movement in Singapore.

The demystification of sexual violence had at least three significant implications for change in Singapore. First, information about victims' experiences of sexual assault was incorporated into the therapeutic research process. In this way the women who participated in our project came to see that they were not alone, that their reactions to sexual abuse were normal, and that their feelings and frustrations were shared by others in similar situations. This functioned not only to validate their experiences of sexual abuse, but also, in many cases, to empower women and to facilitate change and the recovery from sexual assault. Secondly, information was disseminated to relevant organizations who shared an interest in violence against women. In this instance facts and figures were used to justify the necessity for improved services and to precipitate institutional changes to meet these needs. The integration of the aims and objectives of the feminist action-oriented research, grass-roots feminist organizations and voluntary social services became a major force in staging social change in Singapore. Thirdly, demystification of sexual violence had obvious implications for the development of training programmes and the formulation of broader policy recommendations. This additionally linked the project to government agencies and public education campaigns. In this way the social action research became intertwined with the broader anti-rape activities in Singapore.

But how does one evaluate this type of feminist research? In contrast to the guidelines provided by social psychologists in their textbooks on psychological research methods, it is difficult to locate a checklist for the assessment of theoretically and methodologically sound feminist studies. Our project encapsulated at least four of the features cited by Shulamit Reinharz (1992) as commonly found in feminist action-oriented research: demystification, action orientation, participatory or collaborative methods, and needs assessment. It also reflected the broader defining features of feminist scholarship: a feminist perspective rather than a specific feminist method; an involved, rather than detached, multi-method approach; a critical analysis of non-feminist scholarship; an interdisciplinary vantage point; a grounding in feminist theory; and a direction toward social change (Reinharz, 1992). But does that make it good feminist research?

Perhaps there is no simple answer to that question. My own readings on feminist research and feminist research methods have guided me to the conclusion that the quality of action-oriented research is best assessed in relation to its applied objectives. The underlying theory and the application of specific methods may have a bearing on this issue, but the ultimate evaluative yardstick is related to the achievement of proposed social change. In that sense, our project, set in the context of the larger anti-rape movement, was successful. It demonstrated that the personal is political and that people can change, attitudes can change and social systems can change.

How does this link back to social psychology and its theory and research on attitude change? Although the overall approach in feminist action-oriented research is quite different from that of experimental studies of persuasion and attitude shifts, and the understanding and operationalization of 'attitudes' vary, there is still a certain consistency between feminist perspectives on social movements and psychological theories of attitude formation and change. First, psychologists, like feminists, have emphasized the association between attitudes and behaviour (Abelson, 1972). While psychologists' attention has been focused on the individual level, feminists have noted a similar association on the societal level. Feminist scholars have highlighted the broader connection between societal attitudes and societal behaviours, or, more specifically, between rape myths and institutional responses to sexual violence. Secondly, psychologists have argued that discrepancies between attitudes and behaviours induce a state of psychological discomfort, or cognitive dissonance, and that individuals are motivated to alter either their behaviour or their attitudes to promote consistency (Festinger, 1957). Likewise, feminists have maintained that there is a consistency between social attitudes and socio-political responses to rape, and that changes in one of these domains affect changes in the other. For example, if institutional policies and procedures in the management of rape cases are changed in a way that reflects greater sympathy and understanding of victims, the attitudes of relevant professionals are likely to fall in line. Alternatively, if consciousness-raising precipitates public attitude change toward rape, there is likely to be a demand for improving institutional care and treatment of victims.

A third point relates more broadly to consciousness-raising and attitude change. Feminists have noted that patriarchal ideology is so widespread and pervasive that it is rarely questioned or criticized. To counter these effects they have traditionally advocated massive public education programmes as a means of increasing awareness and facilitating attitude change. The effectiveness of this strategy receives some support from psychological theory and research; social psychological studies have demonstrated that mere repeated exposure to a persuasive message can alter perceptions and attitudes (Cialdini et al., 1981). Feminist speak-outs, public forums, educational packages and effective use of the media can effectively contribute to improved attitudes toward victims of sexual violence.

While there is certainly a theoretical convergence between feminist approaches to social change research and social psychological studies of attitudes, methodological issues remain to be considered. No doubt feminist action-oriented research and social psychological studies share an array of methods common to the social sciences; however, with respect to studies of attitude change, methodological preferences vary. Certainly there is a preference in social psychology for experimental studies and the establishment of cause and effect relationships. This has not received such high priority in feminist research, which relies on more field-based studies and naturalistic methods. In addition, there are aspects of feminist implementation of standard research techniques which may prove unsettling to social psychologists. Along these lines, Michele Fine and Virginia Vanderslice (1992) have argued that social action research challenges the epistemological assumptions of traditional social psychology in three ways, by: (1) transforming the role of researcher, (2) reconceptualizing data collection and (3) relying on grounded theory.

In the first instance, feminist researchers acknowledge their values and biases, incorporate them into the research process and allow them to guide social change. Furthermore, they become involved with social change rather than remain disinterested and constrained by observational activities. This obviously challenges the traditional assumptions about detachment and objectivity in the scientific enterprise. On the second count, data collection is implemented as intervention. Incorporating multiple methods and qualitative data in action-oriented research, data collection becomes an interactive process and an impetus for social change. This diverges from the social psychological preference for experimental methods, quantitative data and externally manipulated rather than internally motivated change. Finally, in social action research, theory derives from practice and incorporates politics. It is grounded in the real world and recognizes the political dimensions of social change. This is discomforting to social psychologists, who believe that researchers should be apolitical and that politics and science do not mix. Nevertheless, despite these underlying epistemological conflicts, on the more pragmatic level it is easy to recognize the complementarity of social psychological and feminist research on attitude change.

In Conclusion

Feminist research on sexual violence and attitude change has been largely situated in the context of feminist activism and a broader anti-rape movement. Such action-oriented research has been able to document implicit shifts in attitudes and changes in institutional responses to sexual violence. Personal, institutional and social changes meet the explicit objectives of feminist scholarship and activism. While this line of research might be criticized from a conventional social psychological perspective, the overall social, psychological and political significance of such applied research should not be discounted. Despite their varying points of origin and preferred methodologies, there is some convergence in theoretical perspective, and in the end both feminist and social psychological research give us hope that rape myths can be dispelled, that attitudes can be changed, and that rape victims can receive the care and support that they most certainly deserve.

Notes

1   Publisher's information: this description is found on the cover of *Ask Any Woman*.

2   Indeed rape is a sensitive topic in Singapore, and there are political issues which could be debated, from both feminist and non-feminist perspectives, concerning the involvement of a foreign psychologist in the investigation of sexual violence in the country.

3   The social work staff included Fathiah Inserto and Joyce Tan. The students were Sudha Nair, Esther Goh, Salmiah bte. Mohammad, Nancy Ng, Sukhwinder Kaur, Pang Kee Tai, Gerardine Nonis-Yap and Juliet Tan. In 1986 Ann Wee and Vivienne Wee, academic staff, joined the project.

Conclusion

Ultimately, what can be said about social psychological and feminist theory and research on attitudes toward rape victims? And what comments can be made about the relationship between feminism and psychology?

On Theory . . .

Feminist theorists, in particular, have incorporated the social learning focus on sex role socialization into a social-political-historical account of rape, which emphasizes the overarching construct of the patriarchy. These theorists assumed that patriarchy shapes attitudes and beliefs, women's roles, men's roles, and their relationship to each other, ultimately determining all forms of violence against women. We cannot overestimate the influence of feminist theorists such as Brownmiller upon the thinking of current researchers. (Sorenson and White, 1992, pp. 3–4)

On Method . . .

Each approach for studying sexual aggression has its own strengths and limitations. Empirical analytic methods cannot help us know the phenomenological experience of a beautiful sunset, nor can we know the phenomenological experience of a rape survivor using traditional research paradigms. Conversely, subjective reports shed little light on the incidence and prevalence of sexual assault. There is, however, much that can be learned from both subjective methods and traditional scientific approaches when applied to the study of sexual aggression and victimization. (White and Farmer, 1992, pp. 45–6)

The book has considered *what* we know about attitudes toward rape and rape victims and *how* we acquire that knowledge. In doing so it has compared and contrasted feminist and social psychological approaches to the topic. Such a comprehensive analysis is troublesome to undertake for a number of reasons, the most fundamental problem being the difficulties involved in defining, categorizing and compartmentalizing feminist and social psychological research. Feminist scholarship, for example, is interdisciplinary, and, therefore, crosses boundaries with psychology. To complicate matters further, social psychological research, particularly in the domain of field studies, often merges with related disciplines, especially sociology. While feminist–social psychological distinctions have been drawn in light of several criteria, including research objectives, statements of values, the research context, aspects of research methodologies, theoretical underpinnings and, to some extent, epistemological assumptions, it remains to be considered if these distinctions are ones of relative emphases or qualitative disparities. In the final section a concluding glimpse is offered at the convergences and divergences in feminist and social psychological research on attitudes toward rape victims with special consideration of theoretical, methodological and epistemological issues. In the end it is hoped that conclusions can be drawn about the two bodies of scholarship, how they relate to each other, and what they can tell us about attitudes toward rape victims.

A Word on Theory

Not only has the feminist movement been credited with drawing attention to rape as a major social problem and with encouraging the serious study of sexual violence, but feminist scholars have also been responsible for developing alternative theoretical perspectives for the psychological investigation of sexual assault. In fact, many have argued that the feminist vision of rape has become the dominant theoretical framework in social science research on sexual violence (Donat and D'Emilio, 1992; Ellis, 1989). Feminist theory has positioned rape within a broader socio-cultural context, viewing sexual abuse as only one consequence of socially constructed and constrained gender roles (Rose, 1977). Along these lines rape has been reconceptualized as an act of male power and control, rather than a crime of sexual passion, and has been represented as only one example of men's domination and exploitation of women. Although rape has been interpreted by feminists in a variety of ways – in terms of patriarchal power and authority (Brownmiller, 1975), in terms of sexual access and conflict (LaFree, 1980a, 1980b), and in terms of male ownership of female 'property' (Clark and Lewis, 1977) – a common thread in feminist thought is that rape does not qualitatively differ from other aspects of male and female relations. To the contrary, it may be seen as an extension of typical male–female interactions, reflecting the conventional pattern of male domination and female subordination. This reconceptualization of rape has shifted the psychological study of sexual violence away from the pathological traits of individual offenders and blameworthy victims and has suggested that rape is not an isolated act experienced by some women, but a universal problem for all women (Largen, 1985).

In addition to revising our understanding of what rape is,

feminists have called attention to pervasive rape myths, prejudicial attitudes about rape and rape victims which trivialize sexual violence and reflect victim blame, denigration and disbelief (Brownmiller, 1975; Burt, 1980). They have considered both the origins and the outcomes of these myths, emphasizing the negative consequences for women, men and society. Psychological research has been strongly influenced by the feminist literature on rape myths and has empirically documented the widespread existence of inaccurate and stereotyped beliefs about sexual violence. In the earliest studies psychologists defined, operationalized and measured rape myths, providing empirical support for feminist allegations of prejudice against victims of sexual abuse. In subsequent investigations, they examined antecedents and correlates of attitudes toward sexual violence. In keeping with a long-standing tradition of attitude theory and research, psychologists found that rape attitudes varied between the sexes and across ethnic and cultural groups, that they were affected by education, and that they were linked to personality and other gender-associated attitudes (McGuire, 1985).

The tendency that people have to blame rape victims for their own misfortune has been an object of concern for both feminists and psychologists. The former have concentrated on inaccurate stereotypes of sexual violence and theorized about political dimensions of the blaming process. The latter were quick to note that similar patterns of blame apportionment were observed in other areas of victimology research and turned to the growing field of social cognition to investigate further the situational influences on perceptions of rape and rape victims (Walster, 1966). Consistent with feminist hypothesizing, psychological research demonstrated that characteristics of the victim, the offender and the event influence the definition and perception of rape as well as the assignment of blame, fault and responsibility. In an attempt to explain the patterns of rape-related attributions that they observed, psychologists relied on theories of defensive attribution styles (Shaver, 1970) and the 'just world' hypothesis (Jones and Aronson, 1973). In these cases the motivational foundations and beneficial consequences of attributional explanations, particularly the needs for psychological control and self-esteem, have been highlighted.

What are the actual consequences of rape myths for victims of sexual assault? Feminists and social psychologists have argued that these myths shape the actual treatment of victims on both institutional and interpersonal levels. This is supported on empirical grounds by field investigations and case studies and is further reinforced by mainstream social psychological theory, which posits an attitude–behaviour link (McGuire, 1972). On the institutional count, the insensitive and unfair treatment that victims receive by legal, medical and social service professionals has come under critical scrutiny, and research has confirmed that official processing of rape cases largely conforms to popular myths about sexual violence. For example, successful prosecution of sexual offences is more likely to result in cases where the victim and rapist are strangers, when weapons are used and when the victim has an impeccable moral character. On the interpersonal count, psychologists have also suggested that rape myths induce victim-blaming, limit an individual's capacity to offer social support to survivors of sexual abuse and subsequently affect a victim's recovery from related trauma. In this domain social psychological and clinical theory have converged to elaborate the dynamics of stress and coping in victims of sexual assault (Hobfoll, 1988; Lazarus, 1976) and the impact of mediating variables, including personality, life events and social support, on psychological responses to sexual abuse.

While both feminists and psychologists have been concerned with the effects of rape myths on individuals' recovery from sexual assault, the former have emphasized the political dimensions of the process, and the latter have engaged in more in-depth analysis of the impacts on victims' self-concepts and self-esteem. In this context attribution theory has been merged with social psychological theories of self to explore the negative consequences of rape myths on victims' responses to sexual assault (Merton, 1948). More explicitly, psychologists have argued that pervasive rape myths, in general, and the attitudes and perceptions of significant others, more specifically, are often accepted and internalized by victims themselves. Influenced by societal values and interpersonal interactions, victims frequently blame themselves. The resultant self-blame and -deprecation mitigate against psychological recovery from sexual abuse.

Finally, feminists have consistently advocated social change as a means of empowering women and improving the status quo (Brown-miller, 1975). Psychologists have responded to this challenge by applying cognitive consistency theories to alter attitudes toward rape and rape victims (Festinger, 1957). Along these lines, empirical research has demonstrated that the generation of inconsistent cognitions through informative and experiential attitude change programmes can improve attitudes toward rape victims. This work can be seen to complement the more broad-based feminist approach to changing social systems.

So how do feminist and social psychological theory relate to each other? In the main, it would be accurate to describe feminist scholarship as providing the fundamental theoretical framework for the study of rape and rape myths. The feminist reconceptualization of sexual violence portrays rape as an act of domination and control, posits socio-cultural causes including gender roles and social stratification, and highlights the existence and negative repercussions of inaccurate conceptions of rape and prejudicial attitudes toward rape victims. Psychologists have followed through and empirically documented the existence of rape myths, examining both their causes and consequences. In undertaking this research they have relied on a rich tradition of social psychological theory: attitude formation, measurement and change, attributional thinking, the social construction of self, cognitive dissonance, and others. Obviously, these theories were not originally generated to explain the causes and consequences of rape myths, rather they have been transplanted from mainstream social psychology and applied specifically to this area to elaborate these phenomena.

Despite the differences in origins and disciplinary boundaries, there is a certain consistency between feminist and social psychological theories on rape-related attitudes and a general consensus about what we know about rape and rape myths. Both feminists and psychologists are in agreement about the widespread existence and negative consequences of rape myths. Both recognize the significance of gender and the social construction of self. Both have explored changing negative myths and misconceptions. Although the vantage points are different, feminist scholarship has provided impetus for psychological research, and psychological theory and research have added momentum to the feminist cause. As such, the two approaches may be seen as mutually informing and reinforcing each other.

A Word on Method

In considering *how* we gain information about attitudes toward rape victims, comparisons and contrasts have been drawn between feminist and psychological methodological preferences and their respective evaluations of varied research techniques. As mentioned previously, these feminist–social psychological comparisons are situated on somewhat shaky ground. There are many voices within feminism and arguably different 'cultures' within psychology (Kimble, 1984); neither represents a monolithic approach to the study of attitudes toward rape victims. Despite these definitional difficulties, a concluding comment is warranted about research methods in feminism and psychology.

Although feminist research may be distinguished in terms of its selected topic of investigation, its research objectives, its explicit value statements and its gynocentric perspective (Black, 1989; Lott, 1981), it is not, in the main, differentiated by the *specific* methods or the techniques that it employs. In fact, feminist research relies on an array of methods common to the social sciences, including interviews, surveys, archival research, case studies and participant observational techniques. The data collection strategies are not in themselves inherently feminist or non-feminist (Stanley and Wise, 1983). However, there are aspects of their implementation which distinguish feminist research from mainstream social psychological investigations (Harding, 1987).

One of the most distinctive facets of feminist research is power-sharing between the researchers and the research participants. A major objective of power-sharing activities is to replace the traditional vertical relationship between the researcher and the researched with a more horizontal or egalitarian association. For example, Ann Oakley (1981) has discussed feminist interviewing, arguing that the encounter between the researcher and the research participant should occur in an informal manner, that the interaction should reflect a two-way flow of information, that the respondent may influence the direction and pace of the interview, that she is entitled to ask questions and expect to receive answers, and that the researcher may share her personal experiences in a discussion of the topic of interest. This diverges from the more popular form of structured interview in social psychology, which is directed by a researcher who is expected to remain aloof from the topic of discussion in order to eliminate potential bias in subject responses.

Although interviewing easily lends itself to power-sharing tactics, the same principles may be applied to other aspects of feminist research. In some instances participatory research techniques are used to undermine the distinction between the researchers and the researched. Put in another way, researchers and research participants share a joint responsibility for the design and implementation of the study. Maria Meis (1983), for example, has discussed the formation of Women Help Women and their collective work for the establishment of a refuge in Cologne, Germany. In achieving this goal women from diverse social, economic and educational backgrounds initiated egalitarian-based strategies for research, intervention and social and political change. Along similar lines Joan Acker and colleagues (1991) described power-sharing in the interpretation of data and the dissemination of research findings. In feminist studies, then, researchers are integrated, involved and in a more egalitarian relationship with research participants in comparison with the detached and hierarchical perspective more commonly adopted by psychologists.

In addition to the power-sharing element, feminist studies and social psychological research are often distinguished on the basis of preferences for field- versus lab-based studies and qualitative versus quantitative data. As feminist research aims at both personal consciousness-raising and broader social change, it usually occurs in field settings. Women are studied in their natural environments, and attempts are made to understand wider social and structural issues. Studying women in the real world diverges from the generally preferred lab-based research in experimental social psychology where context-stripping is used as a means of maintaining control over the research setting. The discrepancies between conventional preferences for specific research settings, however, are sometimes exaggerated. Naturalistic field studies have always been an integral part of psychological research, and feminist research is certainly not limited to the field setting.

A similar contrast arises with respect to qualitative and quantitative data. Conventionally, feminist research has been aligned with a preference for qualitative methods while social psychologists are generally more comfortable with quantitative techniques. Feminist scholars, however, have taken a variety of positions on the qualitative–quantitative debate, and although some have recommended the rejection of quantitative methods on the basis of their distortion of women's experiences (Jayaratne, 1983), many have advocated the incorporation of qualitative and quantitative approaches (for example, Jayaratne and Stewart, 1991). A blending of qualitative and quantitative data has also been advocated by some social psychologists, and although, for the most part, quantitative techniques have been traditionally favoured, there are even those who are more strongly allied with qualitative approaches (Harré, 1979; Kimble, 1984).

Given the diversity of methods and approaches in both social psychology and feminist studies, it may be that the apparent discrepancies are less a matter of essence than of emphasis. Feminist research relies on methods common to the social sciences, and social psychology employs techniques simultaneously utilized by feminists. Are there any *unique* feminist methods? While many psychologists would argue that feminist scholarship has not made a unique methodological contribution, there is one possibility that has emerged from research on attitudes toward rape victims. Both Catherine MacKinnon (1983) and Shulamit Reinharz (1992) have cited consciousness-raising as an original feminist research method. This form of data collection enables women to describe, discuss and understand their experiences in their own terms and from their own perspectives. As consciousness-raising facilitates social and personal change, it is used by feminists more often as a political, therapeutic and educational tool. Nevertheless, as evidenced both by Susan Brownmiller's (1975) pioneering work and Ann Bristow and Jody Esper's (1988) more recent study of rape, it also provides powerful information about women's lives, experiences and growth. Having acknowledged the potential of consciousness-raising techniques as a uniquely feminist form of data collection, however, it must also be acknowledged that feminist scholars have largely failed to provide concrete guidelines on how to adopt this technique effectively as a viable research strategy. So is there a methodological divide between feminists and social psychologists? Not necessarily so. The methodological arguments *between* feminism and psychology are, by and large, no greater than the methodological debates *within* each domain. Certainly, there are differences in conventional preferences, but for the most part the actual methods remain the same. However, there are aspects of their implementation which tend to differ between feminism and social psychology, and these differences have implications for underlying epistemological assumptions.

A Word on Epistemology

Brief comments have been made about feminist and social psychological theories – systems of hypothetical propositions – and methods – procedures by which research is conducted and data are collected and analysed. However, both theories and methods have implications for epistemologies – assumptions about knowledge, including its nature, origins, acquisition and limitations. Given the association between theory, methods and epistemology, and considering the current debates concerning science and feminism, it is appropriate to conclude with some comments about the epistemological underpinnings of social psychological and feminist scholarship.

The philosophical assumptions underlying contemporary psychological research are largely rooted in an epistemological system of logical positivism. Although there is considerable debate as to its precise definition, a number of features have been traditionally associated with the positivist paradigm. These include the assertion that science is objective and value-free, the emphasis placed on empiricism and observation, the separation of the observer and observed, the reliance on the hypothetico-deductive method, the preference for quantitative data as means of enhancing research reliability, the preference for laboratory-based and experimental studies as a means of ensuring research validity, and the capacity for generalization across data (Unger, 1983).

The acquisition of knowledge via psychological investigations which employ conventional scientific methods is consistent with the positivist epistemology. However, early feminist criticism of psychological research on rape and rape victims pointed out certain inconsistencies between theory, method and the tenets of positivism. More specifically, psychological theory and research were anything but value-free; rather they were guided by a pervading sexism found both in science and in society. Consequently, the earliest responses to the feminist critique of psychology were an attempt to correct this bias by making women more visible, by studying more topics of relevance to women, and by eliminating sexist perspectives and procedures. This was pursued without any inherent threat to the positivist epistemology. Standard research methods and techniques were implemented, but with allegedly stricter adherence to the criteria of objectivity, that is, the production of non-sexist research. This epistemological tact has often been referred to as feminist empiricism. The bulk of the social psychological research on attitudes toward rape and rape victims described in this book – survey research on rape myths, experimental investigations of attributions, clinical case studies and field research – represents, in the main, a feminist empiricist approach.

Although failure to adhere to the tenets of logical positivism in psychological research has been noted by both feminist and non-feminist scholars, the positivist paradigm has, on the whole, been accepted and adopted by contemporary social psychologists. This is not to say that the positivist epistemology has been without its critics. Many of the problems cited by feminists, such as the limitations of quantitative data, a reductionist approach and hypothetico-deductive reasoning, the neglect of the contextual understanding of the individual, and the lack of mundane realism, have also been found in 1970s debates in social psychology (for example, Strickland et al., 1976), the humanistic branch of psychology (Kimble, 1984) and among the scientific realists (Greenwood, 1989). Feminists, however, have often framed these criticisms in terms of 'ways of knowing', contrasting the agentic mode of knowledge defined by separating, ordering, quantifying, manipulating and controlling with the communal mode involving naturalistic observation, qualitative analysis, a holistic perspective and personal participation (Carlson, 1972). Some feminists believe these routes to knowledge to be linked to gender, with the former or masculine epistemology defining the knowledge structure of science (Weinreich-Haste, 1986). Whether or not this is the case, feminist scholars who acknowledge dualistic approaches to research and advocate communal methods of knowledge acquisition are typical of the second wave of feminism, a more methodologically innovative perspective, and may be seen as proponents of the standpoint epistemology (Harding, 1986; Lather, 1988).

Scholars are divided as to whether the standpoint epistemology recommends an expansion of traditional science or demands a more fundamental shift. Specifically, can science as we know it accommodate the experiential approach to knowledge? Perhaps the ambivalence is reflected in the current state of affairs in contemporary psychology. Research by Gregory Kimble (1984), for example, indicates that there is already a scientific–humanistic split in the discipline and that the possibilities for epistemic reconciliation are not bright. While the feminist standpoint epistemology, then, may be seen as posing a challenge to the epistemological assumptions of positivist psychology, transforming the role of researcher and reconceptualizing the nature of data collection (Fine and Vanderslice, 1992), it by no means poses radically new challenges. The epistemological assumptions advocated by proponents of the feminist standpoint position have been echoed by dissidents in other branches of psychology and have been accommodated, though perhaps marginalized, by the discipline. Scientific realists, for example, have likewise pushed for generative theory and inductive research, phenomenologists have based their studies on subjective frames of reference, and even Kurt Lewin (1948), acknowledged by many as the father of contemporary social psychology, argued that psychological research should be designed not only for explanation but also for social change.

Much of the feminist research presented in this book is consistent with a standpoint epistemology. Involved participant observation, natural research settings, power-sharing, conscious partiality, emphasis on experience and qualitative analysis, are all characteristic of the communal way of knowing. Susan Brownmiller's (1975) early research, for example, exemplified a standpoint perspective in her feminist ethnography, her association with rape victims, reliance on public speak-outs in the anti-rape movement and qualitative content analysis of the media to generate theories about sexual violence. In some instances feminist scholars merge the more traditional quantitative techniques with qualitative, experiential approaches. Along these lines Andra Medea and Kathleen Thompson (1974) utilized standard survey techniques in their study of women's experiences of sexual violence; however, they combined this with their own experiences in the Women against Rape campaign to produce their rape survival manual. My own research in Singapore also relied upon standard survey techniques and quantitative analysis in conjunction with less conventional research and intervention techniques, including feminist interviewing, advocacy and empowering activities. Although deriving from different sources, it is interesting to note that psychologists have long advocated multi-method and multi-measurement techniques to ensure the validity of their research (for example, Campbell and Fiske, 1959).

There are those, however, who argue that the epistemological assumptions underlying at least a portion of feminist research cannot be accommodated by the standpoint position. Harding (1986), in fact, has suggested that feminists have to reinvent both theory and science to make sense of women's experiences. The most radical feminist epistemology, one which presents a major challenge to science and psychology, is the postmodern perspective. It goes beyond the criticism that we have practised bad science (feminist empiricism) and that we should expand the boundaries of science (feminist standpoint), and claims that there is something inherently wrong with the practice of science as we know it. More specifically, postmodernists argue for a relational world view, maintaining that reality is socially constructed and that there should be a priority of moral and political issues over scientific and epistemological ones (Lather, 1988). Maria Meis (1991), who has made major contributions to the development of feminist method and epistemology, has been particularly forceful in her argument that bits of feminism and positivism can neither be blended nor be seen as complementary because they represent qualitatively different epistemologies. From a postmodern perspective there can never be a feminist epistemology, but only many stories that women tell about the different knowledge that they have. In contrast to the tendency toward reductionism and propensity toward unified generalizations found in logical positivism, postmodernists maintain that these fractured identities represent a major resource in feminist research (Harding, 1986).

Unfortunately, feminist researchers who have investigated rape and attitudes toward rape victims have rarely been explicit about the epistemological position underlying their research. However, a postmodern perspective is implied in research by Ann Bristow and Jody Esper (1988). Not only do they emphasize the significance of consciousness-raising in their work with rape victims, they also argue that ignoring the wide range of women's experiences and failing to recognize and validate the diversity of women's realities subvert the research enterprise. A postmodern perspective also appears to underlie Cathy Roberts' (1989) work with rape victims and the London Rape Crisis Collective. In the introduction to her study she discusses research perspectives, acknowledging that the view from the outside, or the researcher's viewpoint, is *a* valuable perspective. However, she maintains that a major problem in social science is that the researcher's perspective is seen not only as objective but also as representative of *the* truth. In contrast, she argues: 'There is nothing which can make an understanding of rape less subjective or partial. It is an experience, experiences are essentially subjective and each person involved can only describe it partially. So feminist research provided a structure within which to explore the subjectivity and so understand the subject better' (1989, p. 45).

Again, the epistemological debates *within* both feminism and social psychology are similar to the debates *between* the two domains. Feminist empiricism represented the first wave of feminist responses to criticisms of value-laden science. It is consistent with the guiding tenets of logical positivism and is illustrated by the bulk of mainstream social psychological research on attitudes toward rape victims. The feminist standpoint perspective represented a second development in feminist challenges to psychology. This perspective, shared by other alternative voices within psychology, has been accommodated to some extent, although marginalized, within the discipline. Feminist research which has blended objectivity and subjectivity, qualitative and quantitative analysis, conventional and alternative research techniques has been shaped by a standpoint epistemology. However, with the evolution of feminism, postmodernism is becoming the more popular epistemology in feminist scholarship. Research deriving from this epistemological base, although fairly limited with respect to studies of rape, is highly political, subjective, qualitative and inductive; it relies on partial, subjective accounts of reality. In contrast to the feminist empiricist and standpoint perspectives, a viable postmodern epistemology would demand that science and psychology as we know them engage in a major paradigm shift. While these more radical epistemological assumptions have yet to produce practical and significant theory and research on rape and attitudes toward rape victims, with the growth and development of feminist research and scholarship it is difficult to predict how things may change in the future.

In Conclusion

The final analysis of social psychological and feminist understandings of attitudes toward rape and rape victims has suggested that there is much common ground between the two perspectives. Both feminist scholarship and social psychological research tell us that rape myths are widespread and insidious and that they have negative consequences for women, men and society. Both hav similarly demonstrated that attitudes and the social systems whic oppress and constrain women can change. Social psychological an feminist research findings are even more powerful when the conver gence of theory is considered in relation to the apparent diversity c methods, varying preferences for specific research techniques, an the assortment of guiding epistemologies.

While the harmonious co-existence of social psychological an feminist theory seems uncontroversial, methodological and epistemo logical issues pose more complicated questions. On the first count feminists and psychologists appear to use the same research methods but to use them in somewhat different ways. Further analysis however, suggests that psychology has already accommodated these less conventional approaches, at least to some extent, in response to other alternative voices within the discipline. Similar argument about the fluid boundaries of psychology may be presented in relation to feminist and social psychological epistemologies Clearly, traditional positivism and contemporary postmodernism are mutually exclusive. However, the reality of the situation, as it stands now, at least with respect to research on attitudes toward rape victims, is that the epistemological assumptions underlying considerable portion of both social psychological and feminist scholarship fall between these two extremes.

In terms of *making and breaking the circle* feminism and social psychology may be seen to be developing in a symbiotic relation ship, each mutually informing and influencing the other about the causes and consequences of rape myths. In this light they should be viewed as sisters in the pursuit of knowledge and in the precipitation of social change.

APPENDICES

Appendix A
Rape: Fact and Fiction

It is commonly believed that rape is rare, but misconceptions about sexual coercion extend beyond myths about its prevalence. When victim characteristics are highlighted, it is generally believed that young, sexually attractive, and often provocatively dressed women are frequent targets of rape. When offender characteristics are emphasized, it is commonly expected that the perpetrator is a sex-starved deviant. When situational factors are considered, it is usually predicted that rape occurs between strangers in deserted and unsafe public places. And when the aftermath is discussed, it is frequently expected that the innocent victim can achieve compensation and redress in the criminal justice system. This is, of course, only after the reality of rape is acknowledged. It is more often believed that a woman cannot be raped against her will and that accusations should be regarded with scepticism, particularly if the victim does not bear signs of a resistance.

However, the facts are as follows:

1 Rape is a relatively common experience in women's lives. Incidence studies are difficult to implement, and methodological considerations pertaining to sampling and the definitions of sexual offences produce variations in results. Nevertheless, there is substantial evidence to dispel the misconception that rape is rare. Diana Russell's (1982) San Francisco study, for example, reported that 44 per cent of the women surveyed had been victims of rape or attempted rape.

Studies with university women have produced variable results. Muehlenhard and Linton (1987) reported that 14.7 per cent of university women in their study were subjected to unwanted sexual intercourse, and Aizenman and Kelley (1988) found that 29 per cent of university women claimed to have experienced forced sexual intercourse. Koss (1985) found that 38 per cent of university women had experienced rape or attempted rape, but in a later nationwide survey estimated only 76 per 1000 university women had been the victims of rape or attempted rape (Koss et al., 1987).

Reviewing and evaluating a series of incidence studies Koss and Harvey (1991) noted that a prevalence rate of about 20 per cent for adult women had been reported by four independent investigative teams employing legal definitions of rape and working in different regions of the United States. They forcefully argue that when we recognize that one in five American women has experienced rape in her life we must transform the vision of sexual violence as a 'heinous but rare event into a common experience in women's lives' (1991, p. 29). Unfortunately, cross-cultural comparative data are not available on rape victimology.

2   *Any woman may be a victim of rape.* Rape victims come in all sizes, shapes and ages. They are not unusually attractive nor do they generally dress provocatively.

In many countries victims are concentrated in their teens and early twenties; however, the overall age range is enormous. In the United States Herman (1989) documented rape and other forms of sexual abuse in victims ranging in age from six months to 93 years. In our research in Singapore sexual abuse of females between the ages of 2 and 80 was documented (Ward and Inserto, 1990).

There is little evidence that victims are promiscuous or provocative. Rape victims in Singapore are 10 times more likely to be school girls than to work in night-life occupations and are much more likely to be sexually naive than experienced. As in the United States, there is no relationship between attire and likelihood of rape (Rodabaugh and Austin, 1981).

3   *The commission of rape is not confined to abnormal, sick or sex-starved deviants.* To the contrary, sexual coercion appears to be an integral part of male behaviour. On the attitudinal level more than half of the 1700 students in Kikuchi's (1988) study indicated it was acceptable for a man to force sex on a woman who was wearing seductive clothing. Forced sex is also considered justified depending upon women's dress, males' level of sexual arousal, amount of money spent on a woman, and previous sexual intimacy; less than half of the adolescent males in Goodchilds and colleagues' (1988) survey thought forced intercourse was unacceptable if they were sexually aroused.

Not only is sexual coercion considered justified, but men frequently express behavioural intentions to rape if there is assurance that they will not be caught (Malamuth, 1981). Although there is an obvious gap between male attitudes, intentions and behaviours, 23 per cent of college males in Koss and Oros's (1982) study actually admitted to forcing intercourse because they were sexually stimulated. In a second study 12 per cent acknowledged forcing vaginal, oral or anal intercourse (Koss et al., 1985). In a larger nationwide survey of university students 4.4 per cent of men sampled admitted to rape and another 3.3 per cent to attempted rape (Koss et al., 1987). Rapaport and associates found that 64 per cent of college men engaged in some form of sexually coercive behaviour, and 15 per cent committed acquaintance rape, further supporting the feminists' vision of 'normal', rather than 'pathological' rapists (Rapaport and Burkhart, 1984; Rapaport and Posey, 1991).

Unfortunately, there are very few cross-cultural data on these activities. However, a study by Tang and colleagues (1993) reported that 2 per cent of Chinese university men in Hong Kong admitted to forcing intercourse on a female partner.

4 *Most rapes occur between people who know each other*. The majority of victims are at least acquainted with the offender and some know him very well (Parrot, 1985). In Singapore, as in the United States, less than half of the *reported* rapes are committed by unknown assailants (McCahill et al., 1979; Palmer, 1983). In the United Kingdom the figure has been cited as 39 per cent (Lloyd, 1991), and in Malaysia rape by strangers has been estimated to compose 31 per cent of reported rapes (Consumers' Association of Penang, 1988).

However, there is reason to believe that the proportion of stranger rape is even lower when actual, as opposed to reported, cases are considered. In Sweden, for example, rape by unknown assailants is more likely to be reported (Snare, 1983). The same pattern was documented in a Women against Rape report from London (London Rape Crisis Centre, 1982). Although an Australian study (Bonney, 1985) cited 39 per cent of unreported rapes as occurring between strangers, in the United States Russell's (1984) community victimology survey revealed that only 12 per cent of rapes were perpetrated by men who were unknown to the victims. Similarly, Koss and colleagues reported a stranger rape incidence of 11 per cent for university women who had been sexually assaulted (Koss et al., 1987).

5 *Only a minority of rapes occur in deserted public places*. In fact, more rapes occur indoors than outdoors (Bart and O'Brien, 1985). In Singapore about 20 per cent of reported rapes take place in public locations; the majority occur in residences and often in the victim's own home (Palmer, 1983). In Malaysia, 39 per cent of reported rapes occur in residences and an additional 26 per cent in 'safe places' such as populated schools, trains and mosques (Consumers' Association of Penang, 1988). Studies have shown that in Australia more than 30 per cent of reported rapes occurred in the victim's residence (Bonney, 1985), in the United Kingdom 30 per cent of convicted rapes take place in the victim's home (Lloyd,

1991), and in the United States the majority of rapes are committed in the home of the victim or the perpetrator (Parrot and Link, 1983).

6   *Most rape victims do not show signs of physical injury*. Sexual coercion is achieved more often by verbal or psychological techniques rather than the use of weapons; consequently, victims often show no external cuts and bruises (Rapaport and Burkhart, 1984). In the United States victim surveys indicate that about one quarter of rapes and attempted rapes involve the infliction of substantial pain or serious threat of injury (Kirkpatrick and Kanin, 1957). The pattern is similar in Singapore, where assailants are usually able to gain compliance through threats. Published medical studies reveal that only 26 per cent of victims of alleged rapes sustained physical injury (Ng, 1974). In an Australian study 44 per cent of rape victims presented no signs of physical injuries (Bonney, 1985). Ironically, this disadvantages women in terms of the successful prosecution of sexual offences.

7   *Most accusations of rape are true*. It is commonly believed that women fabricate stories of rape based on fantasy if they have consented to sexual relations and have changed their minds afterward, if they are angry and want revenge, or if they are pregnant. In the United States, however, false reports are calculated to be in the region of 1–2 per cent, which is not significantly different from other violent crimes (Brownmiller, 1975; Katz and Mazur, 1979). Our research in Singapore estimated a 3–4 per cent false report rate.

8   *The allegation of rape is difficult to make and easy to disprove*. Quite the contrary to the old legal adage, less than 1 per cent of rapes and attempted rapes result in conviction in the United States (Russell, 1984). New Zealand estimates are as low as a 4 per cent chance for the offender being caught and convicted (Young, 1983). In the United Kingdom Wright's (1984) study revealed a 17 per cent conviction rate for reported rapes and attempted rapes while Lloyd and Walmsley (1989) estimated that only one in 10 reported rapes results in conviction. In Singapore the number of reported rapes is almost 10 times as great as the number of convictions (Ward and Inserto, 1990). In Israel Sebba (1968) found 18 per cent of reported felony sex offences resulted in conviction, but less than one third of the reported offences ever reached the district court. Even if rapes are reported and reach trial, in many instances the chances of criminal conviction are not good. Gulotta and Neuberger (1983), for example, cited a 63–80 per cent acquittal rate in Italian courts.

In conclusion, anyone may be a victim of sexual assault. Contrary to popular stereotypes, sexual violence often occurs between 'normal', everyday people. Raped women generally talk, act, dress and look like any other women. Rapists cannot be recognized at twenty paces. They are rarely criminally insane or sex-starved deviants. The most common pattern of rape is one where the victim knows, and often trusts, the offender. Sexual coercion generally occurs in private places, indoors, often in the home of the victim or assailant. Sexual compliance is obtained with verbal threats or psychological tactics rather than physical force, and victims often bear no observable signs of resistance. Given that the common pattern does not match the popular stereotype, women who experience sexual assault are often disbelieved and discredited.

This is not to suggest that rape myths and ideologies are completely unfounded. Sexual violence occurs in many forms and fashions. Women are sometimes assaulted by strangers, and rapes may occur in deserted public places. Women are occasionally dressed in a seductive fashion and may be drinking at the time of the offence. Men who commit acts of sexual violence sometimes have inadequate or antisocial personalities. Violence may be inflicted; some women are beaten, strangled, knifed, shot and murdered. These cases catch the public eye; they often appear more dramatic and, indeed, comprehensible to us. Stereotypes about sexual violence also allow us to cling to the misguided notion that sexual coercion is far removed from conventional male–female relations, that it is something which is both unusual and pathological.

Appendix B
Assessment Instruments:
Reliability and Validity Issues

This appendix is provided for those with a technical interest in psychometrics and the reliability and validity of those instruments which are used to assess attitudes toward rape and rape victims.

Attitudes toward Rape Scale

The first psychometric instrument constructed to measure attitudes toward rape was published by Hubert Feild in 1978. Barnett and Feild (1977) initially tested a pool of 75 items pertaining to rape, rape victims and sexual offenders on 400 university students and subsequently developed the Attitudes toward Rape Scale (ATR). The ATR is composed of 32 statements presented in an agree/disagree six-point Likert format. Factor analysis indicates that the ATR contains eight subscales: sex as motivation for rape, power as motivation for rape, normality of rapists, severity of punishment for rape, victim precipitation of rape, women's resistance during rape, women's responsibility in rape prevention and favourable perceptions of rape victims. Feild (1978a, p. 161) noted that five of the eight factors (excluding sex and power motivations and normality of rapists) can be scored as a 'pro- or anti-' rape attitude, although this is more accurately described as a pro- or anti-victim attitude.

From a psychometric perspective the eight factors appear robust, accounting for a combined total of 50 per cent of the variance. With perhaps only one exception each of the 32 items clearly loads on only one of the eight factors (> .45). However, because Feild (1978a, p. 165) employed what he refers to as 'converted factor scores' in subsequent analyses, he indicated that this 'precludes direct reliability estimates'; mean estimated factor reliability, however, is .62. No test–retest indices are available.

The validity of Feild's (1978a) scale is supported by reported sex differences in expected directions (see also Barnett and Feild, 1977). For example, men are more likely to indicate that women have greater responsibility in rape prevention, that women precipitate rape by their appearances and behaviours and that women are less desirable after sexual abuse. Feild also reported that rapists and counsellors differ in their attitudes, with counsellors being more supportive toward victims in terms of issues of provocativeness, victim desirability and prevention responsibility. Some significant relationships were additionally found between knowledge about rape, attitudes toward women and rape attitudes. All in all, Feild's scale has appeared robust and is widely used. It has formed a starting point for the construction of other scales such as Burt's (1980) Rape Myth Acceptance Scale and Ward's (1988a) Attitudes toward Rape Victims Scale. Its items are generally short, concise and well written. The ATR serves the function of broadly assessing various rape-related attitudes; this advantage may simultaneously be a limitation for the researcher interested more specifically in attitudes toward and perceptions of rape victims.

Attribution of Rape Blame Scale

Ward and Resick (1979) constructed the Attribution of Rape Blame Scale (ARBS) after pre-testing the 20-item instrument with 409 women from the University of South Dakota. In their 1979 conference presentation they reported the findings from both sexually assaulted and non-assaulted samples. Although the patterns of scale factors differed slightly in the two groups, the data cited here are based on the total sample.

The final version of the Attribution of Rape Blame Scale consists of 19 items to which subjects indicate their agreement/disagreement on a six-point scale. Factor analysis reveals four substantial factors which account for 55.3 per cent of the variance: Factor I (26.9 per cent) contains items reflecting victim blame (for example, women entice men to rape them); Factor II (13.2 per cent) concerns offender qualities (for example, most rapists are mentally ill or psychologically disturbed); Factor III (9.9 per cent) reflects event characteristics (for example, alcohol and drugs are significant factors in the occurrence of rape); and Factor IV (5.3 per cent) deals with societal blame (for example, rape is the product of a sexually unhealthy society). The factor loadings are substantial, and the scale appears robust. It is particularly attractive in that the ARBS reflects the various blame models of rape described by Brodsky (1976) and utilized in subsequent research.

The ARBS items are generally concise and well written, and the scale has good potential for further development; however, more substantial work on establishing its reliability and validity is demanded. Published work with the ARBS was provided by Resick and Jackson (1981) in their study of mental health professionals. The research corroborated scale validity via sex differences in attitudes (for example, the tendency for women to rely more on societal blame models than men); however, as the sample was very small ($N = 38$), firm conclusions could not be drawn about the scale's psychometric properties.

Rape Myth Acceptance Scale

Excellent work on attitudes toward rape victims has been under-taken by Burt (1980) in her study of cultural myths and supports for rape. The Rape Myth Acceptance Scale (RMAS) consists of 19 items which measure 'prejudicial, stereotyped or false beliefs about rape, rape victims and rapists' (Burt, 1980, p. 217). Subjects express their agreement/disagreement on a seven-point scale with state-ments such as 'Any female can get raped', and the scale scores reflect the degree of rape myth acceptance.

Burt (1980) has produced some impressive reliability and validity data for her scale (Cronbach alpha = .875, reflecting good internal consistency). With reference to construct validity, RMAS scores are significantly related to gender stereotyping, adversarial sexual beliefs and acceptance of interpersonal violence; that is, the myth accepter holds more traditional stereotypes, has a stronger belief that male–female relations are fundamentally exploitative and is more inclined to tolerate interpersonal violence.

Burt's scale has proven popular and may currently be the most widely used instrument for the assessment of rape-related attitudes. Her initial work deserves commendation particularly as the scale construction was based on a sample of almost 600 randomly selected adults from the Minnesota population. Later research has further documented the RMAS's validity in its correlation with dogmatism (Ashton, 1982) and its relationship to rape definitions as derived from the interpretation of sexual assault vignettes (Burt and Albin, 1981). The scale has also been successfully employed cross-culturally in the United Kingdom (Krahé, 1988).

Despite the RMAS accolades, there are perhaps two noteworthy shortcomings. A number of the 19 statements contain ambiguous components (for example, implying rape by terms such as 'deserves to be taught a lesson' or 'asking for trouble'), and others are occasionally awkwardly worded and clumsy in their constructions (for example, 'If a woman gets drunk at a party and has intercourse with a man she has just met there, she should be considered "fair game" to other males at the party who want to have sex with her too whether she wants to or not'). In addition, it would be desirable to have test–retest reliability figures. This is particularly important if the RMAS is to be used in studies of attitude change.

Rape Empathy Scale

The Rape Empathy Scale (RES) was constructed by Deitz and colleagues and was 'specifically designed to assess empathy for the rape victim, as well as the defendant, [in a style which] might represent more adequately the complex manner in which information is presented to jurors' (1982, p. 373). The format of the RES is explicitly arranged to reflect the adversarial legal process – that is, dual perspectives (victim–defendant) on each aspect of a rape incident – and as such includes 19 pairs of items reflecting victim versus offender empathy. Subjects are asked to choose the preferred statement from each pair and to indicate the extent of their preference on a seven-point scale (for example, 'I feel that the situation in which a man compels a woman to submit to sexual intercourse against her will is an unjustifiable [justifiable] act under any [certain] circumstances'). Item scores are then coded in terms of strong empathy with the rapist versus strong empathy with the victim.

The RES was initially piloted with 639 Colorado State University students and 170 randomly selected citizens from the county's jury list. Item to total correlations range from .33 to .75 for jurors and .18 to .52 for students, and alphas were .89 and .84, respectively. The scale also boasts of sound empirical, convergent and discriminant validity. First, women exhibit greater rape empathy (that is, more empathy with victims) than men. In addition, women who had experienced a rape situation evidence more empathy than those who had not. Empathetic men report less desire to rape than other men. Rape empathy is positively correlated with liberal attitudes toward women's roles and support for enactment of a marital rape law and the Equal Rights Amendment. Green (cited by Deitz et al., 1982) further reported that RES scores are negatively correlated with five of the ATR factors – women's responsibility for rape prevention, sex as a motivation for rape, victim precipitation of rape, normality of rapists, and power as a motivation for rape. Rape empathy, however, is not related to social desirability.

The RES is certainly an impressive piece of work, and with the exception of the standard criticism involving the need for test–retest reliability for these types of instruments, the scale seems essentially sound.

Attitudes toward Rape Victims Scale

Ward's (1988a) Attitudes toward Rape Victims Scale (ARVS) was designed to quantify favourable versus unfavourable attitudes toward victims of sexual violence, particularly attitudes that blame or denigrate victims, trivialize victims' experiences, highlight victims' deservingness or undermine victims' credibility. The scale was constructed from pilot testing on over 400 students at the National University of Singapore and further tested with 510 police officers, psychologists/social workers, lawyers and doctors in Singapore and 572 university students in the United States. The ARVS consists of 25 statements (for example, 'a raped woman is usually an innocent victim') to which subjects indicate their agreement/disagreement on a five-point scale; the scores range from 0 to 100 with higher scores indicating more negative attitudes toward victims.

Psychometric reliability appears strong with alphas of .83 and .86 in Singaporean and United States student samples, respectively. The scale is essentially unidimensional with a single factor accounting for 21–25 per cent of the variance. Test–retest reliability with a sample of 48 students is .80, with no significant differences between first and second testings. Validity was assessed by work modelled on Burt (1980) with ARVS scores significantly related to adversarial sexual beliefs, acceptance of interpersonal violence and attitudes toward women, but not sexual conservatism. Sex differences were documented in all samples, with women being more supportive of victims than men. Similarly, in line with Feild's research, police were least supportive of victims and social workers/psychologists most supportive, with doctors and lawyers falling between the two extremes. A modest but significant relationship between rape knowledge and supportive attitudes toward victims also emerged in this study.

A major advantage of the ARVS has been its construction for use with cross-cultural populations (Ward et al., 1988). To date samples have been collected from 15 countries (Singapore, United States, United Kingdom, Germany, New Zealand, Australia, Canada, Barbados, Israel, Turkey, India, Hong Kong, Malaysia, Zimbabwe and Mexico). The ARVS has also been translated into four languages: Spanish, German, Chinese and Turkish. On the whole the scale has remained psychometrically robust. Cronbach alphas ranged from .66 in Mexico to .89 in New Zealand and the United Kingdom; 10 of the 15 countries produced alphas > .80. (Shortened versions of the ARVS have been recommended for use in Mexico and Malaysia to increase the scale's internal consistency.) Construct validity has also been corroborated by sex differences, with women holding more favourable attitudes toward rape victims than men in all countries except India. In addition, work in the United Kingdom, former West Germany and New Zealand tentatively suggests that the ARVS predicts behavioural intentions towards victims of sexual assault (Baker and Ward, 1988; Krahé, 1988).

Other Scales

Hall and colleagues (1986) produced a 14-item Rape Attitudes Scale (RAS) designed to measure rape tolerance. The RAS includes RMAS items as well as items from previous research which had differentiated sexual and violent offenders from a male control group (for example, 'often girls falsely report rape to get attention'). The RAS was subsequently tested with 973 adolescents and 293 university students. Despite the fact that RAS scores relate to heterosexual relationship attitudes, overall the scale's reliability and validity are not impressive. Alphas are reported as .66 and .78 for the two samples, and there were no sex differences in the attitudes of adolescent males and females. Validity was appraised in a rather naive, superficial manner by asking 20 students to distinguish items from a list of statements as those that measured attitudes toward male–female relations or attitudes toward rape. Howard (1984), however, did report that individuals with liberal rape attitudes attributed more blame to an assailant in a hypothetical sexual assault case.

Young and Thiessen (1992) compiled the Texas Rape Scale, designed to measure attitudes towards rape, sexual aggression and defence against rape. The scale is composed of 96 statements to which subjects indicate their agreement/diasgreement on five-point scales. The psychometric analysis and development of the TRS are based on responses from 520 students at the University of Texas. Unfortunately, the TRS is problematic in that the authors claim four subscales: a 10-item Rape Intensity Scale, a 15-item Rape Resistance Scale (active avoidance attitudes toward rape), an 11-item Sexual Aggression Scale (aggressive attitudes toward potential victims) and a five-item Rape Propensity Scale (willingness to force sex on a partner). However, the internal consistency of the subscales is poor: intensity (.64), resistance (.47), aggression (.55) and propensity (unreported). Furthermore, factor analysis generated only three major factors: aggression, rationalization and punishment. To confuse issues even more, the Intensity Scale was developed separately through the method of equal appearing intervals, and although the authors maintain that the scale can be scored as a whole, it is not clear what that score is assumed to represent. Despite comparative data which support the conceptual validity of the subscales, such as women having more intense attitudes toward rape than men, and men having a greater rape propensity than women, there are major psychometric limitations of the instrument.

Riger and Gordon (1979) utilized a nine-item Rape Prevention Belief Scale (RPBS) in their research with 1600 adults randomly sampled from the Chicago area. They reported that two factors emerged from the nine items – one domain dealing with the restriction of female behaviours and the other which related to rapist control strategies, including victim assertiveness. However, the alphas for the two 'subscales' are unimpressive at .52 and .59, and altogether the scale appears to be a substandard version of the Attribution of Rape Blame Scale.

Finally, Tolor (1978) and Bunting and Reeves (1983) describe a Rape Inventory and a Rape Beliefs Scale. The first is associated with victim strategies in response to an attempted rape, and the latter allegedly deals with certain rape myths such as rape as a sexual act, women ask for it, etc. In neither case, however, do the researchers corroborate their scales' reliability and validity.

References

Abbey, A. (1987) Perceptions of personal avoidability versus responsibility: How do they differ? *Basic and Applied Social Psychology* 8, 3–19.

Abelson, R.P. (1972) Are attitudes necessary? In B.T. King and E. McGinnies (eds), *Attitudes: Conflict and Social Change* (pp. 19–32). New York: Academic Press.

Acker, J., Barry, K. and Essevald, J. (1991) Objectivity and truth: Problems in doing feminist research. In M.M. Fonow and J.A. Cook (eds), *Beyond Methodology: Feminist Scholarship as Lived Research* (pp. 133–153). Bloomington, IN: Indiana University Press.

Acock, A.C. and DeFleur, M.L. (1975) Reply to Susmich, Elliot-Schwartz. *American Sociological Review* 40, 687–90.

Acock, A.C. and Ireland, N.K. (1983) Attribution of blame in rape cases: The impact of norm violation, gender, and sex role attitude. *Sex Roles* 9, 179–93.

Aizenman, M. and Kelley, G. (1988) The incidence of violence and acquaintance rape in dating relationships among college men and women. *Journal of College Student Personnel* 29, 305–311.

Albin, R. (1977) Psychological studies of rape: A review essay. *Signs: Journal of Women, Culture and Society* 3, 423–35.

Alexander, C. (1980) The responsible victim: Nurses' perceptions of victims of rape. *Journal of Health and Social Behavior* 21, 22–33.

Allport, G.W. (1935) Attitudes. In C. Murchinson (ed.), *A Handbook of Social Psychology* (pp. 798–894). Worcester, MA: Clark University Press.

Amir, M. (1971) *Patterns in Forcible Rape*. Chicago: University of Chicago Press.

Ashton, N.L. (1982) Validation of the Rape Myth Acceptance Scale. *Psychological Reports* 50, 252.

Ashworth, C.D. and Feldman-Summers, S. (1978) Perceptions of the effectiveness of the criminal justice system: The female victim's perspective. *Criminal Justice and Behavior* 5, 227–40.

Atkeson, B.M., Calhoun, K.S., Resick, P.A. and Ellis, E.M. (1982) Victims of rape: Repeated assessment of depressive symptoms. *Journal of Consulting and Clinical Psychology* 50, 96–102.

Bailey, S.D. (1985) The effects of exposure to rape victims on men's attitudes toward women and attitudes toward rape. *Dissertation Abstracts International* 45, 3927B.

Baker, S.A. (1987) Testing a Model of Persuasion: Improving Attitudes toward Rape Victims. Unpublished honours thesis. University of Canterbury, Christchurch, New Zealand.

Baker, S.A. and Ward, C. (1988) Improving Attitudes toward Rape Victims. Paper presented at the XXIV International Congress of Psychology, September, Sydney, Australia.

Bankoff, E.A. (1986) Peer support for widows: Personal and structural characteristics related to its provision. In S. Hobfoll (ed.), *Stress, Social Support and Women* (pp. 207–20). Washington, DC: Hemisphere.

Barber, R. (1974) Judge and jury attitudes to rape. *Australian and New Zealand Journal of Criminology* 7, 157–72.

Barnett, N.J. and Feild, H.S. (1977) Sex differences in university students' attitudes toward rape. *Journal of College Student Personnel* 18, 93–6.

Bart, P. and O'Brien, P. (1984) Stopping rape: Effective avoidance strategies. *Signs: Journal of Women in Culture and Society* 10, 83–101.

Bart, P. and O'Brien, P. (1985) *Stopping Rape: Successful Survival Strategies.* Elmsford, NY: Pergamon.

Bartky, S.L. (1990) *Femininity and Domination.* New York: Routledge.

Beaver, E.D., Gold, S.R. and Prosco, A.G. (1992) Priming macho attitudes and emotions. *Journal of Interpersonal Violence* 7, 321–33.

Bem, D. (1972) Self-perception theory. In L. Berkowitz (ed.), *Advances in Experimental Social Psychology* (Vol. 6, pp. 2–63). New York: Academic Press.

Berger, V. (1977) Man's trial, woman's tribulation: Rape cases in the courtroom. *Columbia Law Review* 1, 1–103.

Berkowitz, A.D. and Capraro, R.L. (1989) Acquaintance Rape as a Men's Issue: Strategies for Effective Programming for Men. Paper presented at the Conference of the Acquaintance Rape and Sexual Prevention on College Campuses, Albany, NY.

Best, C.L. (1983) Attitudes and treatment knowledge by medical students regarding rape. *Dissertation Abstracts International* 44, 84B.

Best, C.L., Dansky, B.S. and Kilpatrick, D.G. (1992) Medical students' attitudes about female rape victims. *Journal of Interpersonal Violence* 7, 175–88.

Best, J.B. and Demmin, H.S. (1982) Victim's provocativeness and victim attractiveness as determinants of blame in rape. *Psychological Reports* 51, 255–8.

Black, N. (1989) *Social Feminism.* Ithaca, NY: Cornell University Press.

Blum, M. and Foos, P. (1986) *Data Gathering: Experimental Methods Plus.* New York: Harper & Row.

Bohmer, C. (1974) Judicial attitudes toward rape victims. *Judicature* 57, 303–7.

Boldero, J. and Guiliano, D. (1990) Attitudes toward Rape Victims and the Attribution of Responsibility. Unpublished manuscript, University of Melbourne.

Bonney, R. (1985) *Bureau of Crime Statistics and Research Crimes: Sexual Assault Amendment Act.* Sydney: Attorney General's Department.

Borden, L.A., Karr, S.K. and Caldwell-Colbert, A.T. (1988) Effects of a university rape prevention program on attitudes and empathy toward rape. *Journal of College Student Development* 29, 132–6.

Borgida, E. and White, P. (1978) Social perception of rape victims: The impact of legal reform. *Law and Human Behavior* 2, 339–51.

Bourque, L.B. (1990) *Defining Rape.* Durham, NC: Duke University Press.

Brady, E.C., Chrisler, J.C., Hosdale, D.C., Osowiecki, D.M. and Veal, T.A. (1991) Date rape: Expectations, avoidance strategies and attitudes toward victims. *Journal of Social Psychology* 13, 427–9.

Brakensiek, L.S. (1983) The effect of an educational program in reducing rape myth acceptance. *Dissertation Abstracts International* 43, 3405B.

Bridges, J.S. (1991) Perceptions of date and stranger rape: A difference in sex role expectations and rape supportive beliefs. *Sex Roles* 24, 291–307.

Bristow, A.R. and Esper, J.A. (1988) A feminist research ethos. In The Nebraska Sociological Feminist Collective (eds), *A Feminist Ethic for Social Science Research* (pp. 67–81). Lewiston, NY: Edwin Mellen Press.

Brodsky, S.L. (1976) Sexual assault: Perspectives on prevention and assailants. In

M. Walker and S.L. Brodsky (eds), *Sexual Assault: The Victim and the Rapist* (pp. 1–7). Lexington, MA: Lexington Books.

Brodyaga, L., Gates, M., Singer, S., Tucker, M. and White, R. (1975) *Rape and its Victims: A Report for Citizens, Health Facilities and Criminal Justice Agencies.*

Brown, G.W. and Andrews, B. (1986) Social support and depression. In M.H. Appley and R. Trumbull (eds), *Dynamics of Stress* (pp. 257–82). New York: Plenum.

Brown, W. (1970) Police–victim relationships in sex crimes investigations. *Police Chief* 47, 20–4.

Brownmiller, S. (1975) *Against Our Will: Men, Women and Rape.* Toronto: Bantam Books.

Bruyere, C., Kendall, N., Neville, K. and Shandell, T. (1982) *Rape: Face to Face* [Film]. Seattle: University of Washington.

Buchele, B.J.C. (1985) Attitudes toward rape, violence, and sex role stereotyping in rapists, violent offenders and non-violent offenders. *Dissertation Abstracts International* 45, 2696E.

Bunting, A.B. and Reeves, J.B. (1983) Perceived male sex orientation and beliefs about rape. *Deviant Behavior* 4, 281–95.

Burgess, A.W. and Holmstrom, L.L. (1973) The rape victim in the emergency ward. *American Journal of Nursing* 73, 1740–5.

Burgess, A.W. and Holmstrom, L.L. (1974a) *Rape: Victims of Crisis.* Bowie, MD: Brady.

Burgess, A.W. and Holmstrom, L.L. (1974b) Rape Trauma Syndrome. *American Journal of Psychiatry* 131, 981–6.

Burgess, A.W. and Holmstrom, L.L. (1978) Recovery from rape and prior life stress. *Research in Nursing and Health* 1, 165–71.

Burgess, A.W. and Holmstrom, L.L. (1979a) Rape: Sexual disruption and recovery. *American Journal of Orthopsychiatry* 49, 648–57.

Burgess, A.W. and Holmstrom, L.L. (1979b) *Rape: Crisis and Recovery.* Bowie, MD: Robert Brady.

Burgess, A.W. and Holmstrom, L.L. (1979c) Adaptive strategies and recovery from rape. *American Journal of Psychiatry* 136, 1278–82.

Burkhart, B. and Fromuth, M.E. (1991) Individual psychological and social psychological understandings of sexual coercion. In E. Grauerholz and M.A. Koralewski (eds), *Sexual Coercion* (pp. 75–90). Lexington, MA: Lexington Books.

Burt, M.R. (1980) Cultural myths and supports for rape. *Journal of Personality and Social Psychology* 38, 217–30.

Burt, M.R. (1982) Justifying Personal Violence: A Comparison of Rapists and the General Public. Paper presented at the Third International Study Institute on Victimology, July, Bellagio, Italy.

Burt, M.R. and Albin, R.S. (1981) Rape myths, rape definitions and probability of conviction. *Journal of Applied Psychology* 11, 212–30.

Burt, M.R. and Estep, R.E. (1977) Who is a Victim: Definitional Problems in Sexual Victimization. Paper presented at the Society for the Study of Social Problems Annual Meeting, Chicago.

Byers, E.S. and Eno, R.J. (1991) Predicting men's sexual coercion and aggression from attitudes, dating history and sexual response. *Journal of Psychology and Human Sexuality* 4, 55–70.

Calhoun, L.G., Cann, A., Selby, J.W. and Magee, D.L. (1981) Victim emotional response: Effects on social reactions to victims of rape. *British Journal of Social Psychology* 20, 17–21.

Campbell, D.T. and Fiske, D.W. (1959) Convergent and discriminant validation by the multi-trait-multimethod matrix. *Psychological Bulletin* 56, 81–105.

Cann, A., Calhoun, L.G., and Selby, J.W. (1979) Attributing responsibility to a victim of rape: Influence of information regarding past sexual experience. *Human Relations* 32, 57–67.

Carlson, R. (1972) Understanding women: Implications for personality theory and research. *Journal of Social Issues* 28, 17–32.

Chaiken, S. and Eagly, A.H. (1976) Communication modality as a determinant of message persuasiveness and message comprehensibility. *Journal of Personality and Social Psychology* 34, 605–14.

Chancer, L.S. (1987) New Bedford, Massachusetts, March 6, 1983–March 22, 1984: The 'before and after' of a group rape. *Gender and Society* 1, 239–60.

Cheung, F.M. (1988) Changing attitudes: The War-on-Rape campaign. *Hong Kong Psychological Society Bulletin* 19/20, 41–8.

Cialdini, R.B., Levy, A., Herman, P., Kozlowski, L. and Petty, R.E. (1976) Elastic shifts of opinion: Determinants of direction and durability. *Journal of Personality and Social Psychology* 34, 663–72.

Cialdini, R.B., Petty, R.E., and Cacioppo, J.T. (1981) Attitude and attitude change. *Annual Review of Psychology* 32, 357–404.

Clark, L. and Lewis, D. (1977) *Rape: The Price of Coercive Sexuality*. Toronto: Women's Press.

Coates, D., Wortman, C.B. and Abbey, A. (1979) Reactions to victims. In I.H. Frieze, D. Bar-Tal and J.S. Carroll (eds), *New Approaches to Social Problems* (pp. 21–52). San Francisco: Jossey Bass.

Cochrane, D.A. (1987) Emergency nurses' attitudes toward the rape victim. *American Association of Registered Nurses Newsletter* 43, 14–18.

Cohen, L.J. and Roth, S. (1987). The psychological aftermath of rape: Long-term effects and individual differences in recovery. *Journal of Social and Clinical Psychology* 5, 525–34.

Coleman, J.C. (1979) *Contemporary Psychology and Effective Behavior*. London: Scott Foresman.

Consumers' Association of Penang (1988) *Rape in Malaysia*. Penang: CAP.

Cooley, C.H. (1922) *Human Nature and Social Order*. New York: Scribner's.

Coons, P.M. and Milstein, V. (1984) Rape and post-traumatic stress in multiple personality. *Psychological Reports* 55, 839–45.

Costin, F. (1985) Beliefs about rape and women's social roles. *Archives of Sexual Behavior* 14, 319–25.

Costin, F. and Schwarz, N. (1987) Beliefs about rape and women's social roles. *Journal of Interpersonal Violence* 2, 46–56.

Crenshaw, T.L. (1978) Counseling family and friends. In S. Halpern (ed.), *Rape: Helping the Victim* (pp. 51–65). Oredell, NJ: Medical Economics, Book Division.

Criminal Investigation Division (1994) [Rape cases, recorded and convicted, 1985–93]. Unpublished data.

Damrosch, S.P. (1985a) How perceived carelessness and time of attack affect nursing students' attributions about rape victims. *Psychological Reports* 56, 531–6.

Damrosch, S.P. (1985b) Nursing students' assessments of behaviorally self-blaming rape victims. *Nursing Research* 34, 221–4.

Dane, F.C. (1990) *Research Methods*. Pacific Grove, CA: Brooks/Cole.

Dawes, R.M. and Smith, T.L. (1985) Attitude, opinion and measurement. In G. Lindzey and E. Aronson (eds), *Handbook of Social Psychology: Vol. 1. Theory and Method* (3rd edn, pp. 509–66). New York: Random House.

Deitz, S.R. and Byrnes, L.E. (1981) Attribution of responsibility for sexual assault: The influence of observer empathy and defendant occupation and attractiveness. *Journal of Psychology* 108, 17–29.

Deitz, S.R., Blackwell, K.T., Daley, P. and Bentley, B.J. (1982) Measurement of empathy toward rape victims and rapists. *Journal of Personality and Social Psychology* 43, 372–84.

Deitz, S.R., Littman, M. and Bentley, B.J. (1984) Attribution of responsibility for sexual assault: The influence of observer empathy, victim resistance, and victim attractiveness. *Sex Roles* 10, 261–80.

Deming, M.B. and Eppy, A. (1981) The sociology of rape. *Sociology and Social Research* 65, 357–80.

Deutsch, H. (1944) *Psychology of Women.* New York: Grune & Stratton.

Donat, P.L. and D'Emilio, J. (1992) A feminist redefinition of sexual assault: Historical foundations and change. *Journal of Social Issues* 48, 9–22.

Dukes, L. and Mattley, L. (1977) Predicting rape victim reportage. *Sociology and Social Research* 62, 63–84.

Dull, R.T. and Giacopassi, D.J. (1987) Demographic correlates of sexual and dating attitudes: A study of date rape. *Criminal Justice and Behavior* 14, 175–93.

Dunkel-Schetter, C. and Wortman, C.B. (1982) The interpersonal dynamics of cancer: Problems in social relationships and their impact on the patient. In H.S. Friedman and M.R. DiMatteo (eds), *Interpersonal Issues in Health Care* (pp. 69–100). New York: Academic Press.

Dye, E. and Roth, S. (1990) Psychotherapists' knowledge about and attitudes toward sexual assault victim clients. *Psychology of Women Quarterly* 14, 191–212.

Eagly, A.H. (1978) Sex differences in influenceability. *Psychological Bulletin* 85, 86–116.

Ellis, E.M. (1983) A review of empirical rape research: Victim reactions and response to treatment. *Clinical Psychology Review* 3, 473–90.

Ellis, E.M., Atkeson, B.M. and Calhoun, K.S. (1981) An assessment of long-term reaction to rape. *Journal of Abnormal Psychology* 90, 263–6.

Ellis, E.M., Atkeson, B.M. and Calhoun, K.S. (1982) An examination of differences between multiple- and single-incident victims of sexual assault. *Journal of Abnormal Psychology* 91, 221–4.

Ellis, K.L., Carroll, L., McCrea, S., Hershey, B. and Beaudoin, C. (1991) Strategies from the Heart: Guiding Student Action Against Sexual Assault. Paper presented at the Conference of the American College Personnel Association, March, Atlanta, GA.

Ellis, L. (1989) *Theories of Rape: Inquiries into the Causes of Sexual Aggression.* New York: Hemisphere.

Fazio, R.H. and Zanna, M.P. (1981) Direct experience and attitude–behavior consistency. In L. Berkowitz (ed.), *Advances in Experimental Social Psychology* (Vol. 14, pp. 161–202). New York: Academic Press.

Fazio, R.H., Effrein, E.A. and Falender, V.J. (1981) Self-perceptions following social interaction. *Journal of Personality and Social Psychology* 41, 232–42.

Feild, H.S. (1978a) Attitudes toward rape: A comparative analysis of police, rapists, crisis counsellors and citizens. *Journal of Personality and Social Psychology* 36, 156–79.

Feild, H.S. (1978b) Juror background characteristics and attitudes toward rape. *Law and Human Behavior* 2, 73–93.

Feild, H.S. (1979) Rape trials and jurors' decisions. *Law and Human Behavior* 3, 261–84.

Feild, H.S. and Barnett, N. (1978) Forcible rape. *Journal of Criminal Law and Criminology* 68, 146–59.

Feldman-Summers, S. and Lindner, K. (1976) Perceptions of victims and defendants in criminal assault cases. *Criminal Justice and Behavior* 15, 457–66.

Feldman-Summers, S. and Norris, J. (1984) Differences between rape victims who report and those who do not report to a public agency. *Journal of Applied Social Psychology* 14, 562–73.

Feldman-Summers, S. and Palmer, G.C. (1980) Rape as viewed by judges, prosecutors and police officers. *Criminal Justice and Behavior* 7, 19–40.

Feldman-Summers, S., Gordon, P.E. and Meagher, G.R. (1979) The impact of rape on sexual satisfaction. *Journal of Abnormal Psychology* 88, 101–5.

Festinger, L. (1957) *A Theory of Cognitive Dissonance*. Stanford: Stanford University Press.

Fine, M. and Vanderslice, V. (1992) Qualitative activist research: Reflections on methods and politics. In F.B. Bryant, J. Edwards, R.S. Tindale, E.J. Posanac, L. Heath, E. Henderson and Y. Suarez-Balcazar (eds), *Methodological Issues in Applied Social Psychology* (pp. 199–218). New York: Plenum.

Firth, A. (1975) Interrogation. *Police Review* 28 November, 1507.

Fischer, G.J. (1986) College student attitudes toward forcible date rape: Cognitive predictors. *Archives of Sexual Behaviors* 15, 457–66.

Fischer, G.J. (1987) Hispanic and majority student attitudes toward forcible date rape as a function of differences in attitudes toward women. *Sex Roles* 17, 93–101.

Fischer, G.J. (1991) Cognitive predictors of not-guilty verdicts in a simulated acquaintance rape trial. *Psychological Reports* 68, 1199–206.

Fischer, G.J. (1992) Sex attitudes and prior victimization as predictors of college student sex offences. *Annals of Sex Research* 5, 53–60.

Fishbein, M. and Ajzen, I. (1972) Attitudes and opinions. *Annual Review of Psychology* 23, 487–544.

Fishbein, M. and Ajzen, I. (1975) *Belief, Attitude, Intention and Behavior*. Reading, MA: Addison-Wesley.

Fonow, F.M., Richardson, L. and Wemmerus, V.A. (1992) Feminist rape education: Does it work? *Gender and Society* 6, 108–21.

Frank, E., Turner, S.M. and Duffy, B. (1979) Depressive symptoms in rape victims. *Journal of Affective Disorders* 1, 269–77.

Frank, E., Turner, S.M. and Stewart, B.D. (1980) Initial response to rape: The impact of factors within the rape situation. *Journal of Behavioral Assessment* 2, 39–53.

Frankl, V. (1963) *Man's Search for Meaning*. New York: Washington Square Press.

Friere, P. (1970) *Pedagogy of the Oppressed*. New York: Seabury Press.

Fulero, S.M. and DeLara, C. (1976) Rape victims and attributed responsibility: A defensive attribution approach. *Victimology: An International Journal* 1, 551–63.

Galton, E. (1975–6) Police processing of rape complaints: A case study. *American Journal of Criminal Law* 4, 15–30.

Geis, R., Wright, R. and Geis, G. (1984) Police officer or doctor? Police surgeons' attitudes and opinions about rape. In J. Hopkins (ed.), *Perspectives on Rape and Sexual Assault* (pp. 56–66). London: Harper & Row.

Giacopassi, D.J. and Dull, R.T. (1986) Gender and racial differences in the acceptance of rape myths within a college population. *Sex Roles* 15, 63–75.

Girelli, S.A., Resick, P.A., Marhoefer-Dvorak, S. and Hutter, C.K. (1986) Subjective distress and violence during rape: Their effects on long-term fear. *Victims and Violence* 1, 35–46.

Goffman, E. (1963) *Stigma: Notes on the Management of Spoiled Identity*. Englewood Cliffs, NJ: Prentice Hall.

Golden, C. (1981) Psychology, Feminism and Object Relations Theory. Paper presented at the Eighth Annual National Conference on Feminist Psychology, March, Boston.

Goodchilds, J., Zellman, G., Johnson, P.B. and Giarrusso, R. (1988) Adolescents and their perceptions of sexual interactions. In A.W. Burgess (ed.), *Rape and Sexual Assault* (Vol. 2, pp. 245–70). New York: Garland.

Gorsuch, R.L. and Ortberg, J. (1983) Moral obligation and attitudes: Their relation to behavioral intention. *Journal of Personality and Social Psychology* 44, 1025–28.

Gottesman, S.T. (1977) Police attitudes toward rape before and after a training program. *Journal of Psychiatric Nursing and Mental Health Services* December, 14–18.

Greenwood, J.D. (1989) *Explanation and Experiment in Social Psychological Science*. New York: Springer.

Griffin, S. (1971) Rape: The all-American crime. *Ramparts* September, 26–35.

Griffin, S. (1979) *Rape: The Power of Consciousness*. New York: Harper & Row.

Gulotta, G. and Neuberger, L. de C. (1983) A systematic and attributional approach to victimology. *Victimology: An International Journal* 8, 5–16.

Hall, E.R., Howard, J.A. and Boezio, S.L. (1986) Tolerance of rape: A sexist or antisocial attitude? *Psychology of Women Quarterly* 10, 101–18.

Hall, R.E. (1985) *Ask Any Woman: A London Inquiry into Rape and Sexual Assault*. Bristol: Falling Wall Press.

Halleck, S. (1962) The physician's role in management of victims of sex offenders. *Journal of American Medical Association* 180, 273–8.

Hamilton, M. and Yee, J. (1990) Rape knowledge and propensity. *Journal of Research in Personality* 24, 111–22.

Hanmer, J. and Saunders, S. (1983) Blowing the cover of the protective male: A community study of violence to women. In E. Gamarnikow, D.H.J. Morgan, J. Purvis and D. Taylorson (eds), *The Public and Private* (pp. 28–46). London: Heinemann.

Hanson, D.J. (1980) Relationship between methods and findings in attitude-behavior research. *Psychology* 17, 11–13.

Harding, S. (1986) *The Science Question in Feminism*. Ithaca, NY: Cornell University Press.

Harding, S. (ed.) (1987) *Feminism and Methodology*. Bloomington, IN: Indiana University Press.

Harré, R. (1979) *Social Being*. Oxford: Basil Blackwell.

Harrison, P.J., Downes, J. and Williams, M.D. (1991) Date and acquaintance rape: Perceptions and attitude change strategies. *Journal of College Student Development* 32, 131–9.

Harvey, J.H., Orbuch, T.L., Chwalisz, K.D. and Garwood, G. (1991) Coping with sexual assault: The roles of account-making and confiding. *Journal of Traumatic Stress* 4, 515–31.

Harvey, M.D. and Rule, B.G. (1978) Moral evaluations and judgments of responsibility. *Personality and Social Psychology Bulletin* 4, 583–8.

Heath, L. and Davidson, L. (1988) Dealing with the threat of rape: Reactance or learned helplessness? *Journal of Applied Social Psychology* 18, 1334–51.

Heider, F. (1958) *The Psychology of Interpersonal Relations.* New York: Wiley.

Herman, D. (1989) The rape culture. In J. Freeman (ed.), *Women: A Feminist Perspective* (pp. 20–44). Mountain View, CA: Hayfield Publishing.

Hibey, R.A. (1973) The trial of a rape case: An advocate's analysis of corroboration, consent and character. *American Criminal Law Review* 11, 309–34.

Hight, D. and Skinner, J. (1991) Nuts and Bolts for a Volunteer Peer Education Program in Sexual Assault. Paper presented at the American College Personnel Association Conference, March, Atlanta, GA.

Hilberman, E. (1977) Rape: A crisis in silence. *Psychiatric Opinion* September/October, 32–5.

Hobfoll, S.E. (1988) *The Ecology of Stress.* New York: Hemisphere.

Hofstede, G. (1984) *Culture's Consequences: International Differences in Work-Related Values.* Beverly Hills, CA: Sage.

Holcomb, D.R., Holcomb, L.C., Sondag, K.A. and Williams, N. (1991) Attitudes about date rape: Gender differences among college students. *College Student Journal* 25, 434–9.

Holmstrom, L.L. and Burgess, A.W. (1978) *The Victim of Rape: Institutional Reactions.* New York: Wiley.

Holmstrom, L.L. and Burgess, A.W. (1979) Rape: The husband's and boyfriend's initial reactions. *The Family Coordinator* July, 321–30.

Hovland, C.I. and Mandell, W. (1952) An experimental comparison of conclusion-drawing by the communicator and by the audience. *Journal of Abnormal and Social Psychology* 47, 581–8.

Howard, J.A. (1984) Societal influences on attribution: Blaming some victims more than others. *Journal of Personality and Social Psychology* 47, 494–504.

Howard, J.A. (1988) A structural approach to sexual attitudes: Interracial patterns in adolescents' judgments about sexual intimacy. *Sociological Perspectives* 31, 88–121.

Howells, K., Shaw, F., Greasley, M., Robertson, J., Gloster, D. and Metcalfe, N. (1984) Perceptions of rape in a British sample: Effects of relationship, victim status, sex and attitudes to women. *British Journal of Social Psychology* 23, 35–40.

Interpol (1988) [International statistics on sexual offences]. Unpublished data.

Intons-Peterson, M.J., Roskos-Ewoldsen, B., Thomas, L., Shirley, M. and Blut, D. (1989) Will educational materials reduce negative effects of exposure to sexual violence? *Journal of Social and Clinical Psychology* 8, 256–75.

Jacobson, M.B. and Popovich, P. (1983) Victim attractiveness and perceptions of responsibility in an ambiguous rape case. *Psychology of Women Quarterly* 8, 100–4.

Janoff-Bulman, R. (1979) Characterological versus behavioral self-blame: Inquiries into depression and rape. *Journal of Personality and Social Psychology*, 37, 1798–809.

Janoff-Bulman, R. (1982) Esteem and control bases of blame: 'Adaptive' strategies for victims versus observers. *Journal of Personality* 50, 180–92.

Jayaratne, T.E. (1983) The value of quantitative methodology for feminist research. In G. Bowles and R. Duelli Klein (eds), *Theories of Women's Studies* (pp. 140–61). Boston: Routledge & Kegan Paul.

Jayaratne, T.E. and Stewart, A.J. (1991) Quantitative and qualitative methods in social sciences: Current feminist issues and practical strategies. In M.M. Fonow and J.A. Cook (eds), *Beyond Methodology: Feminist Scholarship as Lived Research* (pp. 85–106). Bloomington, IN: Indiana University Press.

Jeffords, C.R. and Dull, R.T. (1982) Demographic variations in attitudes towards marital rape immunity. *Journal of Marriage and the Family* 44, 755–62.

Jenkins, M.J. and Dambrot, F.H. (1987) The attribution of date rape: Observer's attitudes and sexual experiences and the dating situation. *Journal of Applied Social Psychology* 17, 875–95.

Johnson, J.D. and Jackson, Jr, A. (1988) Assessing the effects of factors that might underlie differential perception of acquaintance and stranger rape. *Sex Roles* 19, 37–45.

Johnson, J.D. and Russ, I. (1989) Effects of salience of consciousness-raising information on perceptions of acquaintance versus stranger rape. *Journal of Applied Social Psychology* 19, 1182–97.

Jones, C. and Aronson, E. (1973) Attribution of fault to a rape victim as a function of respectability of the victim. *Journal of Personality and Social Psychology* 26, 415–19.

Kalven, H. and Zeisel, H. (1966) *The American Jury*. Boston: Little Brown.

Kanekar, S. and Kolsawalla, M.B. (1980) Responsibility of a rape victim in relation to her respectability, attractiveness and provocativeness. *Journal of Social Psychology* 112, 153–4.

Kanekar, S., and Vaz, L. (1983). Determinants of perceived likelihood of rape and victim's fault. *Journal of Social Psychology* 120, 147–148.

Kanekar, S., Kolsawalla, M.B. and D'Souza, A. (1981) Attribution of responsibility to a victim of rape. *British Journal of Social Psychology* 20, 165–70.

Kanekar, S., Pinto, N.J. and Mazumdar, D. (1985) Causal and moral responsibility of victims of rape and robbery. *Journal of Applied Social Psychology* 15, 622–37.

Kanekar, S., Shaherwalla, A., Franco, B., Kunju, T. and Pinto, A.J. (1991) The acquaintance predicament of rape. *Journal of Applied Social Psychology* 21, 1524–44.

Kanin, E.J., Jackson, E.C. and Levine, E.M. (1987) Personal sexual history and punitive judgments for rape. *Psychological Reports* 61, 439–42.

Kaplan, A.G. and Sedney, M.A. (1980) *Psychology and Sex Roles: An Androgynous Perspective*. Boston: Little, Brown & Co.

Karuza, J. and Carey, T.O. (1984) Relative preference and adaptiveness of behavioral blame for observers of rape victims. *Journal of Personality* 52, 249–60.

Katz, B.L. (1991) The psychological impact of stranger versus nonstranger rape on victims' recovery. In A. Parrot and L. Bechhofer (eds), *Acquaintance Rape: The Hidden Crime* (pp. 251–69). New York: Wiley.

Katz, S. and Mazur, M. (1979) *Understanding Rape Victims*. New York: Wiley.

Keating, J.P. and Latane, B. (1976) Politicians on TV: The image is the message. *Journal of Social Issues* 32, 116–32.

Kelley, H.H. (1973) The process of causal attribution. *American Psychologist* 28, 107–28.

Kessler, R.C. and Essex, M. (1982) Marital status and depression: The importance of coping resources. *Social Forces* 61, 484–507.

Kikuchi, J.J. (1988) What do Adolescents Know and Think About Sexual Abuse? Paper presented at the National Symposium on Child Victimization, April, Anaheim, CA.

Kilpatrick, D.G., Veronen, L.J. and Resick, P.A. (1979) The aftermath of rape: Recent empirical findings. *American Journal of Orthopsychiatry* 49, 658–69.

Kilpatrick, D.G., Resick, P.A. and Veronen, L.J. (1981) Effects of a rape experience: A longitudinal study. *Journal of Social Issues* 37, 105–22.

Kimble, G.A. (1984) Psychology's two cultures. *American Psychologist* 39, 833–9.

King, H.E., Rotter, M.J., Calhoun, L.G. and Selby, J.W. (1978) Perceptions of the rape incident: Physicians and volunteer counsellors. *Journal of Community Psychology* 6, 74–7.

Kirkpatrick, C. and Kanin, E. (1957) Male sexual aggression on a university campus. *American Sociological Review* 22, 52–8.

Koh, S.-K. (1977) The need for corroboration in rape cases. *Singapore Police Journal* 8, 138–9.

Koss, M.P. (1985) The hidden rape victim: Personality, attitudinal and situational characteristics. *Psychology of Women Quarterly* 9, 193–212.

Koss, M.P. and Burkhart, B.R. (1989) A conceptual analysis of rape victimization. *Psychology of Women Quarterly* 13, 27–40.

Koss, M.P. and Harvey, M. (1991) *The Rape Victim: Clinical and Community Interventions*. Newbury Park, CA: Sage.

Koss, M.P. and Oros, C. (1982) Sexual experiences survey: A research instrument investigating sexual aggression and victimization. *Journal of Consulting and Clinical Psychology* 50, 455–7.

Koss, M.P., Leonard, K.E., Beezley, D.A. and Oros, C.J. (1985) Nonstranger sexual aggression: A discriminant analysis of the psychological characteristics of undetected offenders. *Sex Roles* 12, 981–92.

Koss, M.P., Gidycz, C.A. and Wisniewski, N. (1987) The scope of rape: Incidence and prevalence of sexual aggression and victimization in a national sample of students in higher education. *Journal of Consulting and Clinical Psychology* 55, 162–70.

Koss, M.P., Dinero, T.E., Seibel, C.A. and Cox, S.L. (1988) Stranger and acquaintance rape: Are there differences in the victim's experience? *Psychology of Women Quarterly* 12, 1–24.

Krahé, B. (1988) Victim and observer characteristics as determinants of responsibility attributions to victims of rape. *Journal of Applied Psychology* 18, 50-8.

Krahé, B. (1991) Police officers' definitions of rape: A prototype study. *Journal of Community and Applied Social Psychology* 1, 223–44.

Krulewitz, J. (1981) Sex differences in evaluations of female and male victims: Responses to sexual assault. *Journal of Applied Social Psychology* 11, 460–74.

Krulewitz, J. (1982) Reactions to rape victims: Effects of rape circumstances, victim's emotional response, and sex of helper. *Journal of Counseling Psychology* 29, 645–54.

Krulewitz, J. and Kahn, A.S. (1983) Preferences for rape reduction strategies. *Psychology of Women Quarterly* 7, 301–12.

Krulewitz, J. and Nash, J. (1979) Effects of rape victim resistance, assault outcome and sex of observer on attributions about rape. *Journal of Personality* 47, 557–74.

Krulewitz, J. and Payne, E. (1978) Attributions about rape: Effects of rapist force, observer sex and sex role attitudes. *Journal of Applied Social Psychology* 8, 291–305.

LaFree, G.D. (1980a) Variables affecting guilty pleas and convictions in rape cases: Toward a social theory of rape processing. *Social Forces* 58, 833–50.

LaFree, G.D. (1980b) The effect of sexual stratification by race on official reactions to rape. *American Sociological Review* 45, 842–54.

LaFree, G.D., Reskin, B.F. and Visher, C.A. (1985) Jurors' responses to victims' behavior and legal issues in sexual assault trials. *Social Problems* 32, 389–407.

L'Armand, K. and Pepitone, A. (1982) Judgments about rape: A study of victim–rapist relationship and victim sexual history. *Personality and Social Psychology Bulletin* 8, 134–9.

L'Armand, K., Pepitone, A. and Shanmugam, T.E. (1982) The role of chastity in judgments about rape: A comparison of attitudes in India and the United States. In R. Rath, H.S. Asthana, D. Sinha and J.B.H. Sinha (eds), *Diversity and Unity in Cross-Cultural Psychology* (pp. 329–38). Lisse: Swets & Zeitlinger.

Largen, M.A. (1985) The anti-rape movement: Past and present. In A.W. Burgess (ed.), *Rape and Sexual Assault* (pp. 1–13). New York: Garland.

Larsen, K.S. and Long, E. (1988) Attitudes toward rape. *Journal of Sex Research* 24, 299–304.

Lather, P. (1988) Feminist perspectives on empowering research methodologies. *Women's Studies International Forum* 11, 569–81.

Lazarus, R.S. (1976) *Patterns of Adjustment*. New York: McGraw-Hill.

Lazarus, R.S. and Folkman, S. (1984) *Stress, Appraisal and Coping*. New York: Springer.

Leavy, R.L. (1983) Social support and psychological disorder: A review. *Journal of Community Psychology* 11, 3–21.

LeBourdais, E. (1976) Rape victims: The unpopular patients. *Dimensions of Health Services* 53, 12–14.

LeDoux, J.C. and Hazelwood, R.R. (1985) Police attitudes and beliefs toward rape. *Journal of Police Science and Administration* 13, 211–20.

Lee, H.B. and Cheung, F.M. (1991) The Attitudes toward Rape Victims Scale: Reliability and validity in a Chinese context. *Sex Roles* 24, 599–603.

Lee, L. (1987) Rape prevention: Experiential training for men. *Journal of Counseling and Development* 66, 100–1.

LeGrand, C. (1973) Rape and rape laws: Sexism in society and law. *California Law Review* 63, 919–41.

Lenihan, G.O., Rawlins, M.E., Eberly, C.G., Buckley, B. and Masters, B. (1992) Gender differences in rape supportive attitudes before and after a date rape education intervention. *Journal of College Student Development*, 33, 331–8.

Lerner, M.J. and Simmons, C.H. (1966) The observer's reaction to the 'innocent victim': Compassion or rejection? *Journal of Personality and Social Psychology* 4, 203–10.

Lester, D., Gronau, F. and Wondrack, K. (1982) The personality and attitudes of female police officers: Needs, androgyny, and attitudes toward rape. *Journal of Police Science and Administration* 10, 357–60.

Levett, A. and Kuhn, L. (1991) Attitudes toward rape and rapists: A white, English-speaking South African student sample. *South African Journal of Psychology* 21, 32–7.

Levine, S. and Koenig, J. (eds) (1983) *Why Men Rape: Interviews with Convicted Rapists*. London: W.H. Allen.

Lewin, K. (1948) *Resolving Social Conflicts*. New York: Harper.

Libow, J. and Doty, D. (1979) An exploratory approach to self-blame and self-derogation by rape victims. *American Journal of Orthopsychiatry* 49, 670–9.

Linz, D. (1989) Exposure to sexually explicit materials and attitudes toward rape: A comparison of study results. *Journal of Sex Research* 26, 50–84.

Linz, D., Fuson, I.A. and Donnerstein, E. (1990) Mitigating the negative effects of sexually violent mass communications through pre-exposure briefings. *Communication Research* 17, 641–74.

Litman, T.J. (1974) The family as a basic unit in health and medical care: A social-behavioral overview. *Social Science and Medicine* 8, 494–519.

Lloyd, C. (1991) The offence: Changes in pattern and nature of sex offences. *Criminal Behavior and Mental Health* 1, 115–22.

Lloyd, C. and Walmsley, R. (1989) Changes in rape offences and sentencing. *Home Office Research Study No. 105*. London: HMSO.

London Rape Crisis Centre (1982) *Annual Report*. London: Rape Crisis Centre.

Lott, B. (1981) *Becoming a Woman: The Socialization of Gender*. Springfield, IL: Charles C. Thomas.

Lottes, I.L. (1991) Belief systems: Sexuality and rape. *Journal of Psychology and Human Sexuality* 4, 37–59.

Luginbuhl, J. and Mullin, C. (1981) Rape and responsibility: How and how much is the victim blamed? *Sex Roles* 7, 547–59.

McCahill, T.W., Meyer, L.C. and Fischman, A.M. (1979) *The Aftermath of Rape*. Lexington, MA: D.C. Heath.

McCombie, S.L. (1975) Characteristics of rape victims seen in crisis intervention. *Smith College Studies in Social Work* 46, 137–58.

McDermott, M.J. (1979) *Rape Victimization in 26 American Cities*. Washington, DC: Government Printing Office.

McGuire, C. and Stern, D. (1976) Survey of incidence of and physicians' attitudes toward sexual assault. *Public Health Services* 91, 103–9.

McGuire, W.J. (1961) Resistance to persuasion conferred by active and passive prior refutation of the same and alternative counter-arguments. *Journal of Abnormal and Social Psychology* 63, 326–32.

McGuire, W.J. (1972) Attitude change: An information processing paradigm. In C.G. McClintock (ed.), *Experimental Social Psychology* (pp. 108–41). New York: Holt Rinehart & Winston.

McGuire, W.J. (1981) The probabilogical model of cognitive structure and attitude change. In R.E. Petty, T.M. Ostrom and T.C. Brock (eds), *Cognitive Responses in Persuasion* (pp. 291–307). Hillsdale, NJ: Erlbaum.

McGuire, W.J. (1985) Attitudes and attitude change. In G. Lindzey and E. Aronson (eds), *Handbook of Social Psychology: Vol. 2. Special Fields and Applications*. (3rd edn, pp. 233–346). New York: Random House.

MacKinnon, C. (1983) Feminism, Marxism, method and the state: An agenda for theory. In E. Abel and E.K. Abel (eds), *The Signs Reader* (pp. 227–56). Chicago: University of Chicago Press.

McMillan, P. (1976) Rape. *New York Sunday News* December 5, 8–10.

Mahoney, E.R., Shively, M.D. and Traw, M. (1986) Sexual coercion and sexual assault: Male socialization and female risk. *Sexual Coercion and Assault* 1, 2–8.

Malamuth, N.M. (1981) Rape proclivity among males. *Journal of Social Issues* 37, 138–57.

Malamuth, N.M. and Check, J.V.P. (1984) Debriefing effectiveness following exposure to pornographic rape depictions. *Journal of Sex Research* 20, 1–13.

Mandoki, C.A. and Burkhart, B.R. (1991) Women as victims: Antecedents and consequences of acquaintance rape. In A. Parrot and L. Bechhofer (eds), *Acquaintance Rape: The Hidden Crime* (pp. 176–91). New York: Wiley.

Manicas, P.T. and Secord, P.F. (1983) Implications for psychology of the new philosophy of science. *American Psychologist* 38, 399–413.

Margolin, L., Miller, M. and Moran, P.B. (1989) When a kiss is not just a kiss: Relating violations of consent in kissing to rape myth acceptance. *Sex Roles* 20, 231–43.

Mathiasen, S.E. (1974) The rape victim: A victim of society and law. *Willamette Law Journal* 11, 36–55.

Mazelan, P. (1980) Stereotypes and perceptions of the victims of rape. *Victimology: An International Journal* 5, 121–32.

Mead, G.H. (1934) *Mind, Self and Society*. Chicago: University of Chicago Press.

Medea, C. and Thompson, K. (1974) *Against Rape: A Survival Manual for Women* New York: Farrar, Straus, & Giroux.

Mehrhof, B. and Kearon, P. (1973) Rape: An act of terror. In A. Koedt, E. Levine and A. Rapone (eds), *Radical Feminism* (pp. 228–33). New York: Quadrangle Books.

Meis, M. (1983) Towards a methodology for feminist research. In G. Bowles and R. Duelli Klein (eds), *Theories of Women's Studies* (pp. 117–39). London: Routledge & Kegan Paul.

Meis, M. (1991) Women's research or feminist research? The debate surrounding feminist science and methodology. In M.M. Fonow and J.A. Cook (eds), *Beyond Methodology: Feminist Scholarship as Lived Research* (pp. 60–84). Bloomington, IN: Indiana University Press.

Merton, R. (1948) The self-fulfilling prophesy. *Antioch Review* 8, 193–210.

Meyer, C.B. and Taylor, S.E. (1986) Adjustment to rape. *Journal of Personality and Social Psychology* 50, 1226–34.

Miller, F.D., Smith, E.R., Ferree, M.M. and Taylor, S.E. (1976) Predicting perceptions of victimization. *Journal of Applied Social Psychology* 6, 352–9.

Miller, W.R., Williams, A.M. and Bernstein, M.H. (1982) The effects of rape on marital and sexual adjustment. *American Journal of Family Therapy* 10, 51–8.

Millett, K. (1969) *Sexual Politics*. London: Abacus.

Muehlenhard, C.L. and Falcon, P.L. (1990) Men's heterosocial skill and attitudes toward women as predictors of verbal sexual coercion and forceful rape. *Sex Roles* 23, 241–59.

Muehlenhard, C.L. and Linton, M.A. (1987) Date rape and sexual aggression in dating situations: Incidence and risk factors. *Journal of Counseling Psychology* 34, 186–96.

Muehlenhard, C.L. and MacNaughton, J.S. (1988) Women's beliefs about women who 'lead men on'. *Journal of Social and Clinical Psychology* 7, 65–79.

Muehlenhard, C.L., Friedman, D.E. and Thomas, C.M. (1985) Is date rape justifiable? The effects of dating activity, who initiated, who paid, and men's attitudes toward women. *Psychology of Women Quarterly* 9, 297–310.

Myers, M.A. and LaFree, G.D. (1982) Sexual assault and its prosecution: A comparison with other crimes. *Journal of Criminal Law and Criminology* 73, 1282–305.

Mynatt, C.R. and Allgeier, E.R. (1990) Risk factors, self-attributions and adjustment problems among victims of sexual coercion. *Journal of Applied Social Psychology* 20, 130–53.

Nawal El Saadawi (1980) *The Hidden Face of Eve: Women in the Arab World.* London: Zed Books.

Nelson, E.S. and Torgler, C.C. (1990) A comparison of strategies for changing college students' attitudes toward acquaintance rape. *Journal of Humanistic Education and Development* 29, 69–85.

Ng, A.Y.H. (1974) The pattern of rape in Singapore. *Singapore Medical Journal* 15, 49–50.

Norris, J. and Cubbins, L.A. (1992) Dating, drinking and rape: Effects of victim's and assailant's alcohol consumption on judgments of their behavior and traits. *Psychology of Women Quarterly* 16, 179–91.

Norris, J. and Feldman-Summers, S. (1981) Factors related to psychological impacts of rape on the victim. *Journal of Abnormal Psychology* 90, 562–7.

Nuckolls, K.G., Cassel, J. and Kaplan, B.H. (1972) Psychosocial assets, life crisis and the prognosis of pregnancy. *American Journal of Epidemiology* 95, 431–41.

Oakley, A. (1981) Interviewing women: A contradiction in terms. In H. Roberts (ed.), *Doing Feminist Research* (pp. 30–61). London: Routledge & Kegan Paul.

Orlando, J.A. and Koss, M.P. (1983) The effect of sexual victimization on sexual satisfaction: A study of the negative-association hypothesis. *Journal of Abnormal Psychology* 92, 104–6.

Pallak, S.R. and Davies, J.M. (1982) Finding fault versus attributing responsibility: Using facts differently. *Personality and Social Psychology Bulletin* 8, 454–9.

Palmer, G. (1983) Violence against Girls. Paper presented at the National Crime Prevention Council and Singapore Council of Women's Organizations Forum on 'Violence against Girls', June, Singapore.

Parrot, A. (1985) Comparison of Acquaintance Rape Patterns among College Students in a Large Co-ed University and a Small Women's College. Paper presented at the Annual Meeting of the Society for the Scientific Study of Sex, November, San Diego, CA.

Parrot, A. and Link, R. (1983) Acquaintance Rape in a College Population. Paper presented at the Eastern Regional Meeting of the Society for the Scientific Study of Sex, April, Philadelphia, PA.

Paulsen, K. (1979) Attribution of fault to a rape victim as a function of locus of control. *Journal of Social Psychology* 107, 131–2.

Pearlin, L.I., Leiberman, M.A., Menaghan, E.G. and Mullan, J.T. (1981) The stress process. *Journal of Health and Social Behavior* 22, 337–56.

Popiel, D.A. and Susskind, E.C. (1985) The impact of rape: Social support as a moderator of stress. *American Journal of Community Psychology* 13, 645–76.

Pugh, M.D. (1983) Contributory fault and rape convictions: Loglinear models for blaming the victim. *Social Psychology Quarterly* 46, 233–42.

Quackenbush, R.L. (1989) A comparison of androgynous, masculine sex-typed and undifferentiated males on dimensions of attitudes toward rape. *Journal of Research in Personality* 23, 318–42.

Raden, D. (1977) Situational thresholds and attitude-behavior consistency. *Sociometry* 40, 123–9.

Rapaport, K.R. and Burkhart, B.R. (1984) Personality and attitudinal characteristics of coercive college males. *Journal of Abnormal Psychology* 93, 216–21.

Rapaport, K.R. and Posey, C.D. (1991) Sexually coercive college males. In A. Parrot and L. Bechhofer (eds), *Hidden Rape: Sexual Assault among Acquaintances, Friends and Intimates.* New York: Wiley.

Reibstein, J. (1981) *Adjustment to the Maternal Role in Mothers Leaving Careers:*

The Impact of their Interaction with Role Colleagues. Doctoral dissertation, University of Chicago.

Reilly, M.E., Lott, B., Caldwell, D. and DeLuca, L. (1992) Tolerance for sexual harassment related to self-reported victimization. *Gender and Society* 6, 122–38.

Reinharz, S. (1992) *Feminist Methods in Social Research*. New York: Oxford University Press.

Resick, P.A. and Jackson, T.L. (1981) Attitudes toward rape among mental health professionals. *American Journal of Community Psychology* 9, 481–90.

Resick, P.A., Calhoun, K.S., Atkeson, B.M. and Ellis, E.M. (1981) Social adjustment in victims of sexual assault. *Journal of Consulting and Clinical Psychology* 49, 705–12.

Rich, R.F. and Sampson, R.J. (1990) Public perceptions of criminal justice policy: Does victimization make a difference? *Violence and Victims* 5, 109–18.

Richardson, D. and Campbell, J.L. (1982) Alcohol and rape: The effect of alcohol on attributions of blame for rape. *Personality and Social Psychology Bulletin* 8, 468–76.

Riger, S. and Gordon, M.T. (1979) The structure of rape prevention beliefs. *Personality and Social Psychology Bulletin* 5, 186–90.

Roberts, C. (1989) *Women and Rape*. New York: Harvester Wheatsheaf.

Robin, G.D. (1977) Forcible rape: Institutional sexism in the criminal justice system. *Crime and Delinquency* 23, 136–53.

Rodabaugh, B. and Austin, M. (1981) *Sexual Assault*. New York: Garland Press.

Rook, K.S. (1985) The functions of social bonds: Perspectives from research on social support, loneliness and social isolation. In I.G. Sarason and B.R. Sarason (eds), *Social Support: Theory, Research and Applications* (pp. 243–67). The Hague: Martinus Nijhoff.

Rose, V.M. (1977) Rape as a social problem: A byproduct of the feminist movement. *Social Problems* 25, 75–89.

Rose, V.M. and Randall, S.C. (1982) The impact of investigator perceptions of victim legitimacy on the processing of rape/sexual assault cases. *Symbolic Interaction* 5, 23–36.

Rosenthal, R. and Rubin, D.B. (1978) Interpersonal expectancy effects: The first 345 studies. *Behavioral and Brain Sciences* 3, 377–415.

Rubin, Z. and Peplau, L. (1975) Who believes in a just world? *Journal of Social Issues* 31, 65–89.

Ruch, L.O. and Chandler, S.M. (1983) Sexual assault trauma during the acute phase: An exploratory model and multivariate analysis. *Journal of Health and Social Behavior* 24, 174–185.

Rumsey, M.G. and Rumsey, J.M. (1977) A case of rape: Sentencing judgments of males and females. *Psychological Reports* 41, 459–65.

Russell, D.E. (1975) *The Politics of Rape: The Victim's Perspective*. New York: Stein & Day.

Russell, D.E. (1982) *Rape in Marriage*. New York: Macmillan.

Russell, D.E. (1984) *Sexual Exploitation*. Beverly Hills, CA: Sage.

Russell, D.E. and Van de Ven, N. (eds) (1976) *Proceedings of the International Tribunal on Crimes against Women*. Millbrae, CA: Les Femmes.

St Lawrence, J.S. and Joyner, D.J. (1991) The effects of sexually violent rock music on males' acceptance of violence against women. *Psychology of Women Quarterly* 15, 49–63.

Saks, M.J. and Krupat, E. (1988) *Social Psychology and Its Applications*. New York: Harper & Row.

Sales, E., Baum, M. and Shore, B. (1984) Victim readjustment following assault. *Journal of Social Issues* 40, 117–36.

Saltzstein, H.D. and Sandberg, L. (1979) Indirect social influence: Change in judgmental process or anticipatory conformity. *Journal of Experimental Social Psychology* 15, 209–16.

Sample, J. and Warlund, R. (1973) Attitude and prediction of behavior. *Social Forces* 51, 292–304.

Sanday, P.R. (1981) The socio-cultural context of rape. *Journal of Social Issues* 37, 5–27.

Schwartz, S.H. (1973) Normative explanations of helping behavior: A critique, proposal amd empirical test. *Journal of Experimental Social Psychology* 9, 349–64.

Schwendinger, J. and Schwendinger, H. (1974) Rape myths in legal, theoretical and everyday practice. *Crime and Social Justice* 1, 18–26.

Schwendinger, J. and Schwendinger, H. (1983) *Rape and Inequality*. London: Sage.

Sealy, A.P. and Wain, C.M. (1980) Person perception and juror decisions. *British Journal of Social and Clinical Psychology* 19, 7–16.

Sebba, L. (1968) The requirement of corroboration in sex offences. *Israel Law Review* 3, 67–87.

Selby, J.W., Calhoun, L.G. and Brock, T.A. (1977) Sex differences in the social perception of rape victims. *Personality and Social Psychology Bulletin* 3, 412–15.

Seligman, C., Brickman, J. and Koulack, D. (1977) Rape and physical attractiveness: Assigning responsibility to victims. *Journal of Personality* 45, 555–63.

Seligman, M.E.P. (1975) *Helplessness: On Depression, Development and Death*. San Francisco: Freeman.

Shainess, N. (1976) Psychological significance of rape. *New York State Journal of Medicine* 76, 2044–8.

Shaver, K.G. (1970) Defensive attribution: Effects of severity and relevance of responsibility assigned for an accident. *Journal of Personality and Social Psychology* 14, 101–13.

Shepard, S.D., Lynch, S.K. and Scott, J. (1991) Coercive Sexual Behavior: Incidence and Implications for Campus Leadership. Paper presented at the Conference of the American College Personnel Association, March, Atlanta, GA.

Shotland, R.L. and Goodstein, L. (1983) Just because she doesn't want to doesn't mean it's rape: An experimentally based causal model of the perception of rape in a dating situation. *Social Psychology Quarterly* 46, 220–32.

Silver, R.L. and Wortman, C.B. (1980) Coping with undesirable life events. In J. Garber and M.E.P. Seligman (eds), *Human Helplessness* (pp. 279–375). New York: Academic Press.

Silver, R.L., Boon C. and Stones, M.H. (1983) Searching for meaning in misfortune: Making sense of incest. *Journal of Social Issues* 39, 81–102.

Silverman, D. (1978) Sharing the crisis of rape: Counseling the mates and families of victims. *American Journal of Orthopsychiatry* 48, 166–73.

Sivard, R. (1985) *Women: A World Survey*. Washington, DC: World Priorities.

Skinner, L.J., Becker, J.V., Abel, G.G. and Cichon, J. (1982) Sexual Dysfunctions in Rape and Incest Survivors. Paper presented at the Ninetieth Annual Convention of the American Psychological Association, August, Washington, DC.

Smith, R.E., Keating, J.P., Hester, R.K. and Mitchell, H.E. (1976) Role and justice considerations in the attribution of responsibility to a rape victim. *Journal of Research in Personality* 10, 346–57.

Smith, W.R. and Ousley, N.K. (1982) Social and Psychological Consequences of Different Types of Sexual Assault. Paper presented at the Ninetieth Annual Convention of the American Psychological Association, August, Washington, DC.

Snare, A. (1983) Sexual violence against women. In *Sexual Behavior and Attitudes and Their Implications for Criminal Law, Report of the 15th Criminological Research Conference*. Strasbourg: Council of Europe.

Sng, S.P. and Ng, K.C. (1978) A study of alleged rape cases in Singapore. *Singapore Medical Journal* 19, 160–5.

Snyder, M. and Swann, W.B., Jr (1978) Behavioral confirmation in social interaction: From social perception to social reality. *Journal of Experimental Social Psychology* 14, 148–62.

Sommerfeldt, T.G., Burkhart, B.R. and Mandoki, C.A. (1989) In Her Own Words: Victims' Descriptions of Hidden Rape Effects. Paper presented at the Annual Convention of the American Psychological Association, August, New Orleans.

Sorenson, S.B. and White, J.W. (1992) Adult sexual assault: Overview of research. *Journal of Social Issues* 48, 1–8.

Spanos, N.P., Dubreuil, S.C. and Gwynn, M.I. (1991–2) The effects of expert testimony concerning rape on the verdicts and beliefs of mock jurors. *Imagination, Cognition and Personality* 11, 37–51.

Stanley, L. and Wise, S. (1983) *Breaking Out: Feminist Consciousness and Feminist Research*. London: Routledge & Kegan Paul.

Stanley, L. and Wise, S. (1991) Feminist research, feminist consciousness, and experiences of sexism. In M.M. Fonow and J.A. Cook (eds), *Beyond Methodology: Feminist Scholarship as Lived Research* (pp. 265–83). Bloomington, IN: Indiana University Press.

Statistical Report on Crime in Singapore (1981) Singapore: Singapore Criminal Intelligence Unit, CID.

Strickland, L.H., Aboud, F.E. and Gergen, K.J. (eds) (1976) *Social Psychology in Transition*. New York: Plenum.

Swann, W.B. and Predmore, S.C. (1985) Intimates as agents of social support: Sources of consolation or despair? *Journal of Personality and Social Psychology* 49, 1609–17.

Tang, C. S.-K., Critelli, J.W. and Porter, J.F. (1993) Motives in sexual aggression: The Chinese context. *Journal of Interpersonal Violence* 8, 435–45.

Task Force for the Prevention of Violence against Women (1988) *Men, Women and Violence: A Handbook for Survival*. Singapore: AWARE and SAWL.

Taylor, S.E., Wood, J.V. and Lichtman, R.R. (1983) It could be worse: Selective evaluation as a response to victimization. *Journal of Social Issues* 39, 19–40.

Temkin, J. (1986) Women, rape and law reform. In S. Tomaselli and R. Porter (eds), *Rape* (pp. 16–40). Oxford: Basil Blackwell.

Tetreault, P. and Barnett, M.A. (1987) Reactions to stranger and acquaintance rape. *Psychology of Women Quarterly*, 11, 353–8.

Thornton, B. and Ryckman, R.M. (1983) The influence of a rape victim's physical attractiveness on observer's attributions of responsibility. *Human Relations* 36, 549–62.

Thornton, B., Robbins, M.A. and Johnson, J.A. (1981) Social perception of rape victim's culpability: The influence of respondents' personal–environmental causal attribution tendencies. *Human Relations* 34, 225–37.

Thornton, B., Ryckman, R.M. and Robbins, M.A. (1982) The relationship of observer characteristics to beliefs in causal responsibility of victims of sexual assault. *Human Relations* 35, 321–30.

Thornton, B., Ryckman, R.M., Kirchner, G., Jacobs, J., Kaczor, L. and Kuehnel, R.H. (1988) Reaction to self-attributed victim responsibility: A comparative analysis of rape crisis counselors and lay observers. *Journal of Applied Social Psychology* 18, 409–22.

Tieger, T. (1981) Self-rated likelihood of raping and the social perception of rape. *Journal of Research in Personality* 15, 147–58.

Tolor, A. (1978) Women's attitudes toward forcible rape. *Community Mental Health Journal* 143, 116–22.

Unger, R.K. (1983) Through the looking glass: No wonderland yet! *Psychology of Women Quarterly* 8, 9–32.

Walster, E. (1966) Assignment of responsibility for an accident. *Journal of Personality and Social Psychology* 3, 73–9.

Walter-Brooks, T., Jaynes, J. and Marshall, D. (1990) Acquaintance Rape Education and Prevention: A Peer Programming Model. Paper presented at the American College Personnel Association Conference, April, St Louis, MO.

Ward, C. (1988a) The Attitudes toward Rape Victims Scale: Construction, validation and cross-cultural applicability. *Psychology of Women Quarterly* 12, 127–46.

Ward, C. (1988b) Stress, coping and adjustment in victims of sexual assault: The role of psychological defense mechanisms. *Counselling Psychology Quarterly* 1, 165–78.

Ward, C. (1992) [Interviews with sexual assault victims in New Zealand]. Unpublished data.

Ward, C. and Inserto, F. (1990) *Victims of Sexual Violence: A Handbook for Helpers*. Singapore: Singapore University Press.

Ward, C., Newlon, B., Krahé, B., Myambo, K., Payne, M., Taştaban, Y., Yuksel, Ş., Ghadially, R., Kumar, U., Lee, H.B., Cheung, F.M., Upadhyaya, S., Patnoe, J., Kirby, C., Vasquez Gomez, A., Parra, E. and Colosio, C. (1988) The Attitudes toward Rape Victims Scale: Psychometric data from 14 countries. *Social and Behavioral Sciences Documents* 18, No. 2877.

Ward, M.A. and Resick, P.A. (1979) Relationships between Attitudes toward Rape and Sex Role Perception. Paper presented at the meeting of the American Psychological Association, September, New York.

Weinreich-Haste, H. (1986) Brother sun, sister moon: Does rationality overcome a dualistic world view? In J. Harding (ed.), *Perspectives on Gender and Science* (pp. 113–31). London: Falmer Press.

Weir, J.A. and Wrightsman, L.S. (1990) The determinants of mock jurors' verdicts in a rape case. *Journal of Applied Social Psychology* 20, 901–19.

Weis, K. and Borges, S.S. (1973) Victimology and rape: The case of the legitimate victim. *Issues in Criminology* 8, 71–115.

White, J.W. and Farmer, R. (1992) Research methods: How they shape views of sexual violence. *Journal of Social Issues* 48, 45–60.

Wiener, R.L. and Rinehart, N. (1986) Psychological causality in the attribution of responsibility for rape. *Sex Roles* 14, 369–82.

Wilcox, P.L. and Jackson, T.T. (1985) Fact variation: A study of responsibility versus fault. *Psychological Reports* 56, 787–90.

Williams, A.W., Ware, J.E. and Donald, C.A. (1981) A model of mental health, life events and social supports applicable to general populations. *Journal of Health and Social Behavior* 22, 324–36.

Williams, J.E. (1979) Sex role stereotypes, women's liberation and rape: A cross-cultural analysis of attitudes. *Sociological Symposium* 25, 61–97.

Williams, K.M. (1976) The effects of victim characteristics on the disposition of violent crimes. In W.F. McDonald (ed.), *Criminal Justice and the Victim* (pp. 171–203). Beverly Hills, CA: Sage.

Williams, K.M. (1978) *The Role of the Victim in the Prosecution of Violent Crime.* Washington, DC: Institute for Law and Social Research.

Willis, C.E. (1992) The effect of sex role stereotypes, victim and defendant race, and prior relationship on rape culpability attributions. *Sex Roles* 26, 213–26.

Wood, P.L. (1973) The victim in a forcible rape case: A feminist view. *American Criminal Law Review* 11, 335–54.

Wright, R. (1984) A note on the attrition of rape cases. *British Journal of Criminology* 24, 399–400.

Wyatt, G.E., Notgrass, C.M. and Newcomb, M. (1990) Internal and external mediators of women's rape experiences. *Psychology of Women Quarterly* 14, 153–76.

Wyer, R.S., Bodenhausen, G.V. and Gorman, T.F. (1985) Cognitive mediators of reactions to rape. *Journal of Personality and Social Psychology* 48, 324–38.

Yarmey, A.D. (1985) Older and younger adults' attributions of responsibility towards rape victims and rapists. *Canadian Journal of Behavioral Science* 17, 327–38.

Young, R.K. and Thiessen, D. (1992) The Texas Rape Scale. *Ethnology and Sociobiology* 13, 19–33.

Young, W. (1983) *Rape Study: A Discussion of Law and Practice.* Wellington, New Zealand: Department of Justice and Institute of Criminology.

Zajonc, R.B. (1968) Attitudinal effects of mere exposure. *Journal of Personality and Social Psychology Monograph Supplement* 9, 2–27.

Name Index

Acker, J., 185
Albin, R., 30–1
Amir, M., 31
Aravjo, C., 107–9
Aronson, E., 71, 84
Ashworth, C., 132

Baker, S., 149–50
Barber, R., 101–2
Bartky, S.L., 19
Bem, S., 125
Blum, M., 35
Bohmer, C., 96, 105–6
Borden, L., 139
Borges, S., 31
Borgida, E., 110
Bristow, A., 157, 190
Brodsky, S., 72
Brownmiller, S., 9, 18, 19–20, 21,
    23–4, 28–9, 44, 56, 156–7, 189
Bunting, A., 52, 204
Burgess, A., 120, 123
Burkhart, B., 53, 127
Burt, M., 25, 47, 51, 61, 200
Byers, S., 52

Campbell, J., 76
Carey, T., 85
Chancer, L., 107–10
Cheung, F., 52, 59, 161, 165
Cialdini, R., 152
Cooley, C., 121
Costin, F., 52
Crenshaw, T.L., 131

Deitz, S., 79, 201
Deutsch, H., 30, 31
Doty, D., 124
Dull, T., 42, 46, 48, 49
Dye, E., 57, 97

Eno, R., 52
Esper, J., 157, 190
Estep, R., 25

Falcon, P., 53
Feild, H., 38, 43–4, 58, 61, 198–9
Feldman-Summers, S., 58, 124, 132

Festinger, L., 140, 142
Fine, M., 178
Fischer, G., 49, 52
Fonow, M., 144–5
Foos, P., 35
Freud, S., 9–10, 30

Galton, E., 99–100
Giacopassi, D., 46, 49
Gordon, M.T., 204
Griffin, S., 9, 18, 26

Hall, E.R., 203
Harding, S., 190
Harrison, P., 145–6, 151
Harvey, J., 123
Harvey, M., 159, 173–4, 194
Hazelwood, R., 56
Heider, F., 70, 71
Hilberman, E., 25, 31–2
Hofstede, G., 55
Holstrom, L., 120, 123
Howard, J., 49–50
Howells, K., 82

Intons-Peterson, M., 147

Jackson, T., 57–8
Janoff-Bulman, R., 124–5, 126
Jeffords, C., 42, 48
Johnson, J., 148
Jones, C., 84

Kalven, H., 104
Kanekar, S., 81, 82
Karuza, J., 85
Katz, B., 126
Kelley, H., 70
Kimble, G., 189
Koss, M., 123, 159, 173–4, 194
Krahé, B., 56–7, 82
Krulewitz, J., 81

LaFree, G., 96, 102–5
L'Armand, K., 82
LeDoux, J., 56
Lee, B., 52, 59
LeGrand, C., 31, 34–5, 105

Lenihan, G., 146
Lerner, M., 71
Lewin, K., 189
Libow, J., 124
Linz, D., 147–8
Lottes, I., 52
Luginbuhl, J., 85

McCombie, S., 125
McDermott, M.J., 48
McGuire, L.S., 57
MacKinnon, C., 186
McMillan, P., 131
Mandoki, C., 127
Margolin, L., 52
Mead, G.H., 121
Medea, A., 50, 52, 159–60, 189
Meis, M., 157, 165, 185, 190
Merton, R., 121
Meyer, B., 125, 127
Millett, K., 30
Muehlenhard, C., 53, 79
Mullin, C., 85
Myers, M.A., 104–5

Newlon, B., 38–9
Norris, J., 124

Oakley, A., 157, 185
Ousley, N.K., 125

Palmer, G., 58
Payne, E., 81
Peplau, L., 85
Popiel, D., 133

Quackenbush, R., 51

Randall, S., 96, 100–1, 113
Rapaport, K., 53
Reeves, J., 52, 204
Reinharz, S., 22, 176, 186
Resick, P., 57–8, 199
Rich, R., 45, 48

Richardson, D., 76
Riger, S., 204
Roberts, C., 159, 160–1, 190–1
Robin, G., 105
Rook, K.S., 129
Rose, V., 96, 100–1, 113
Roth, S., 57, 97
Rubin, Z., 85
Russ, I., 148

Sales, E., 133
Sampson, R., 45, 48
Schwendinger, J., 24
Selby, J., 47
Shaver, K., 72
Silver, R., 123
Silverman, D., 130–1
Smith, W.R., 125
Sommerfeldt, T.G., 125
Stanley, L., 35–6
Stern, M., 57
Susskind, E., 133

Taylor, S., 120, 125, 127
Theissen, D., 203
Thompson, K., 50, 52, 159–60, 189
Tolor, A., 204

Vanderslice, V., 178

Walster, E., 71
Ward, C., 38–9, 72, 164–8, 174–6, 201–2
Ward, M.A., 199
Weis, K., 31
White, P., 110
Williams, J., 48
Wise, S., 35–6
Wood, P.L., 25, 27, 31
Wyatt, G., 125, 126, 127–8

Young, R.K., 203

Zeisel, H., 104

Subject Index

academic literature, and rape myths, 4, 9–10, 25, 30–1
account making, 123
acquaintance rape
  attitudes to victim of, 68, 75, 76–7, 91, 92
  and conviction, 102, 104, 111
  definitions of, 57, 74
  patterns of, 195
  victim responses to, 118, 126
  see also date rape
action-oriented research, 13, 22, 138, 154, 155, 156–8, 174–8
  evaluation of, 36–7, 176
  in Hong Kong, 161–2
  in Singapore, 163–74
  WAR campaign, 154–5
  and women's movement, 158–63
adjustment *see* stress and coping
adversarial sexual beliefs, 51–2, 53, 62, 200
Against Our Will (Brownmiller), 9, 19–20, 157
Against Rape (Medea and Thompson), 160
age, and attitudes, 47–8, 49
alcohol *see* intoxication
androcentrism, 10
Anglo-Saxon law, 23
anti-rape campaigns *see* action-oriented research
appearance of victim
  and definitions of rape, 73, 84
  in media, 29–30
  and victim blame, 27–8, 57, 75, 76, 77, 84
applied research, 16, 110, 143–4, 152
Arab world, 23
archival research, 13, 21, 28–32, 36, 95, 96, 112, 113
Ask Any Woman (Hall), 154–5
attitude change, 41, 137, 183
  empirical research in, 139, 140, 144–50
  evaluation of research on, 148–9, 150–2
  factors affecting, 139–40, 142–52

feminist means of, 137–8, 156, 176, 177
  methods of, 143–4
  permanence of, 152
  theories of, 140–3
attitude scales, 42, 63, 144, 198–204
  Attitudes toward Rape, 42, 198–9, 201
  Attitudes toward Rape Victims Scale, 42, 46, 51, 58–9, 149–50, 199, 201–3
  Attribution of Rape Blame Scale, 199–200, 204
  Rape Attitudes Scale, 203
  Rape Beliefs Scale, 204
  Rape Empathy Scale, 79, 144, 201
  Rape Inventory, 204
  Rape Myth Acceptance Scale, 42, 51, 144, 146, 199, 200
  Rape Prevention Beliefs, 204
  Texas Rape Scale, 203–4
attitudes toward rape
  age and educational differences in, 47–8
  and attribution, 78–9
  of community, 107–10
  cultural differences in, 39, 54–5
  ethnic differences in, 48–50
  of family and friends, 130–2
  of offenders, 61, 62
  and personality, 43, 50–3
attitude theory, 15, 40–1
attitudes
  and behaviour, 41, 62–3, 92–4, 95, 97, 99, 111, 134, 136–7, 176–7
  theories of, 10–11, 15–17, 40–1, 61–3
  professional and institutional, 56–61, 62–3, 97–107
  and related attitudes, 51–3
  research on, 38–9, 41–3, 44–5, 63–4
  sex differences in, 45–7, 48–9
Attitudes toward Rape Scale (ATR), 42, 198–9, 201
Attitudes toward Rape Victims Scale (ARVS), 42, 46, 51, 54, 58–9, 149–50, 199, 201–3

attractiveness
  of offender, 77
  of victim, 73, 75, 77, 84
Attribution of Rape Blame Scale
    (ARBS), 199–200
attribution theory, 70–3, 83–6
attributions
  and attitudes, 78–9
  and behaviour, 70–1, 84, 86, 88–9
  and blame, 72, 80–2, 83, 86, 125–6
  cultural differences in, 82–3
  experimental research on, 73–8, 87–8
  and individual differences, 78–9
  sex differences in, 80–2, 85–6
  see also victims, behaviour of
Australia, 54, 101–2, 195, 196, 202
authorities *see* institutional responses to
    rape
AWARE (Singapore), 170–1, 174

Barbados, 39, 54–5, 202
beauty *see* attractiveness
behaviour
  and attitudes, 41, 62–3, 92–4, 97, 99,
    111, 134, 136–7, 176–7
  and attributions, 70–1, 84, 86, 88–9
  of victim *see* provocation; victims
behavioural self-blame, 124–5, 126–7
blame
  attributions of, 72, 75, 76, 80–2, 83,
    86, 125–6
  behavioural, 126–7
  characterological, 126–7
  definition and models of, 72–3, 80–2
  offender, 72, 77–8, 80
  self-blame, 124–8
  societal, 58, 72–3, 127
  victim *see* victims
  see also fault; responsibility
Brownmiller, S.
  Against Our Will, 9, 18, 19–20
  epistemology, 189
  identification of rape myths, 23–4,
    28–9, 44, 56
  reflexivity, 21, 156–7

Canada, 39, 54–5, 202
case studies, 116–18
clinical case studies, 117–18
cognitive dissonance, 140–1
cognitive responses to rape, 122–3
cognitive theory
  and social psychology, 15–16, 117
community responses to rape, 107–10
community surveys, 117
conflict theory, 22–3, 94, 110

consciousness-raising
  in feminist theory and research, 13,
    22, 36, 138, 158, 159, 186–7
  as means of social change, 47, 156,
    170–1, 177, 186–7
consent, 26, 33–4, 99–100, 101
consistency theories of attitude change,
    140, 183
content analysis, 12, 13, 21–2, 29
conviction of offender, 32, 96, 101,
    102–4, 106, 110–11, 173, 174, 196
  see also trial outcomes
coping *see* stress and coping
counselling for victims, 58–9, 165–6,
    169, 171
  psychotherapeutic intervention, 97,
    112, 175
credibility, 33–4, 46, 58, 73–4, 105–6
criminal justice system, 98–9
  case management, 90, 91
  conviction, 32, 96, 102–4, 110–11,
    173, 174, 196
  mitigation and aggravation, 91,
    101–2
  myths in, 25, 32–5
  in New Bedford gang rape, 108
  professional attitudes, 58–9, 108
  and race, 50, 102–3
  research on, 96
  responses to rape, 27, 31, 101–7
  in Singapore, 162, 173
  victim experience of, 27, 132–3
  see also investigation procedures;
      police; prosecution of sexual
      offences, trial outcomes
cross-cultural differences, 52, 57, 202
  in attitudes to rape, 39, 54–5, 202
  in attributions, 82–3

date rape, 46, 67, 74, 76, 77, 145–6
  see also acquaintance rape
defensive attribution styles, 71, 72,
    85–6, 182
deductive research, 35, 188–98
delayed reporting, 100, 101, 106
demystification, 23, 156, 175, 176
  see also education and training (rape
      awareness)
denigration, 75, 162
deservingness, 46, 71, 75
dispositions, 15, 40, 71, 78, 86
dissonance, 93, 140–1
doctors *see* medical profession

education and training (rape
    awareness), 139–40, 144–52, 162,
    167–8, 170, 174, 175–6

educational background, and attitudes, 43, 47, 48

empathy, 71–2, 79, 111, 201
  see also identification, with victim

epistemology, 12, 178, 187–91

ethnicity
  and attitudes, 48–50
  and community responses to rape, 108–9
  and criminal justice system, 50, 95, 102–3
  and media, 29

ethnography, 12–13, 21, 26–8, 95–6, 138

evaluation apprehension, 63

evidence of rape, 105, 124

expectations, and self-concept, 121

experimental research
  on attitude change, 137, 143–4
  on attribution, 73–83
  methods of, 13–14, 68–70, 87–8
  quasi-experimental, 13, 96, 112–14

experts *see* professionals

external validity, 63, 70, 87–8, 114

family
  social support by, 3, 129, 130–2
  trauma associated with rape, 130–2

fault, 80–2
  offender, 77–8, 80
  victim, 48–9, 75–7, 80, 81
  see also blame; responsibility

feminism
  contribution and influence of, 5, 11, 19–20, 36, 37, 43–4, 159, 181–2, 192
  critique of science, 9–10, 87–8, 157, 188
  relationship with psychology, 6–7, 9–12, 11–12, 19, 37, 64, 87–8, 95–6, 111, 117, 137–8, 157–8, 176–8, 180–88, 191–2

feminist consciousness, 19–20

feminist empiricism, 188

feminist epistemology, 12, 187–91

feminist literature on rape, 18–20, 22–35

feminist movement
  and feminist scholarship, 158–63

feminist research
  methodology and methods, 6, 12–13, 14, 21–3, 36–7, 64, 95–6, 138, 157–8, 175, 177–8, 184–7
  power-sharing in, 6, 157–8, 185
  and social change, 137–8, 156, 158–63, 170–1, 175–6

see also action-oriented research; archival research; content analysis; ethnography

feminist theory, 10–11, 22–3, 35–7, 93–5, 155–6, 175, 180, 181–4

field research, 14, 91, 92, 95–7, 111–14, 186
  on community responses to rape, 107–10
  on institutional responses to rape, 97–108
  theory underpinning, 92–5, 110–12

force, used in rape, 67, 73, 77–8, 99–100, 102, 110, 118, 124, 196

friends, social support by, 131

gang rape, 102, 107–10

gender roles, 23, 51–2, 53, 76, 88–9, 94, 103–4, 134, 181

general public *see* public attitudes to rape

generalizability *see* external validity

Germany, 39, 52, 54–5, 56–7, 165, 185, 202

guilt *see* blame; conviction of offender

health *see* medical profession

hitch-hiking, 76, 104

Hong Kong, 32, 54–5, 59, 161–3, 165, 195, 202

husbands *see* partners, social support by

identification, with victim, 45–6, 71–2, 75, 86
  see also defensive attribution styles; empathy

India, 54–5, 81–2, 83, 202

inductive research, 35, 188–9

information *see* education and training; knowledge

injury *see* force, used in rape

institutional responses to rape, 4, 91–5, 110–12, 132–3, 161, 177, 182–3
  field research on, 97–107
  research in Singapore, 164, 166–7, 171, 172–3
  victim experiences of, 26–8, 132–3, 182–3
  see also criminal justice system; medical profession; police; social services

interpretive studies, 14

interviews, 95, 112, 114, 117, 137, 157, 166, 185

intoxication, 74, 76–86, 102, 103, 125–6

investigation procedures, 98–9
Israel, 39, 52, 54–5, 196, 202
Italy, 96

judges, responses to rape, 27–8, 101–2, 105–7, 112
juries, responses to rape, 101, 102, 103–4, 201
'just world' hypothesis, 84–6, 182

'kissing violations', 52
knowledge
    and attitudes, 58–9, 63
    see also education and training; epistemology

lawyers
    attitudes toward rape, 59–61
    responses to rape, 112
'leading men on', 79
learning, of roles and attitudes, 23, 41
legal system *see* criminal justice system; police
legislation, 23, 162, 173
literary criticism *see* content analysis
locus of control, 53, 78
logical positivism, 187–8
London Rape Crisis Centre and Collective, 160, 190, 195
'looking glass' self, 121

'macho' orientation, 52, 78
Malaysia, 39, 54,–5, 99, 189, 195, 202
male-female relationships, 29, 50–3, 62, 181, 194
    women as men's property, 23, 28, 94–5, 112
marital rape, 23, 42, 48, 95
media presentation of rape, 28–30, 108, 109, 170–1
medical profession
    attitudes and responses to rape, 25, 26, 31–2, 57–8, 59–61, 112, 172–3
    mental health professionals, 57–8, 59–61, 97, 112
    victim experience of, 26, 133
men
    attitudes to rape, 45–7, 146, 150–1, 194–5
    and attributions, 80–2, 85–6
    and gender roles, 51–2, 53
    see also male-female relationships
Men, Women and Violence (Task Force), 170
mental health professionals, 57–8, 59–61, 97, 112
methodology *see* feminist research;

social psychological research methods
action-oriented *see* action-oriented research
archival and content analysis, 13, 21–2, 28–32, 36, 113
case studies, 117–18
ethnography, 12–13, 21, 26–8, 95–6
experimental, 13–14, 68–70, 73, 87–8, 143–4
field research, 14, 91, 95–7, 112–14
interviews, 95, 111–14, 117, 157, 166, 185, 186
naturalistic observations, 95, 113, 117
survey, 13, 41–3, 63–4, 88, 117
    see also feminist research; social psychological research
Mexico, 39, 54–5, 202
moral character *see* respectability; victims character, responsibility and credibility of
multi-methods
    in field research, 95–7, 114–15
    feminist research, 21–2

National Crime Prevention Council (NCPC), 163, 164, 166, 171
naturalistic observations, 95, 113, 117
networking, 171
'Networking for Families in Crisis', 171
New Bedford gang rape, 107–10
New Zealand, 54–5, 149, 196, 202

observational methods, 96, 113
offenders
    attitudes of, 61, 62
    blame and responsibility of, 72, 77–8, 80
    characteristics of, 9, 72, 73, 87, 102–3, 104, 194–5
    relationship to victim *see* acquaintance rape; stranger rape
oppression *see* social control and oppression of women

partners, social support by, 3, 131–2, 134–5
patriarchy and social control, 4, 22–3, 45, 50, 94, 180
Penal Code (Singapore), 173
penis envy, 8
personality and attitudes, 43, 50–3, 78–9
persuasion *see* attitude change
police
    attitudes, 26–7, 56–7, 58, 59–61, 63

police, *cont.*
    responses to rape, 26–7, 96, 98,
        99–101
    responses to research in Singapore, 171
    victim experience of, 132, 133
popular press *see* media presentation of
    rape
pornography, 147–8
positivism, 187–8, 190, 192
post-traumatic stress disorders (PTSD),
    118
postmodernism, 190–2
power *see* social control and oppression
    of women
power-sharing in feminist research, 6,
    157–8, 185
praxis, 137, 155–8, 174–8
precipitation *see* victims
premeditation, 78
professional literature, and rape myths,
    18, 25, 30–2
professionals
    attitudes and responses of, 56–61,
        62–3, 97–107
    education and training of, 162,
        167–8, 169–70
    see also criminal justice system;
        medical profession; police; social
        services
property, women as men's, 23, 28,
    94–5, 112, 181
prosecution of sexual offences, 98–9
provocation, 79
    victim appearance as, 27–8, 30, 57,
        75–6, 84
    victim behaviour as, 27, 57, 67, 75–6,
        77
psychoanalytic literature, rape myths
    in, 9–10, 30–1, 97
psychological adjustment *see* stress and
    coping
psychology *see* social psychology,
    relationship with feminism
psychotherapy for victims, 97, 112, 175
    see also counselling for victims
public attitudes to rape, 3–4, 61, 161

race
    and attitudes, 48–50
    and criminal justice system, 50, 95,
        102–3
    and media, 29
rape
    attempted, 77, 131
    definitions of, 32, 67–8, 73–4, 79, 80,
        105–6, 123–4

education on *see* education and
    training
facts of, 193–7
false accusations of, 30–1, 32–3, 57,
    99, 100, 196
incidence of, 164, 193–4
intentions, 194
justification, 194
location of, 195–6
perceived psychological effects of,
    68, 74, 80, 83, 84
and physical injury, 196
psychological effects of, 118–20
reporting of, 100–1, 106, 124, 195
    see also rape myths
Rape Attitudes Scale (RAS), 203
Rape Beliefs Scale, 204
Rape Empathy Scale (RES), 79, 144,
    201
Rape Inventory Scale, 204
Rape Myth Acceptance Scale, 42, 51,
    144, 146, 199, 200
rape myths, 2–5, 23–5, 37, 123, 133–4
    in academic literature, 30–2
    acceptance, 45–55, 145, 147–8
    acceptance by professionals, 56–61
    antecedents and consequences, 17,
        34–5
    effect on institutional responses to
        rape, 26–8, 31–3, 110–11, 132, 177,
        182–3
    effect on victims' responses to rape,
        28, 116–17, 122–33, 135, 183
    identification and research on, 23–5,
        38–9, 44–5, 182, 185
    in popular media, 28–30
    rape = sex myth, 24, 27, 30, 50, 53,
        74, 84, 91, 99
    and rape facts, 193–7
Rape Prevention Belief Scale (RPBS),
    204
Rape Prevention Education Project,
    144
Rape Study Committee (Singapore),
    171
rape-supportive cultures, 10
Rape Trauma Syndrome, 120
rapists *see* offenders
reflexivity in feminist research, 21, 36,
    156–7
relationship with offender *see*
    acquaintance rape; date rape;
    stranger rape
relationships, and social support, 3,
    129–32, 134–5
reliability, 42, 113, 117, 187, 198–204

research
  types of, 14–15, 16
  see also feminist research; methods,
    social psychological research
resistance by victim, 57, 67, 73, 77,
  100, 110, 111
respectability, 68, 74, 75, 76, 84, 85,
  110
response bias, 63
responsibility
  and attribution, 79, 80–2, 86
  offender, 77–8, 79, 80
  victim, 30–1, 68, 72, 75–7, 79, 81–2
  see also blame; fault

SAFV (Society against Family
    Violence, Singapore), 171, 174
Samaritans of Singapore (SOS), 168,
  169, 171
sampling, 43, 63, 87, 113
SAWL (Singapore Association of
    Women Lawyers), 170, 171
science, feminist critique of, 9–10,
  87–9, 157, 187–8
scientific realists, 188, 189
SCWO (Singapore Council of Women's
    Organizations), 163, 164, 166,
    170, 171
self-blame of victim, 28, 124–8
self-concept of victim, 28, 121–8, 130,
  132
self-fulfilling prophecy, 121
sex differences
  in attitude change, 146, 150–1
  in attitudes to rape, 45–7, 48–9
  in attribution, 80–2, 85–6
sexual access, 95
sexual experience of victim
  and blame, 34, 76, 77, 83, 101, 110
  and trivialization of rape, 74, 83
Sexual Politics (Millett), 30
sexually coercive behaviours, 148, 194,
  195
similarity *see* identification
simulation studies, 110, 111
Singapore, 39, 52, 54–5, 59–60, 90–1,
  96, 106, 107, 165, 167, 168, 169,
  171, 172, 173, 195–6, 202
  feminist research in, 106, 163–74
Singapore Association of Women
    Lawyers (SAWL), 170, 171
Singapore Council of Women's
    Organizations (SCWO), 163, 164,
    166, 170, 171
situational factors

in attributing blame, 72, 75, 80, 87,
  104
in defining rape, 16, 68, 74, 86, 87
myth and fact, 193, 195–6
social change and feminism, 6, 47, 53,
  137–8, 156, 158–63, 170–1,
  176, 177, 183, 186–7
  see also action-oriented research
social cognition, 15–16
social control and oppression of
    women, 22–3, 24, 29, 45, 50, 62,
    94, 109–10, 112, 148, 155–6
social desirability, 63, 152, 181
social learning, 23, 41
social psychological research
  epistemology, 187–91
  feminist critique of, 9–10, 87–8, 188
  methodology, 6, 12, 184–7
  methods, 13–14, 63–4, 95–6, 137,
    184–7
  response to feminist influences, 5
  topics of, 51, 82
  see also case studies; experimental
    research; field research; survey
    research
social psychological theory, 15–17,
  40–1, 61–3, 70–3, 83–6, 92–3,
  112–14, 137
social psychology, relationship with
    feminism, 6–7, 9–12, 11–12, 19,
    37, 64, 87–8, 95–6, 111, 112–14,
    176–7, 180–4, 191–2
social services, 124, 165–6, 169–70
social support
  and psychological responses, 128–33,
  of significant others, 130–2
  from institutions, 132–3
  see also psychotherapy for victims
societal
  blame, 58, 72–3, 125, 127
  responses to rape, 107–10
Society against Family Violence
    (SAFV) (Singapore), 171, 174
sociological literature, rape myths in,
  31
SOS (Samaritans of Singapore), 168,
  169, 171
speak-outs, 13, 20, 22, 177, 189
standpoint epistemology, 188–90
stereotypes *see* gender roles; rape
  myths
stranger rape, 57, 68, 74, 75, 77, 84,
  118, 124, 126, 195
stress and coping, 117–20
  self-concept in, 121–8

stress and coping, *cont.*
  social support in, 128–33
support *see* psychotherapy for victims;
    social support
survey research, 13, 41–3, 63–4, 88, 95,
    96, 112, 138
  community surveys, 117
  on rape attitudes, 38–9, 41–61
Woman's Safety Survey, 154–5
survivors *see* victims
Sweden, 195
symbolic interactionism, 121

Texas Rape Scale (TRS), 203–4
theory *see* feminist theory; social
    psychological theory
therapy *see* psychotherapy for victims
training *see* education and training
traits *see* personality and attitudes
trial outcomes
  and defendant characteristics, 102,
    103
  and juror characteristics, 103, 104,
    111
  rape compared to property crimes,
    104–4
  in simulation studies, 110
  and victim characteristics, 106–7
  see also conviction of offender
trivialization, 39, 46, 74, 84
Turkey, 39, 54–5

UK (Britain, England), 39, 52, 54–5,
    57, 82, 154–5, 160–1, 195, 196,
    200, 202

validity, 42, 113, 117, 187, 198–204
  external, 70, 87–8, 114
verdict *see* conviction of offender
victimization
  ethnic differences in, 48
  primary and secondary, 120
victims
  behaviour of
    role in attribution of, 72, 75, 76,
      80, 81, 82, 84–5, 88–9, 124–5,
      126–7
    role in defining rape of, 34, 73,
      101, 102, 110
    see also provocation; sexual
      experience of victim
  blame of, 27–8, 52, 72, 75–7, 80–1,
    108–9, 121–2, 124–8, 134, 182
  character, responsibility and
    credibility of, 33–4, 68, 71–2, 73–4,
    75, 76, 80, 84–5, 101–2, 110

characteristics of, 194
    role in attribution, 68, 80, 81, 84–5
    role in defining rape, 100–1, 103–4
    see also appearance of victim
  cognitive appraisal of rape, 122–3
  consent and perceived fabrication by,
    26, 32–4, 57, 99–100, 101, 196
  coping responses and self-concept of,
    3, 28, 74, 75, 77, 118–28, 132, 183
  experiences with social institutions
    of, 26–8, 132–3, 182–3
  fault of, 48–9, 75–7, 80, 81
  precipitation and responsibility of,
    9–10, 30–1, 34, 57, 68, 72, 75–7,
    79, 81–2
  support and therapy for, 97, 112,
    128–33, 175
Victims of Sexual Violence (Ward), 168
violence
  attitudes to interpersonal, 50, 51–2,
    53, 148
  see also force, used in rape
'Violence against Girls', 166
'Violence against Women', 176

War on Rape Committee (Hong
    Kong), 161–2
Ward, C.
  research in Singapore, 164–8, 174–6
weapons used in rape, 98, 99, 100, 101,
    103, 104, 196
Woman's Safety Survey, 154–5
women
  attitudes to rape, 45–7, 48–9, 146,
    150–1
  and attributions, 80–2, 85–6
  male-female relationships, 29, 50–3,
    62, 181, 194
  psychological characteristics of, 9–10,
    30, 51–2
  role and status of, 23, 28, 54–5, 62,
    76, 88–9, 94–5, 112, 134, 148
  social control and oppression of,
    22–3, 24, 45, 62, 94–5, 109–10,
    112, 181
Women against Rape (WAR), 154–5,
    159, 189, 195
Women Help Women (Germany), 185
women's movement, and feminist
    research, 158–63, 169, 170–2
Working Committee on Rape,
    Molestation and Sexual Assault
    (Singapore), 172–3

Zimbabwe, 39, 54–5

DATE DUE

DEC 1 8 2006			